NORTH KOREA UNDER C(

After the collapse of the Soviet world North Korea has continued alone on the rigid communist way, in spite of its economic consequences that have led the state beyond ruin – to famine. What are the reasons behind this peculiar choice of direction? Why did the leaders in Pyongyang pursue a policy abandoned not only by the Soviet Union but also by China and Vietnam?

The author of this book spent three years as Head of the Embassy of Sweden in Pyongyang – which, until a few years ago, was the only Western embassy in North Korea. His unique experiences are related with descriptions of day-to-day life and with analyses of economic, political and ideological conditions. A picture is drawn of a society and a political order that defy both human nature and common sense.

Erik Cornell opened the Embassy of Sweden in North Korea in 1975 and served there as Chargé d'Affaires until 1977. He was commissioned into the Royal Svea Life Guards in 1953 before entering the University of Stockholm, where he gained a Masters Degree in Political Science. Joining the Swedish Royal Ministry for Foreign Affairs in 1958, Cornell has served in Bonn, Warsaw, Addis Ababa, Rome and Pyongyang. He was appointed Minister to Geneva in 1977 and Ambassador to West Africa in 1982 and to Turkey in 1990. He is the author of *Turkey in the Twenty-first Century*, Curzon Press 2001.

NORTH KOREA UNDER COMMUNISM

Report of an Envoy to Paradise

Translated by Rodney Bradbury

Erik Cornell

RoutledgeCurzon
Taylor & Francis Group

LONDON AND NEW YORK

First published 2002
by RoutledgeCurzon
2 Park Square, Milton Park, Abingdon, Oxon, OX14 4RN

Simultaneously published in the USA and Canada
by RoutledgeCurzon
270 Madison Ave, New York NY 10016

RoutledgeCurzon is an imprint of the Taylor & Francis Group

Transferred to Digital Printing 2005

© 2002 Erik Cornell

Translated by Rodney Bradbury from the Swedish *Nordkorea: Sändebud
till Paradiset*, Studentlitteratur, Lund 1999

Typeset in Times by
Prepress Projects Ltd, Perth, Scotland

British Library Cataloguing in Publication Data
A catalogue record for this book is available from the British Library

Library of Congress Cataloging in Publication Data
A catalog record for this book has been requested

ISBN 0–7007–1692–0 (hbk)
ISBN 0–7007–1697–1 (pbk)

CONTENTS

CONTENTS

Part I

REPORT OF AN ENVOY TO
PARADISE

1

HISTORICAL REVIEW

During the last few centuries, the Kingdom of Korea could have been regarded as virtually a vassal of the Emperor of China. It had contact only with Beijing and was so isolated from other parts of the world that it came to be known as the Hermit Kingdom. Koreans were not even prepared to become involved with shipwrecked foreigners, nearly always preferring to keep them in confinement until they could be sent across the border to China. When evaluating North Korean attitudes and North Korea's foreign policy, it is helpful if one understands that the regime in Pyongyang has still not been able to break with this tradition, but has, to a considerable degree, endeavoured to maintain its isolation from the surrounding world.

In the 1850s, the US Navy had forced Japan to open its borders to trade, and in 1866 it made an unsuccessful attempt to do the same with Korea. However, the Koreans managed to sink the warship *General Sherman* and kill the crew. Instead, it was Japan that successfully completed the task in 1876, and for a few decades Korea was opened up to the world. But, at the same time, Japan was gradually colonizing Korea, a process that was completed in 1910 when the peninsula was once again closed to foreign influence. It was not until Japan's defeat in the Second World War that Korea regained its independence from Japan. While South Korea, after liberation in 1945, was progressively integrated into world society, North Korea's isolation continued, albeit as a rather odd member of the communist world.

The victorious allies had agreed that Korea should be divided along the thirty-eighth parallel, with the northern part being liberated by the Soviet Union and the southern part by the USA. The advent of the Cold War, and the increasingly strained relations between the superpowers, meant that the free elections intended for the whole of Korea never took place. Instead, the Republic of Korea (South Korea) and the Democratic People's Republic of Korea (DPRK; North Korea) were established in 1948. The frontline of the Cold War cut right across Korea, much as it did in Germany. However, in Korea this division led to the outbreak of war in 1950, during which the northern side rapidly captured all of the peninsula with the exception of the south-eastern corner. The Soviet Union was opposed to Taiwan representing China in the United Nations (UN) and therefore refused to take part in Security Council meetings, which meant that it was unable to use its veto. This made it possible for the USA to push through a resolution in which North Korea was branded as the aggressor. UN troops were sent in, and in a few months they not only recaptured South Korea but pushed on northwards towards the Chinese border. Then China intervened – and it may be noted here that China has put up with a number of foreign concessions (such as Hong Kong and Macao) on its territory, but on two occasions, in 1895 and 1950, it went to war to prevent foreign control of northern Korea. On this occasion, the UN troops were pushed back and the front gradually stabilized, for the most part just north of the thirty-eighth parallel, which has since been the border between the two Korean states. Between the two states lies a depopulated area several kilometres wide.

The armistice agreement was not signed until 1953 and there has never been any peace treaty. To ensure that the agreement was followed an armistice commission was appointed, and because of its combatant status the UN could not be a member. Instead, four neutral countries were chosen: Sweden and Switzerland by the UN, and Poland and Czechoslovakia by North Korea. Since that time, Sweden has always been represented in the little negotiating village of Panmunjom, which is situated on the border and the only contact point between the two states. The members of the commission have lived on their own sides of the border. Passage between North and South Korea via Panmunjom has, in effect, been limited to members of the commission in the strict sense, that is only properly accredited members and no other citizens from the commission's member states. Following the collapse of Soviet power, North Korea sent the Polish and Czech delegations home and is now trying to have the armistice agreement annulled.

The Soviet Union installed a communist regime under Kim Il Sung, who had apparently spent the Second World War in Siberia and advanced to the rank of captain, or possibly major. The historical isolation of the northern area was thus reinforced. Following the immense destruction wreaked during the Korean War, an extraordinary reconstruction programme was embarked upon in the north, resulting in what seemed to be a remarkably successful industrialization programme, plus the development of agriculture. The communist countries rather looked down on their exotic 'poor relation', and wanted to force the country to become a part of the Council for Mutual Economic Assistance (COMECON) cooperation, primarily as a supplier of raw materials. But North Korea refused, because it wanted to develop an all-round economic base with modern industry. In as far as the shifting conditions allowed, North Korea complained about the way in which advantage was taken of the country's isolation, particularly by the Soviet Union, in order to sell at a high price and buy at a low price regardless of world market prices. The antagonism between the Soviet Union and China, which became all the more marked during the 1950s, gave Pyongyang greater freedom to manoeuvre. Furthermore, the Cultural Revolution in China – during which Red Guards were allowed to call North Korea's head of state, Kim Il Sung, 'the fat revisionist' – also made Pyongyang somewhat wary of its dominant Chinese neighbour, which for centuries had been the Koreans' model, gauge and only known part of the outside world, in other words their entire frame of reference.

The time was ripe and the occasion suitable for an attempt to end their isolation through their own efforts. The North Koreans decided to embark upon a major programme of rapid industrial development by importing the most modern technical equipment that the advanced industrial nations in the West could deliver – why pay high prices for poor quality in the East, when cheaper and better products were available in the West? North Korean buyers flocked to Western Europe and Japan in the early 1970s, and signed contracts for enormous sums. From Sweden alone, North Korea committed itself to import contracts worth about one thousand million Swedish krona (SEK) in the currency value of the time. Soon, the hotels in Pyongyang were filled with salesmen and suppliers from virtually every European country and Japan. Trade relations with countries in the communist bloc had, in general, been established long before the socialist takeovers had occurred and this had, if anything, improved their reputations in the West as reliable trading partners. The North Korean newcomer was therefore welcomed to world trade, the rules of which were assumed to be well known. But what little the Hermit Kingdom knew of the ways of the rest of the world, or the world economy, had been gleaned from Marxist textbooks.

North Korea had overspent. The equipment that had been ordered had hardly started being delivered before it became clear that there were delays in payment. The North Koreans had been blinded by twenty years of undeniable success, having picked themselves up by establishing a diversified industrial base, achieving self-sufficiency in agriculture and rebuilding towns and the countryside after the dreadful destruction wrought by the Korean War. A large part of the population that had been forced to seek shelter in earth dwellings had been rehoused and Pyongyang had already been transformed into a modern city, where visitors were shown the three houses that had survived the war undamaged. Their justifiable pride in what had been achieved obscured their sense of proportion on account of the total isolation of the country from the rest of the world, resulting in a complete ignorance of both Western society and the history of industrial development. The North Koreans were convinced that they were on the point of catching up with the developed industrial nations. Their ideology of self-reliance, *Juche*, dominated their minds with the power of religion, and there were neither the conditions nor the space for a sober appraisal of their own capabilities. Expensive machinery was left to rust away in harbour warehouses because its delivery had not been coordinated with the construction of factory buildings, and fully equipped factories could not start production because of lack of planning for energy resources. Similarly, great sums were squandered on flamboyant effects, such as luxurious cars for the *nomenklatura* and fantastic electrical equipment for theatres and museums, while resources out of all proportion were devoted to prestigious monuments glorifying the leader and the ideology. In order to demonstrate a high level of technological attainment, expensive prototypes of technically advanced products were constructed and exhibited as symbols of the country's industrial capacity.

Companies in the West financed their deliveries, to a great extent, with export credits, and payment was to be based on the production that North Korea's new mining and manufacturing industries were to generate. But nothing was produced; meanwhile the payment deadlines passed, and the debts mounted with interest upon interest. No help could be expected from other communist states, as they were of the opinion that Pyongyang was learning a well-deserved lesson as a result of its disloyal attempt to turn its back on the COMECON countries. But in the early 1970s, the rest of the world was blissfully ignorant of these circumstances. Nor could anyone in the West have any idea that the North Koreans had a tendency to believe that their new trading partners had 'seen the light', i.e. gained an insight into what was right and wrong, and now were going to help North Korea fulfil its destiny as a frontline state in the struggle against US imperialism. Under such circumstances, it must surely be regarded as somewhat petty to fuss about the repayment of debts.

Rarely indeed have trading relations been established, and contracts and agreements of this scale and magnitude entered into, between parties wallowing in such monumental delusions with regard to each other's principles, intentions, priorities, production capacity and social mores.

The West's trading relations with North Korea thus came to a sudden halt, more or less immediately, and were transformed into debt negotiations, which were as long drawn out as they were fruitless. North Korea was forced to go back to bartering goods with the communist countries, with strict requirements in the form of punctual deliveries of goods in return. But it was also, not least for the Soviet Union, a matter of pride to protect the reputation of the communist bloc by preventing the nature of the backward momentum of the North Korean economy from becoming too obvious to the rest of the world. The magnitude of Soviet Russian aid is naturally unknown, but it must have been of crucial importance, for, following the dissolution of the Soviet Union, it came to an end, and that was the start of North Korea's rapid downhill slide into the acute crisis of the 1990s.

In the West, North Korea has acquired a certain notoriety but it remains a comparatively unknown country. It has probably only ever been visited by a few thousand Westerners, mainly businessmen, technicians and debt negotiators. A small group of Western countries established diplomatic relations with the country in the 1970s and their Beijing ambassador was also accredited to Pyongyang. Sweden, alone, opened an embassy there in 1975, and Finland and Austria opened trading offices. These had few staff and the accumulated number of resident employees can hardly, family members included, have exceeded 100 in twenty-five years. Towards the end of the 1980s, the UN Development Programme (UNDP) opened an office in Pyongyang and during the crisis years of the 1990s, it was joined by a number of other permanent, as well as temporary, delegations from international aid organisations.

One difficulty in judging North Korean conditions is that literature on the country is, in comparison with virtually all other countries, in very short supply. Reliable statistics are even more difficult to come by. Specialists on East Asia and communism have published a number of basic and often detailed studies, but the very character of the Hermit Kingdom has meant that the authors, particularly in the early years, have seldom had the opportunity to even visit the country, let alone live there. The dissolution of the Soviet Union, the reunion of East and West Germany, and North Korea's increasingly serious problem of feeding its population, have all led to a renewed interest in the country and developments generally on the Korean peninsula. The number of articles, papers and books about the North Korean question has become almost too many to cope with in just a few years. Scenarios have been presented, debated and criticized, there has been speculation over North Korea's intentions and, not least, discussion about how the rest of the world should react in the face of what would appear to be North Korea's death rattle. It has now been realized that the much criticized and despised country must be given a helping hand in order to avoid its collapse, which would force the world to more or less suddenly assume responsibility, and foot the bill, for feeding twenty million people and reorganizing its society. Confronted with these problems, writers have been unable to refrain from complaining about the meagre availability of factual information, of which I can cite a typical example: 'The DPRK's totalitarian features have limited the availability of data and analysis so beloved of social scientists. Despite these handicaps, however, conference participants were able to shed light on one of the world's most closed societies'[1] International aid in the form of emergency supplies to North Korea has led to increased access to, and knowledge of, existing conditions; yet it is unavoidably characterized by the secretiveness and antagonistic attitude adopted by the local authorities towards those from whom they have requested assistance. Although it is now possible to gradually build up a stock of information, the problem of how to comprehend the North Koreans remains.

An in-depth sociological study on North Korea has only recently been published. It is written by a former US intelligence officer, and systematizes all the information on aspects on daily life that has been acquired over the years. This author also underlines the inevitable fact that the study is based on second-hand information.[2]

With this background in mind, perhaps an account written by somebody who has lived in Pyongyang for a couple of years might be of interest. I opened the Swedish Embassy in 1975 and was stationed there until mid-1977, returning for a short period in 1988. This work consists of what is probably a vain attempt to clarify the essence of North Korea and the reasons for the state's rapid rise and predictable fall. The book begins with a description of the human, material and cultural environment with the object of creating an impression of the worldview within which North Koreans thought and acted. What follows immediately is a treatment of the ideological aspects that left their mark upon the North Koreans' inherited attitudes and values, primarily the background of East Asian civilisation.

An Appendix contains a concise presentation of the development of Marxist ideas, from Marx to Gorbachev, as a background to the basic ideological principles within the framework of which Kim Il Sung was trained and which characterized his choice of path for the industrialization and modernization of Korea. The values and economic principles of this ideology bear the responsibility for the failure of North Korea's misguided projects, whereas nationalism and a lack of knowledge of the rest of the world can be blamed for the fact that the chosen path was never subject to question.

2

TO PYONGYANG

In the autumn of 1974, the Swedish Ministry of Foreign Affairs asked me to open an embassy in Pyongyang, which was to be under the auspices of the ambassador in Beijing. At that time, I had spent the previous half-dozen years occupied with matters concerning development cooperation – half of the time in Africa, the other half within the UN system. During these years the revolutionary left-wing ideas, which had fuelled the violent student demonstrations across Western Europe in 1968, became all the more prevalent within the foreign aid establishment, and many embraced the thesis that 'the freedom of the free world was the freedom to starve'. This led to an increased interest in the socialist state of North Korea, which in only two decades seemed to have managed to guarantee its food supply and build up an industrial nation from what had been a colony that supplied raw materials, and one that had also been bombed to destruction and twice over-run by the armies of the Korean War. It was thus with certain expectations that I prepared myself for the move to Pyongyang.

The proposal to establish an embassy in Pyongyang had come from Swedish export companies that had suddenly found themselves in a situation in which they were about to sign contracts with North Korea for the delivery of primarily factory equipment for hundreds of millions of SEK. This also included 1,000 motorcars, which made their mark on the street scene, and heavy lorries, which were never seen because they were allocated to the military. My preparations before departure were mainly devoted to the Swedish Export Council, which was in the process of organizing a large industrial exhibition in Pyongyang, and to visits to companies. A number of company representatives had recently visited North Korea to sign contracts and examine the living conditions for the installation technicians who were to be sent out. They were all both fascinated and somewhat shaken by their impressions, which had evidently been highly contradictory, the essence of which was that they had never experienced anything similar in any other country. I soon grew accustomed to this: each and every person who visited North Korea or had contact with North Koreans could only provide me with the same sort of decidedly unhelpful information. The express interest of the business world to see an embassy in place was in itself a sort of warning signal – embassies are indeed useful to have around, but they are not normally regarded as essential for doing business.

The Swedish National Property Board had already made a journey to reconnoitre the situation and had rented office premises and staff accommodation. Its staff was now occupied with a certain degree of urgency in purchasing furniture, kitchen equipment and other goods necessary in a distant country with poor communications where there was no possibility of buying locally. I was personally responsible for ordering everything that an embassy office could possibly need. All the goods were to be packed along with the industrial exhibition material, and within a few weeks it was all sent via the Trans-Siberian railway.

Pyongyang's transport communications with the rest of the world were restricted, to say the least: two train departures and two flights a week to and from Beijing, and one of each to and from Moscow. In addition, there were two flights a week between Pyongyang and Khabarovsk in eastern Siberia, where one could change to the Soviet Russian domestic network or fly to Niigata in Japan.

As the embassy in Pyongyang was subordinate to the embassy in China, it seemed natural to make the outward journey via Beijing. There we were able to soak up Chinese culture in the Forbidden City, at the Ming graves and the T'ien T'an, the Temple of Heaven, as well as in museums and antique shops. We were later to discover that the North Korean equivalents were almost systematically hidden away. In the company of Dr Torbjörn Lodén, the embassy sinologist, we gained a glimpse of everyday China at a popular restaurant where city dwellers in their eternal blue clothes sat preparing piles of sliced meat in Mongolian pots – a memory of the transitional period between the Cultural Revolution and the 'Gang of Four' which, during the years in North Korea, I came to regard all the more clearly as a symbol of both relative affluence and individual consumer freedom.

Impressed and replenished by Chinese civilization, exotic in our eyes, we got on the train a week later, which took twenty-four hours to transport us via Shenyang, the former Mukden, and across the Jalu river into North Korea. Little did we then realize that in the future, from a Pyongyang horizon, we would come to realize that we were back in the West when we crossed the Jalu river and returned to China. The very force of this – by definition – unreasonable impression bears witness to the doubt surrounding all evaluations of North Korea.

The night train on the Manchurian railway was an agreeable experience, with its roomy and comfortable compartments. The pleasant restaurant car was completely furnished in a classical style from the turn of the twentieth century, with little table lamps and silk curtains. The food was excellent. When we later journeyed westward, we noticed that all the Pyongyang foreigners rushed to it as soon as the carriage was joined to the train after arriving at Shenyang. It is said that the kitchen was run by one of China's best chefs. That would not surprise me, because the Chinese are masters when it comes to demonstrating their superiority and finesse by subtle means. The Chinese passport police officer at the border – whom we gradually got to know a little – was exceedingly polite, helpful and approachable. One time, he welcomed us back to China with the words, 'How is it over there?' He spoke at least three European languages, English, French and Spanish, the last presumably on account of the Cuban Embassy in Pyongyang. The station also had a pleasant little souvenir shop with a surprisingly wide range of products.

Early next morning, the train slowly crossed the bridge over the Jalu river, close to the foundations of the previous bridge that had been bombed to destruction during the war. On the Korean side, the station was very spacious but deserted. A number of large steam locomotives were standing beside the platforms letting off steam, or puffing back and forth – a dream for railway enthusiasts. The passport police were armed, reserved, stern, taciturn and painstaking – from the very first, the traveller was to be instructed that he had entered a country in a state of war. This lesson in the difference between the Chinese and Korean attitudes was continued in the restaurant car. It comprised a kitchen section and a part of the carriage without any fittings, in which some chairs and tables with white cloths had been placed. It gave the impression of a provisional solution that had become permanent. The food was mediocre, and for foreigners it consisted of soup and rice with a few pieces of meat. After a while, representatives of the country's *nomenklatura* turned up and were served a decidedly better meal with the typical Korean first course dishes and chicken.

The journey took us through a colourless winter landscape, which appeared to be without interest. But when one travelled there during the green season of the year, it was hilly and beautiful. Then, its primary characteristic was that every little plot of land was cultivated, even between the railway lines, where this was at all possible. And on the slopes of the hills, apple trees had been planted close together. In contrast to China, the country seemed depopulated.

Pyongyang was entirely newly built and reminded me of the rather boring and nondescript suburbs that grew up like mushrooms around most expanding European cities in the 1950s. During the Korean War, the city had been totally destroyed by aerial bombardment and the fact that it had changed hands several times. Large areas of the city that had been rebuilt with traditional single-storey dwellings in long rows still remained. Each house had three rooms in a row, and an outside fireplace against one of the short walls. This also served as a sort of central heating because the smoke was channelled under the house to the chimney situated by the opposite short wall. These houses were now continually being replaced by large buildings of several storeys. Those that faced the wide streets had decorated façades. The quality was perhaps not of the very best, but it was undeniably a great achievement to actually house the population in such a short time. On one of the few journeys we were permitted to undertake in the country, we could see that all the towns looked the same. In addition, there were a number of monumental buildings such as government ministries, museums, theatres and hotels. Some of these had been built in a traditional temple style with curved roofs, particularly by the river that flowed through the city. There too, a pair of old city gates had been reconstructed. In front of the Museum of the Revolution, the urban scene was dominated by a statue of Kim Il Sung, so huge that his feet were the size of beds. The streets were of three types: narrow with single lanes, medium-sized with two lanes and large with three lanes in each direction. With the advent of spring, the richness of blossom was overwhelming. Fruit trees came into flower virtually everywhere, and the parks in the hilly landscape became enchantingly beautiful. But, unfortunately, the spring season in Korea only lasts a week or two.

The comparison with Beijing was striking. In the main, the Chinese capital consisted of an infinite number of low, small buildings and seemed more old-fashioned and dusty. It was packed with people who stared unabashed at foreigners with friendly curiosity and could often point them out to their children. The traffic was intense and there were innumerable cyclists, with noise everywhere. In Pyongyang there was not a single bicycle, cars were very limited in number and silent traffic was the order of the day (and this was obeyed); pedestrians were few and far between, and most of them were in uniform and seemed to be going somewhere. The inhabitants generally ignored the presence of foreigners, although occasionally it felt as though someone was trying to sneak a look out of the corner of an eye. As opposed to the ubiquitous blue cotton clothes of the Chinese, Korean women often wore traditional wide dresses fastened under their bosoms while the men wore a suit, shirt and tie, or a jacket buttoned up to the neck and made in a synthetic material called vinalon, which was manufactured from limestone by a special Korean method. There did not seem to be any shops. Many of the people waiting at bus stops squatted on their haunches, and young mothers carried tiny children in a harness on their backs. In winter the babies were so well wrapped up that you could only see their eyes. In all, the city and the population gave the impression of a higher standard of living than in Beijing – but the atmosphere was in some way lifeless.

We were keen to see our future home and we made our way to the suburb where most of the embassies were concentrated. At one end of a long and wide street were a number of buildings with flats for embassy staff, and along the street were three types of building, depending on the size and requirements of the embassies. There were not many, little more than twenty. But new blocks were being constructed, as more embassies were expected – although very few were actually to come, despite North Korea having been recognized by about eighty nations. Above the embassy office, we fitted out the accommodation – one could hardly call it a diplomatic residence as in many respects it was like the flat I had rented in a Stockholm suburb in the 1960s. However, it turned into a pleasant little dwelling where we were to spend the two strangest years of our lives.

Exactly one week after our arrival, Ambassador Björk came from Beijing to hand over his credentials. The Korean authorities had supplied us with cars and drivers, which was absolutely necessary as there were neither taxis nor car rental firms and we were not allowed to use the buses or the underground railway. The

Ministry of Foreign Affairs arranged a comprehensive introduction programme. One of the first items on the agenda was, suitably enough, a visit to Kim Il Sung's birthplace, which was a humble dwelling, a sort of porter's lodge. It was a typical Korean house, as previously described, which had evidently stood at the entrance to a country estate. The surroundings had now been landscaped so that the house lay in a little park. In an outhouse one could observe various sorts of household equipment, including man-size earthenware pots, used for storage. One of them had been unsuccessfully fired and was grotesquely deformed – a sign of the family's meagre circumstances.

The Commander-in-Chief of the armed forces, an ascetic, weatherbeaten, elderly, four-star general, was perhaps the only person not to ward off political questions by resorting to propaganda lectures. But that by no means implied that he was ready to discuss North Korea's stance in any way. The ambassador's cautious attempts at achieving some sort of exchange of ideas were rejected with the observation that such views may well suit a Swede but that Sweden was a country without any problems. As a comment, this was in itself not incorrect, but it ignored the fact that it is possible to try to even out disagreements with one's neighbours.

At the Planning Commission, our primary purpose was to acquire information on North Korea's payment commitments and its economic situation. Our worries were dismissed, as these were said to only be temporary difficulties. Instead, we were served a long description, which, to judge by the way it was presented, was considered very humorous, of the South Korean president's ten-point plan for fleeing to the USA with great riches. A number of further visits of this type reinforced the impression that, wherever one went, one was presented the same standard lesson describing the production capacity of North Korea in contrast to the misery in US imperialist-dominated South Korea.

The university vice-chancellor gave us a long lecture about the students' eagerness to contribute to the fulfilment of the planning targets, and how they were inspired by the writings and thoughts of Kim Il Sung, always referred to as the Great Leader. The ambassador asked whether the teaching even included a study of the works of Mao. Our appointed interpreter did not understand the question – it actually seemed as if she did not know who Mao was. The vice-chancellor, who had already reacted to the interpreter's deficient language skills by correcting her, interrupted our attempts to clarify the question – and thereby its implications – for the interpreter by simply and conclusively answering the question with a 'no'.

The visit to a children's nursery was a rather unnerving experience. The children were certainly well cared for. There was no shortage of pedagogical toys, and the fittings were specially designed for children with rooms and furniture in children's sizes, so that we adults had to crouch down. And the food seemed to be first class. But both children and staff seemed altogether too perfect and obviously well trained. The children did not seem like children at all, more like professional actors. The dance numbers were indescribably cute but about as spontaneous as a military parade. Three-year-olds with pointers in front of a miniature landscape in a sandbox described the Leader's birthplace and showed us where he had played as a child and how he was so much cleverer than his elder playmates. Five-year-old boys were drilled with toy rifles and taught to shoot down American warplanes. After a successful exercise, they all sat in a little tram that crossed the room where they were then united with the children in South Korea. It was like coming across Kafka in a children's picture book.

We were also invited to watch a performance of a revolutionary opera, *The Flower Girl*. This was typical of all the operas and films we were to see later. The plot was melodramatic and the message simple, with variations on one and the same theme: how people and entire families were subjected to the most dreadful sufferings during the Japanese occupation, as well as those currently caused by capitalists and imperialists in South Korea, but under socialism in North Korea they achieve a better material standard of living and are reunited and happy, for which they sing their inexpressible praise for the Great Leader. The performances were magnificent and stirring, and the singers were brilliant, no doubt about that, but then it was said that each work was performed by a special, full-time ensemble. The audience followed wholeheartedly the switches of fate, cried uncontrollably when a landowner's wife threw boiling water over a servant's four-year-old daughter, blinding her, and cheered when Kim Il Sung's partisans justly punished the Japanese occupiers and their Korean upper-class collaborators. The music was somewhat special or, rather, it was not really special at all. It was not East Asian but clearly European, and if one was at all musical one could recognize many tunes from Western operas and operettas. The general impression was a mixture of *Swan Lake* and a romantic Viennese operetta. And the personality cult naturally was always present in the form of choruses or songs full of phrases such as 'the rich blossom of the magnolias expresses an endless and unlimited gratitude to the great Sun of the Fatherland', which, of course, referred to the Great Leader. On such occasions, the audience would rise up from their seats and loudly express their approval, clapping their hands above their heads.

The intended climax was the handing over of the ambassador's credentials to the president. Kim Il Sung gave an unexpected impression. He was jovial and relaxed. He gave the impression of apparent intellectual flexibility and became almost enthusiastic when he started talking about current development plans. He was fairly natural and unaffected, albeit aware of his position, and there was undoubtedly something of a twinkle in his eye. When one experienced this, one could only marvel at how the personality cult worked – evidently its objects have a character weakness and are flattered and (in the beginning) appreciative, but they become all the more demanding over time. But the question is whether it is not the only-too-willing careerists who are the biggest crooks for taking advantage of their leader's weaknesses in order to further their own advancement – and in a dictatorship who dares to say otherwise when the price may be loss of freedom or even life, whereas in a democracy it may only end one's career. For it was hardly on the personal orders of Kim Il Sung that on the evening before our audience with the president we were visited by a doctor and a nurse. Although only two of us were to meet the president, we were all given a medical examination in order to… yes, what exactly? Perhaps we were suspected of being carriers of infectious diseases, from which the Great Leader must be protected!

We later experienced how the prudery of the interpreters made it difficult for them to translate bodily functions, and this undeniably made consultations with local doctors more difficult. If the need arose, we therefore preferred to call upon the services of the Soviet Russian Embassy's doctor. When the Swedish Foreign Service medical officer visited us to gain an understanding of local conditions, he got the impression that a whole hospital ward was kept empty in readiness for the treatment of embassy staff. We never had cause to use it, but when our little boy once suddenly went down with a high fever, a local doctor came accompanied by an elderly nurse. They gave him an injection of some excellent medicine, which reduced his temperature in a few minutes and cured him. The nurse was very impressive, she seemed to radiate calm and sagacity and had the wisest face we had ever seen anywhere.

At the Military Museum – which is entirely devoted to the Korean War – we were received by two colonels and a competent lady interpreter. A proper visit, it was explained, required two days and we would only be given a concentrated tour of four hours. The museum was technically impressive with constructed landscapes in which, for example, one could stand in a bunker and look out over the battlefield. In another room, a curtain was opened to show a miniature landscape in which lorries crossed rivers and mountains to transport supplies to the front. There were memorial plaques everywhere and pictures of fallen heroes. Showcases displayed clothes, binoculars and other equipment that had been used by the Great Leader when he had visited the front. The cellar was full of bits from American planes that had been shot down, as well as a photomontage of a captured warship, the crew of which had been taken prisoner.

Beside the grandiose museum lay a smaller, circular building. The staircase was in the middle and led up to a platform on which the observer found himself in the midst of the battlefield. On all sides was a ten-metre-wide section of the terrain with trenches, army vehicles and soldiers (life-size models) in battle. The constructed terrain blended invisibly with the panorama-painted background. The focal point was a US general who had just been taken prisoner beside his regimental banner, which was carelessly thrown over the radiator of a jeep. No expense had been spared and it was skilfully done – nor had they missed a single chance of emphasizing the nationalism, devotion and invincibility of the North Koreans.

The circus was perhaps the only occasion on which indoctrination was not in the limelight. The performance was first class, too, and one would be hard put to find better acrobats and jugglers. It confirmed one's impression that the North Koreans felt compelled to show that they were best in virtually every area. But the immense indoctrination and the need they obviously had to assert themselves was so overwhelming that most foreigners reacted in a highly negative fashion by rejecting and suspecting each and every positive impression. This was most particularly the case with the representatives of the communist countries, who regarded North Korea as a newcomer to the socialist camp with much to learn and catch up on, not least on an ideological plane.

3

DIPLOMACY IN THE
TWENTIETH CENTURY

One of my first duties on behalf of the embassy was to open a bank account to pay for overheads and everyday expenses. So off I went to the Central Bank, the only bank there was. It was a modest building in the centre of the city, consisting mainly of a small bank hall with a high, U-shaped marble counter. With the help of the interpreter, I presented the letter of credit, made out in Swiss francs, that the Swedish Foreign Ministry had sent with me. This was passed from the hands of one bank officer to the other, held under a lamp, up against the light and thoroughly examined from both back and front. In the end it became clear that I would not be able to get any money, or open an account. Evidently, no-one had ever seen such a document before. Fortunately, I had some travellers' cheques for my personal expenses and these were accepted. It was not until several weeks later that the letter of credit was accepted. Thus, the book-keeping of the Royal Swedish Embassy in Pyongyang started with a temporary loan from me.

After a few weeks, the joint freight transport via the Siberian railway arrived with all the products for the industrial exhibition as well as the equipment for the office and accommodation, and we could move into the embassy premises. We had to do most of the work ourselves, because the local labour force was flummoxed by Western goods. The 'Bureau for Services for the Diplomatic Corps' had a monopoly on all practical help that we needed, regarding both personnel and material. They were obliging and, to an even greater extent, curious about what we were unpacking and were keen to get hold of various ingenious gadgets, such as door-closers, in order to copy them.

Staff could be employed by registering a request with the Service Bureau mentioned above, after which household helps, cleaners, gardeners, drivers, etc. turned up for duty. There was no question of any selection procedure. The cleaner was a youngish, reserved but agreeable lady who was treated with great respect by the others. The gardener once came in with a dirty lamp globe that needed cleaning. When he realized that it was she – and not one of the foreign women – that he had to ask for help, he crouched down and respectfully lifted up the globe towards her. We came to the conclusion that she was an intelligence officer. She also served at table when we gave formal dinner parties, and then wore the traditional wide Korean dress of beautiful silk cloth. On one of the first times, as ill-luck would have it, a sudden crackling noise emanated from under her skirts as she was serving dinner – it sounded like someone trying to tune into a station on an old-fashioned radio. She abruptly stopped serving and rushed back into the kitchen – evidently the tape recorder was malfunctioning.

Language difficulties turned out to be an unpredictable factor in all our contacts. The North Koreans were completely self-sufficient when it came to language studies and had never sent their language teachers abroad to round off their studies by actually visiting the country in which the language was spoken. Rather, with their characteristic energy, they had a comprehensive programme that was exclusively on home ground. One unintended result was that they only knew words in a dictionary sense and perhaps in a literary context, and had only a vague awareness of frequency and nuance. A Swedish journalist who visited North Korea shortly before me described a typical example of linguistic problems. The visiting group had been shown a Korean film in which a US missionary in South Korea tried to seduce an unfortunate, impoverished and innocent Korean girl. Their prudish interpreter was very offended when the Swedes burst out laughing after he had explained the situation with the words, 'now she is a victim of his cunning desires'. In a sense, the choice of words was quite right, but as happened so often in North Korea the message was distorted through dissonance. When the Korean authorities offered me the choice of an interpreter who spoke poor English or one who spoke good German, I readily chose the latter. But, even then, nuances caused problems. I always found it hard to accept the unintended self-irony when Mr Ri spoke of the Great Leader as 'unser grosser Führer'.

The Korean language has its own phonetic alphabet (*Hangul*), which was introduced as early as 1446. In North Korea, they use only this; Chinese characters are no longer used. The language was difficult to learn but there were other problems too. Some of the embassy officers engaged the services of a language teacher, who, however, was perplexed by her pupils' wish to have useful words and phrases in the exercises. Her own were all of the type 'the people's courageous soldiers vanquished the miserable lackeys of the USA imperialism'.

An ever-present problem in translation was the rendering of large numbers, such as those discussed in our trade and debt negotiations and in the presentation of financial accounts. After a while I believed I had understood the reason. In Western languages, we use a system with three noughts: thousand, million and thousand million. Korea, however, uses a four-nought system. A number such as 12,968,705,341 would be expressed in Korean as 129,6870,5341 and even the best interpreter could not manage the transformation straight off, so we were presented with obvious absurdities. This explains why 'thousand' in the Swedish sense of 'many' (as in 'tusen tack' – i.e. 'thanks a thousand') becomes 'ten thousand' in Korean.

On the far side of the embassy grounds there were some traditional buildings. Little boys who lived there had constructed some rather primitive homemade fireworks from old tin cans. When they whirled these through the air on the end of a string they ignited and sparkles came out of slits in the cans. I was curious about their construction and asked the interpreter, who at first seemed indignant about such hooligan behaviour and was positively surprised that I was sympathetic towards these snub-nosed, rowdy youngsters with their red, pioneer scarves.

After we had moved in, the neighbouring buildings were evacuated and then demolished, after which crowds of old people were set to work to chip away at the remains and turn them into gravel. And when that had been done, large lumps of concrete were dumped on the site to be subjected to the same treatment. Was this penal labour for the former upper classes? Or simply an expression of their mania for keeping everybody occupied? The area was finally left as a bare and empty plot separating the embassies from the local population, at night lit up by searchlights. On the other side of the plot was the heating and hot water central boiler unit for the embassy district. The pollution and the dirt were annoying. Every morning, there was a layer of dust on all the garden furniture, even when they did not need to stoke the furnace for heating. In the summer, when it was tempting to take a morning swim in the little pool, one had to hose down the garden chairs before sitting on them.

From the very beginning, it was something of a problem getting hold of food. Not that there was any risk of starving, of course, but the quality and variety left a great deal to be desired. In the diplomatic district, there was a little shop which served only foreigners. It had three sections. The upper storey consisted of a large room a bit like a department store but with an extremely limited stock of goods – the book department, for example, sold only works by and about the Great Leader. Half of the ground floor was occupied by a seamstress and tailor's, which proved to have some highly skilled practitioners. We were told that one of the country's four 'honoured people's tailors' (or as the interpreter expressed it, 'verehrter Volksschneider') was at the foreigners' disposal. Local cloth was expensive and of dubious quality, but cheaper and better was available in Beijing.

The other half contained the food department, in which most of the surfaces were of ceramic tiles or stone, giving a very old-fashioned impression. The selection was limited. There were three sorts of vegetable, white cabbage, cucumber and tomato – not as bad as it might sound, because as they had lots of greenhouses they could guarantee the vitamin requirements of the population all year round. The meat counter was a catastrophe. Large pieces of animals hung on the wall. The fillets and other better cuts had been reserved for the party bosses, so there was not much choice for us. All you could do was order a certain amount of meat, whereupon the part of the animal that was hanging closest was taken down and a suitably sized piece chopped off. It was, without exception, so leathery and sinewy that it was only with difficulty one could tackle it with a knife, and it could not be served in slices – it could hardly even be served in pieces but had to be minced. So one of my first imperatives was to requisition a meat mincer by air freight – they were not available locally – and, even when this was used, it was necessary to dismantle and clean the mincer three or four times per kilo.

Fish was regularly available, but the fish were still alive so that only the larger embassies, in which the staff made joint purchases or were served together, could buy ordinary fish – the rest of us had to stick to small fish. One could also find salted Pacific salmon, which it was possible to turn into the marinated favourite dish of many Swedes known as *gravlax*, or at any rate something similar. In winter, salted fish were hung up in trees in the neighbourhood by the locals, like a sort of Christmas tree decoration. The cold weather did service as a deep-freeze and the whole area smelt of fish. In addition, there was, of course, bread and rather flat beer, mineral water and two caramel-flavoured fizzy drinks. Butter had an old-fashioned, stale taste. Rice formed the staple diet of the North Koreans. The apples were excellent and there was also a variety of pear which was quite large and hard with plenty of juice, but virtually tasteless. We called them 'papples'. Buying anything at all was made inexplicably difficult because of language confusion – we have lived in many countries without knowing the local languages, but never has it been such an awkward impediment as it was in Pyongyang. Perhaps it was the authorities' way of inducing foreigners not to wander about the city on their own and only to venture out when accompanied by an appointed interpreter.

At first, we were not allowed to visit the handful of other shops that did exist. However, the regulations were relaxed almost immediately and we could go to one or two but were not allowed to buy anything. The lack of food shops was manifest, the explanation perhaps being that the population obtained food from its workplaces; this is an undeniably effective method of controlling every single individual and tying him or her to a machine or farmland.

At a couple of the larger hotels there were also shops in which some foreign goods, such as spirits and tobacco, and strangely enough motorcycles, could be purchased for 'hard' currency. The prices were comparatively high and often haphazardly set. Some of their deliveries evidently came from the gifts sent to North Korea by the group of loyal Koreans living in Japan. Local officials had little knowledge of various goods and how they should be priced. If one was lucky, one could sometimes find luxury brands of cognac and whisky for the price of standard products, and the Polish ambassador joyfully related how he had bought a new Porsche for 4,000 dollars – it had evidently been priced in accordance with its size. Normally, however, the East Europeans did not have access to hard currency so they were unable to make use of the shops.

On the advice of the interpreter, I made an appointment to visit the police authority in order to request that they man the police box beside our gateway. My reflection was that it might be useful to have someone there should something unexpected happen, such as a fire or an acute appendicitis, and we were on our own and rather cut off out of office hours. Besides which, it was patently obvious that the authorities expected such a request and there was no point being awkward. We were received by a colonel and a captain who, after we had exchanged greetings and a few polite phrases, put on their uniform caps so that we could discuss the matter in question. The colonel nodded deep in thought, and explained that our request was indeed judicious in the light of the threat from the US imperialist infiltrators.

In actual fact, the threat, as far as we were concerned, came rather from the police themselves. One morning when I came out into the stairwell, I noticed the smell of smoke from a fire. I sniffed my way to a hatch in the wall under the stairs from which both the smell and a trace of smoke were seeping in. I immediately alerted the interpreter in order to avert a fire. It turned out to be a false alarm – at least from the point of view of the North Koreans, but hardly from ours. No smoke without fire, and in this case the fire was about 200 metres distant on the building site in the neighbouring plot. There, the workers were said to be constructing foundations and were warming themselves beside a fire they had made below ground level. It was thus revealed that there was a network of tunnels under the embassies so that the police would not need to use the outer doors. The Indonesian ambassador's wife confirmed that she had one day been terrified to see a face that suddenly looked out at her from the equivalent hatch in their house.

Once, when an embassy official was on a Sunday stroll in the neighbourhood, she was seized by the police and locked in a shed for several hours. Even the embassy secretary's wife suffered an unpleasant brush with the police when – wearing breeches (which did not exist in the country) – she was out cycling with her daughter in the diplomatic district. There were simply no bicycles in Korea – in contrast to China – which, if one thought about it, obviously meant they were forbidden. A Norwegian embassy secretary on a business visit from Beijing had taken his bicycle along with him but had been prohibited from using it. He protested loudly and the interpreter joyfully returned with the message, 'I have good news for you. You may use the bicycle during the weekend!'. In cases such as these, we tried to discuss with the Ministry of Foreign Affairs – via the interpreter – just how unreasonable the incidents were and the lack of hospitality that they signified… instead of protesting about the breaches of diplomatic immunity that the events undoubtedly involved. On the North Korean side they always uncompromisingly maintained that they never ever made mistakes, and trying to prove they were wrong led without exception to petty persecution of various sorts.

Foreign driving licences were not accepted; one had to take a driving test. The Service Bureau courteously lent us an English translation of the instruction book. The difficulty was simply that certain parts of it were incomprehensible: 'When policeman hold yellow flag his fronthood' I could understand, and the indecipherable bits I have, of course, now forgotten. With the help of the interpreter, despite his poor English, I made some of the phrases clearer as a token of my appreciation for their lending me the manual. The policeman's manoeuvres with his yellow flag were easy to learn. What was worse was that they had started introducing traffic lights; in the process, the desire to be best outweighed any other considerations. The Koreans were not satisfied with red–amber–green lights, but added a fourth colour, namely blue. When the blue light shone, one could turn at a crossroads if the blue light was in the middle of the post or in a horizontal row with the other lights, otherwise only in the same direction as the side of the post that the light was placed on. In addition, there were special rules for one-, two-

and three-lane streets: on a two-lane street it was mandatory to stay in the left lane even if turning right. Another point was that, at least during my time, it was useless for a foreign woman to try to get a driving licence.

The large industrial exhibition was, in its own way, really quite successful – but was anyone to benefit? It had just started to become apparent that North Korea could not pay for the deliveries already made. There were a lot of visitors, mainly technicians who had a very good knowledge of their fields. But there was really no question of any new contracts – instead, a shameless haggling started as the exhibition closed and the Swedish companies had to decide whether to sell their exhibits on the spot or transport them back to Sweden. When the Swedes refused to sell dirt-cheap, the North Korean authorities turned to me and demanded that I should put my compatriots right. When I retorted that I had no right at all to give orders to Swedish businessmen, the North Koreans doubled up with laughter at the – in their eyes – unreasonable statement that the embassy was not superior to the representatives for foreign trade. Their reaction was a spontaneous expression of how embarrassed they were by what they took to be my lying to them directly in the face. Several North Korean technicians got involved in long conversations, and not just about technical questions, but even serious discussions about the weather, which perplexed the Swedes. Sometimes their purpose was clear, as when some polite visitors ended the conversation by saying, 'Thank you very much, I have understood everything you said.' They had quite simply taken the opportunity to test their linguistic capability.

One morning, the visiting Swedes were not allowed to leave the hotel to travel to their exhibition. Only after waiting for several hours could they set off, and on their arrival they met groups of photographers leaving the building. They had spent the night there documenting all the exhibits but had evidently been delayed. Judging by appearances, they had also taken the machines and instruments apart – proof of this was that they had not been able to put everything back together again.

One afternoon, all the Swedish visitors were taken to the large Children's Palace in the centre of the city. The Swedish company directors were endowed with a red pioneer scarf around their necks and were led round on a tour that ended with a song and dance performance, as always very skilfully executed. In the palace, it was possible for older children to develop their special talents. There were chemistry and electrotechnical laboratories, as well as needlework rooms and music halls and swimming baths – and even firing ranges with targets shaped in the form of American soldiers. In the pingpong hall the visitors could compete against brilliantly drilled and obviously nervous boys, who naturally won without exception.

It was instructive to observe the reactions of visitors of various political shades, be they people from trade and industry or members of parliament. The more conservative their outlook, the less surprised they were, and the more satisfied they seemed to be. All their preconceived opinions were confirmed in a manner they had not dared dream of. However, if visitor considered themselves to be 'radicals' – within Western democratic norms of course, although not even communists could always hide their reactions – one noticed how their discomfort increased to agony. Really, these reactions were strange. Did they not know in advance that they were going to visit an unusually totalitarian society? Did they not know how much deviation from Western democratic ideals they were prepared to accept?

North Korea was a unique example of a non-capitalist development alternative. Particularly for those who had praised the then current thesis that the free world's freedom was – for all too large a part of the population of the underdeveloped countries – purely the freedom to starve, the country was a model by virtue, having achieved rapid development with work for all and a palpable increase in the standard of living for the majority of the population, workers and peasants. The obvious restrictions to the rights and freedoms of the individual were seen as acceptable sacrifices, particularly as they were regarded as being of value to only a limited fraction of the population and not as offering anything of primary interest to the impoverished masses.

It could not be disputed that the North Koreans had achieved great things with regard to living standards, health care, education and housing – especially considering what they started from. But the work input was inconceivable. The population evidently worked twelve to fifteen hours a day, and seemed to have been graced with four or five free days a year. The country had become virtually one huge army camp with the entire population conscripted for service with weapons or tools. Large groups of subjects did not go around singly but, as a rule, moved in square formations. Regulated leisure time was filled with 'voluntary work' and obligatory ideological study. In line with one's position in society, subservient behaviour was expected and material benefits were forthcoming in the form of better clothes, official cars of various sorts with driver, and a better standard of food and housing. In what sense was it a prototype, this society in which the population was indoctrinated to call it the earthly paradise?

During my long stay in North Korea, this problematical question pushed its way to the foreground. Even if one was prepared to tolerate the restrictions on freedom in order to achieve material and egalitarian progress, one was bound to ask whether the people had been forced to pay an unreasonable price. The North Korean example thus showed how essential it is to repudiate the claim that restrictions in civil liberties are the concern only of an exclusive minority. However small this minority is, if its right to make even justifiable criticism is sacrificed, then the floodgates are opened and the possibilities for workers and peasants to defend their rights and their welfare will also have been sacrificed. If one still maintained that the freedom of the free world consisted of a freedom to starve, then it was done in the knowledge that in systems of the totalitarian left, the right to influence society through hunger strike was suppressed. Milovan Djilas expressed this in the 1950s in *The New Class*: 'Thus, by justifying the means because of the end, the end itself becomes increasingly more distant and unrealistic, while the frightful reality of the means becomes increasingly obvious and intolerable.'[1]

The embassy diplomatic bag containing post had to be fetched from Beijing, and on one occasion when I returned I had with me a whole wodge of bills of exchange for a total sum of some tens of millions of SEK. The Swedish company had marked the places at which they should be signed by the relevant North Korean, and they had asked me to check that this was done. The North Koreans' restricted knowledge of trade documents had led to bills often being signed in the wrong place, so that the Swedish exporter could not access the money until all the papers – after long diversions – were in order. The bills that I had with me eventually came back to the embassy duly signed, but then I discovered to my amazement that I also had received an additional wad of bills of exchange for some fifty million SEK, emanating from an entirely different Swedish company, and this without any sort of note or explanation.

4

DAY-TO-DAY LIFE IN PYONGYANG

Social life in Pyongyang was, in a sense, a struggle against all odds as meeting Koreans in private was out of the question and foreigners were a rare breed. In addition, the representatives of the communist countries shied away from establishing contacts of an informal kind with non-communists. There were no restaurants or anywhere else to go to. The Swedish Embassy was really the only Western one because Finland and Austria only had trade representation. But, in practice, it made little difference.

In all, there were twenty-three embassies representing all the communist countries except Laos, but including Cuba, Cambodia and Vietnam. Asia was represented by three countries (India, Indonesia and Pakistan), the Arab world by four (Algeria, Egypt, Iraq and Syria) and Africa by Gabon and Zaire. In addition, there were the two trade offices mentioned above, one Palestinian Liberation Organization mission, and a representative of the Paris Chamber of Commerce. The embassies of the communist countries were often large as the staff included representatives of their nationalized industries' many foreign trade organizations. Other embassies had seldom more than two or three officials. In the early days, the number of resident Westerners was nine in all, and it never exceeded more than thirteen or fourteen, with the occasional addition of a handful of children of nursery school age. Only the Swedish family Sporrong had a slightly older daughter, who was given a place at the East German school and surprised her parents by coming home and singing, 'Hier marschiert die Volkspolizei und wir marschieren fröhlich mit' ('Here march the People's Police, and we march happily along with them').

Considering so few countries were represented, surprisingly many had strained relations with each other. The contacts of the Chinese with the Moscow bloc countries seemed to be limited to handshakes, and the East Germans, among others, were not even allowed to visit China as tourists. The Albanians were more than rigid, and when they met with Russians they kept their hands behind their backs and pretended not to see them. Indonesia's relations with China had been broken off after the massacre of communists in the 1960s. They had to travel to and from Pyongyang via Moscow and maintained their supply of food and other essentials from Helsinki. The Africans' attitude towards the Arabs was, to put it mildly,

25

lukewarm, and in fact they were pretty lukewarm to each other too. It was rather hard to follow the internal relations of the Arabs, unstable and sometimes vehement as they were. The relations between the Indians and the Pakistanis went up and down. However, in a country in which there was a sum total of twenty or so English-speaking colleagues, including the Soviet military attachés, on the whole they realized how much they had in common despite everything. There was a general election in Sweden in 1976 and one in India in 1977, and in both countries new governments came into power. My Indian colleague was, in fact, a supporter of Indira Gandhi, but after she resigned he made sure he always stood beside me in all official contexts – we were the only representatives of countries that had changed their governments by way of a democratic process.

The attitude of the resident foreigners to their host country was, throughout, anything but appreciative. Non-communists were openly critical and gladly told anecdotes about bizarre experiences. The East Europeans were not too eager to share their knowledge of the country but were not against making ironic comments in a superior manner and joking about the North Koreans' need to assert themselves. But the Vietnamese ambassador could be more candid. On one occasion, he told us that he had handed out Vietnamese picture postcards to children on the street outside the embassy. Some adult Koreans had then intervened and taken the cards away from the children, slapping them around the head. Another time, he openly commented upon 'how they falsified historical records in this country'. In this way, he indicated that brotherhood on the anti-imperialist front did not exclude critical judgement.

Informal social meetings between the embassies were fairly restricted. Those who came from outside Europe had really very little in common with each other. The only thing that was shared by the East Europeans was that they were dominated by Moscow though their history was, if anything, one of internal strife – Germans, Poles and Czechs were about as keen to mix with each other as were Hungarians and Romanians. The restricted social life was also, to some extent, due to the fact that the North Koreans had, for some reason or other, long persisted in trying to prevent any socializing by summoning embassy officials to the ministry when they knew there was to be some sort of party. Fortunately, this bad behaviour ceased around the time we arrived. It was replaced by an eccentric service philosophy, which could take the form of their delivering a telegram from your home country directly to you at the embassy to which you had been invited for dinner. The authorities kept themselves informed as to where everyone was. The Indian chargé d'affaires, who was a Sikh and wore a fancy turban, used to joke with the North Koreans about his always being shadowed by the security police: it was not necessary because he had no chance to escape notice wherever he happened to go.

I met my colleagues regularly on account of the abundance of official visits at presidential, prime ministerial or foreign ministerial level, visits which played such an important role in North Korean diplomacy. At short notice, sometimes less than an hour (such as on the evening of one Christmas Day in honour of the president of Sao Tomé and Principe), and only in highly exceptional cases as early as the day before, the heads of mission were summoned on both weekdays and Sundays to see an exhibition, to attend a mass meeting or partake in a banquet.

The mass meetings were dreadful arrangements, at which one had to suffer three- to four-hour speeches in Korean with a translation to, say, Albanian and vice versa, and one was continually expected to get up and applaud. The East Europeans seemed to accept the whole procedure without demur, and the Koreans appeared genuinely perplexed by the vociferous protests of the newcomers. The banquets followed a strict ritual: a speech of welcome devoted just as much to their own leader and state as to those of the visitor, a speech of thanks and four song and music items from each of their own and the guest nation's repertoires. The banquet was regularly followed by a return banquet a couple of days later, at which the procedure was repeated. All the heads of mission sat at small tables in order of rank: first ambassadors, then chargés d'affaires, and last trade representatives.

Knowledge of languages was often limited. The Korean host at the table gave a lecture – via the interpreter – about the leader, US imperialism and the situation in South Korea. All attempts at establishing some exchange of ideas with the North Koreans were fruitless. The Cuban ambassador's wife – herself a committed communist – told of the time she had tried to start a normal conversation with her partner at the table, a senior lady official in the North Korean administration. She remarked that she had noticed that there were no burial grounds in Pyongyang, and asked about Korean burial customs. The Korean lady looked at her seriously and replied, 'You understand, here in the Democratic People's Republic of Korea people do not die so much.' The Cuban gave up, and could not even be bothered to reply that in the countries she knew about the mortality rate was 100%, all people died at some stage or other. Like the other guests at the table, all she could do was lose herself in her own thoughts. Fortunately, the banquets usually lasted only a couple of hours and, when the signal was given that it was time to break up, all the guests rushed towards the doors.

The heads of mission were quite often summoned to file past the bier of some deceased party bigwig. At one time the summonses came so thick and fast that the non-communists wondered if there was a political purge going on. The foreigners gathered in a lobby and then walked in file past the deceased, who lay clothed and with make-up in an open coffin. At its foot, his decorations were displayed on a cushion. We then expressed our condolences to the family. On several occasions, one could tell that the facial features had been tidied up, and it was said that the cause of death had been a car accident.

There was no question of meeting North Koreans in private. A party with Koreans as guests was thus, by definition, official. They invited themselves, and also decided who should be invited along. The usual procedure was that the interpreter – really a sort of Trojan horse that had been placed inside the embassy walls – told the ambassador that he was expected to invite some ministry officials responsible for his particular country, and that their drivers were to be given meal coupons for a restaurant. Social behaviour was very hierarchical and stereotyped. Only the most high-ranking guest (or guests, if several had the same rank) and the host made conversation via the interpreter. The others observed a respectful silence. The words of welcome and the vote of thanks, which were directed only at 'friendly relations', were read from a manuscript and ended with toasts to heads of state, guests of honour and to continued friendship. After two and a half hours, the guests trooped out in order of seniority and drove off in a Mercedes, Volvo or Volga, depending upon rank. A couple of days later, the event was reported on the news agency wires.

The North Korean government was actually called the Administrative Council and it was, in effect, a sort of civil service department. All authority lay with the Communist Party, and it was said to have a section for each ministry. Non-communist embassies had contact only with the Administrative Council, and were never admitted to the real governing powers other than on rare meetings with ministers who were presumed to be anchored in the party hierarchy. The embassies of communist countries, however, had access to party functionaries.[a] This led to increased demands upon formal hospitality.

The East German ambassador gleefully related what happened when he had received hints that it might be suitable to invite the Great Leader's wife to the embassy. This had subjected both his own and his embassy's organizational capabilities to a severe test. The invitation could not be written on a card, but had to be in the form of an official letter. The answer came that the invitation was accepted and that a date would be announced two days in advance. The locally appointed interpreters became dreadfully excited. They asked which film the embassy had planned to screen – the embassy had not planned any at all. They also enquired about the content of the cultural programme that the embassy ladies intended to perform – the embassy had not planned on doing that either, but all the wives rapidly started learning Korean songs, which they intended to sing as a choir with the ambassador's wife as soloist. The embassy was informed that the president's wife would be accompanied by an inner circle of ten or so ladies, including a woman general as adjutant. In addition, there would be a group of about twenty lady attendants. Both these groups, the instructions went, were to be served the same food but in different rooms. Further, an unspecified number of security men and drivers, etc. would be present and would need feeding, but they could be given less fancy food.

The East German had become all the more apprehensive, but had no choice but to see it through to the bitter end. He had liaised with his Yugoslav colleague, who had previously passed the test, and who cheered him up by recounting how

a The last East German ambassador to Pyongyang has described the structure of the North Korean Workers' Party, and he claims that a head of department in the Central Committee of the Party was of higher rank than the equivalent government minister; see Maretzki, H., *Kimismus in Nordkorea*, p. 90.

so many people came that the last guests – by implication the lowest ranking – had to eat their food in the lavatories. The Yugoslav's presentation of the expenses had led to some reproachful questions from his administration at home, wondering if he considered himself some sort of people's tribune as he seemed to be feeding a large number of Koreans. And an Arab ambassador could, in turn, describe how on the occasion of a visit by his own president he had hosted a banquet for 280 guests but been presented with a bill for feeding 1,600 people. The Yugoslav used to say that there were no big problems in Pyongyang – but that everything turned into a problem.

Leisure activities were limited, to say the least. We were not permitted to visit cinemas. We had soon seen every circus performance and revolutionary opera. There was no point in going to restaurants because one had to book a table the day before and was allotted a private room; mixing with either other foreigners or the local populace was not allowed. It was, if anything, even lonelier than sitting at home on one's own. The whole atmosphere in Pyongyang was in some way incompatible with the idea of having a pleasant evening out.

The Ministry of Foreign Affairs occasionally arranged film shows for the embassies, but the unabashed and repetitive propaganda content made them unpalatable despite their being well made and often containing breathtakingly beautiful country scenery. Embassy interpreters sat behind each person and explained what was happening on the white screen. We once had to endure a film six hours long – with a brief teabreak – about the Great Leader's visit to Bucharest, Belgrade and Algiers. On other occasions they were mainly stories about the Leader's revolutionary activity during the Japanese occupation. From one of these, I particularly remember a magnificent scene: as the music of the heavens gradually grew to a crescendo, a figure could be seen coming out of the forest, lit up from behind by the rays of the sun which finally formed a halo around the person's head. When we could eventually discern that it was the Leader's mother, all the Koreans present stood up and joined together in a chorus of cheers, while jumping up and down in front of their seats and clapping their hands with their arms stretched up over their heads.

There were few opportunities to go off anywhere because of the restrictions on our freedom of movement. One could travel as far as the town of Nampo on the coast, several dozen kilometres away, where there was a restaurant by the beach. En route was a recreation area beside an artificial lake cum hydro-electric dam, where one could have a picnic and where the larger embassies had informally staked out their own patches. One could visit the house where the Leader's father had once lived. He had evidently been a village teacher, and I had hoped to see a typical village. But it had been demolished and transformed into a park with the house in its centre as a monument. The guide showed us a roofing tile that could be lifted off. Under it, the Leader's father had hidden compromising documents and thus foiled the Japanese police – a scene that could be observed on reproductions in many places.

Now and then, trips were arranged to Panmunjom. In the mid-1970s, seven

Swedish officers were stationed there. Members of the Neutral Nations' Supervisory Commission (NNSC) were in effect the only people who had the right to cross the borderline between the two halves of the nation. The only exception that I know of was the then Swedish ambassador to China, Mr Lennart Petri, who once, in the 1960s, drove in his own car from Seoul to Panmunjom and then surprised everybody by quite simply crossing the line and continuing on to Beijing. On my visits I was thus unable to go across to my countrymen who lived south of the line; instead we had to meet next to the negotiations barracks. Visits by the East European officers to the South were greatly restricted on account of North Korean aversion to the idea, while Swedes and Swiss were happy to accept journeys in the North. The work of the NNSC consisted largely in simply being present during discussions between the parties, at which they usually dealt with or, more accurately, 'chewed over' violations of the armistice agreement. In 1976, the number of incidents that had occurred since the signing of the armistice in 1953 was given as 180,000 – almost one an hour.

It was remarkable that trips to Panmunjom formed part of the propaganda routines of both the northern and the southern sides. Journeys by car were always tiring, as the cement roads were so bumpy that it took more than three hours to cover the 200 kilometres. (When Volvo was planning its delivery of motor cars, it had offered to install firmer springs, but this had been indignantly rejected by the buyers with reference to their modern roads; by local standards they may well have been epoch-making and that was the frame of reference of the buyers.) Depending on the season, for kilometre upon kilometre, half of the width of the road surface could be covered with grain spread out to dry. It did not really matter, because there was so little traffic.

We travelled in a caravan, with national flags on the cars, to Kaesong, where the flags were removed and the car licence plates unscrewed. Why this was done nobody could understand, as our visit was so impossible to keep secret that our countrymen in Panmunjom had heard about it on Seoul Radio before we had even reached them. We passed the last border outpost, where we stopped to greet the guards. We walked along the row and shook hands with the select, elite soldiers who demonstrated their irrepressible toughness by grasping our hands so hard that all the ladies cried out and for the rest of the day were to be seen massaging their right hands – I had learnt a trick after innumerable welcome ceremonies and that was to fold the joint of the little finger inside the other fingers. We then crossed the 'bridge of no return' – but from the wrong side, so to speak – and passed the northernmost UN outpost, where US soldiers evidently counted how many people passed. We continued up a slope to the North side's large pavilion. If you went out on to the balcony and looked down at the conference barracks, you were immediately photographed by the zealous US military police. We then went down among the buildings to meet the Swedish officers. Our North Korean companions carefully saw to it that we did not transgress the demarcation line by many metres; it went right through the middle of the buildings and inside the conference room it was marked by a loudspeaker cable that ran straight across the negotiating table. We understood why we were being supervised when one of the Swedes asked if we had seen the exhibition behind the barracks that the South had arranged and which contained material that had been taken from captured infiltrators from the North. Our minders were eager for us not to see this. It was of little import, as it was presumably very similar to the exhibition we had just seen a few kilometres to the north, containing items from captured infiltrators from the South.

On our car journeys, we passed a large town and a number of villages. The town, Sariwon, was well planned and tidy, built in the same style as Pyongyang. All the villages consisted of traditional buildings and did not seem to be particularly affluent. They were, however, without exception, electrified, and one could see agricultural machines everywhere. Nevertheless, there were a considerable number of ox-carts. There were few men to be seen, and no old men at all. On the other hand, there were many old women, often carrying heavy loads. The older ones wore traditional dress, while the younger ones had Western-style clothes. There were lots of children everywhere and they bowed like clasp-knives when the black cars passed by. A woman junior officer at the head of her marching platoon saluted us. A decidedly picturesque element was made up of women sailors in their sailor dresses. There were many road blocks at which all traffic was checked and, in general, the police and military were all over the place. They did not seem to be overworked – on one occasion a whole lorry-load of police officers were picking flowers by the roadside.

On our own initiative, we once approached the Foreign Ministry to ask if we could visit industries or farms. After some time, we were informed that a couple of days later we would be welcome at a tractor factory and a farm cooperative. The tractor factory lay just outside the capital, and one morning off we went. As soon as we arrived, we instinctively felt there was something not quite right. We stopped by a large open doorway and were led in to spacious workshop premises, where we were shown round by a junior director. Many tractors were under production. But there was no activity at all. There was not a single worker to be seen. Had the factory been evacuated on account of our visit?

The farm cooperative was even weirder. On the way there we could see a few workers on the flooded ricefields working homemade planting machines, which looked like moped tricycles, steered by a man and with women wading behind feeding the rice plants into the machine. We got out of the cars in a yard with a Party office, dining room and health and child care unit. Beside this was a residential block with traditional houses in a network of parallel small streets. We walked in and had a look around. There was not a soul anywhere. The narrow streets had been swept clean and smartened up, and on one of them lay a somewhat carelessly abandoned child's tricycle. It seemed totally out of place in the simple village, as if it had been placed there by a visiting film director as a prop.

We were taken to the child care unit, which was clean and tidy and properly maintained, and there we met the only adult we saw, a woman who looked after the children. In a large nursery room, babies were having their morning sleep in small cots placed in long rows. They were all sleeping equally peacefully, they all seemed to be exactly the same size, they all looked equally contented and had the same rosy cheeks. I pinched my arm and wondered if I was dreaming or if there were dolls lying in the cots. Then, thank God, one of the dolls moved a fraction and I understood that I was in this world after all. Had all the children been given sleeping pills so that they would behave properly? The children had make-up on to honour the fine guests, there was no doubt about that.

But we had a better time when the diplomatic corps was invited to a harvest celebration at another cooperative. The harvest had been stacked up into an impressive mound, which was decorated with enormous straw effigies. There were speeches and a theatre and dance performance by ethereal girl dancers from the city. A large buffet table had been laden with food and we could mingle with each other around that. This was followed by dancing in a ring and folk dances in which all the old women in the cooperative delighted in taking hold of foreigners and swirling off with us in to the whirls of the dance – this was one of the rare spontaneous moments I experienced in the country. Even the girls danced with us, and what a difference between their soft hands and the callused palms of the working women.

5

THE SONG OF PARADISE
A musical about the social order

In an elevated part of the centre of Pyongyang myriads of workers were busy with an enormous building project for several years. By and by, shining façades with gigantic colourful mosaics could be seen, and a large number of groups of sculptures and aquatic installations behind a high fence of wrought iron. The Mansudae Theatre was meant to have been completed in time for the Communist Party's thirtieth jubilee in 1975. But they did not manage that, and the theatre could not be opened until the beginning of 1977.

One arrived via arched openings into an outer courtyard, and then entered a large marble hall in which innumerable, enormous chandeliers illuminated the mosaics and the aquatic decorations. On one side lay a large stairwell that extended right up to the top of the building. The rear wall was covered with illustrations from the Diamond Mountains with a waterfall that emptied into an artificial lake, accompanied by sounds that were meant to be the noise of the waterfall. Against this background, the stairs branched out above the water surface, covered with thick carpets and with the underside lit up by lamps of all colours. There were escalators at the side. Upstairs were large galleries and reception rooms for dignitaries of varying status. The finest rooms had such thick carpets that it was difficult to walk on them without losing one's balance – ladies with high heels had to be supported. On all sides were the most luxurious wall coverings and chandeliers and more decorative detail than it was possible to take in.

A guided tour of the building gave plentiful cause for astonishment, not least as the North Koreans had not shied away from any expense for importing the luxuries mentioned above, despite the fact that the country was wrestling with serious balance of payments problems and a galloping foreign debt. Down in the basement we were shown a gigantic electricity substation and beside that an equally enormous control centre for temperature and humidity, from which the conditions in every single room could be adjusted. Via a central clock, the time on all 300 clocks in the building could be changed.

One floor consisted solely of a complete TV studio and broadcasting station – also used to monitor the immediate surroundings. Backstage and in the wings, we were given a demonstration of the most modern machinery with every finesse imaginable. Along the whole length of the rear of the theatre auditorium was a built-in control room for stage effects, with electronic manoeuvring panels on both the back wall and all along the front under the windows facing out onto the auditorium and stage, perhaps dozens of metres of them in all. This room also contained the only blemish, for stuck away in a corner was a washbasin in a cupboard obviously put together by a local joiner. All the electrical equipment had Japanese production labels. Behind and above the stage were the actors' dressing rooms with the same high standards of comfort and technical accessories as elsewhere in the building. Every dressing room that we were shown had its own spacious bathroom – a marble dream in shades of pastel.

After we had been on the tour, our surprise was all the greater when we took our seats in the auditorium. Certainly, the carpets here were also deep enough to trip over, the lighting systems expensive and the knee-room for the seated audience was more than generous. But the entrance doors were narrow, and the fittings did not give quite the same sumptuous impression. Perhaps the luxury was reserved for the six exclusive private boxes high up at the rear of the auditorium. But, above all, it was the relatively small size that was surprising – the auditorium could seat 500 spectators at the most.

It was a court theatre.

At the inauguration they performed *The Song of Paradise* and I shall describe it here as it was a typical example of how North Korean indoctrination and propaganda functioned in practice. Theatrical productions of this type were enacted by a permanent ensemble that toured countrywide and formed an essential part of the cultural politics. The audience did not seem to consist of culturally interested 'ordinary people', but it was more of a combined reward and indoctrination for specially invited Party cadres and successful teams of workers. Such performances were also recorded for TV and thus could reach out to a large public. Tickets could not be purchased in the normal manner, and foreigners had to book seats through their appointed interpreters.

The word 'paradise' had been introduced by the authorities and was the generally accepted name for North Korea under the existing regime. The standard revolutionary operas usually recounted heroic episodes in the class struggle and the battle for freedom. By contrast, the new work was a musical with song and dance numbers interspersed with ordinary dialogue that moved the action along. And the story was simple: a young woman journalist travels around visiting farming cooperatives, fishing villages, tourist attractions, steelworks and so on, in order to write a series of articles under the title 'The Song of Paradise', which would illustrate the happiness and welfare of the people guided by the Great Leader. On her travels, she meets some people who decide to investigate the fate of a little girl, the daughter of a fallen war hero who disappeared in the Korean war. The denouement reveals that the journalist herself is the lost daughter.

During the course of the performance, a description of the action in English and French and translations of the song lyrics were projected on to screens beside the stage, making it easy to follow the plot. The opening scene showed a public holiday in Pyongyang with fireworks and citizens who (according to the French screen guide), intoxicated with joy, sing the praises of the socialist paradise on Earth that has been created by Korea's Great Leader. The name of the song was 'My Juche Country'.

The first act continued in the capital city where young women workers danced in a park. The heroine and her adoptive mother sang 'Under the Fatherly Leader's Loving Care' as a declaration of gratitude to the Leader for having helped the orphaned girl to grow up and train as a journalist. The heroine was going to set off on a journey to do a reportage accompanied by a photographer, and it should be noted here that, in puritanical Korea, there was no question of any romance between these young people who were going to cross and recross the country together. The act ended with a duet, 'We Shall Boast of Our Paradise Before the Whole World'.

The second act took place on an apple orchard farm, which was the first station on the reportage journey. The heroine sang the praises of the Great Leader, who sent apples to the children during the anti-Japanese guerilla war. The assistant director showed them the orchards and the pollination process, and in the song 'Let Us Spread the Pollen of Love' the Great Leader, who sent plant cuttings to the farm from the war front, was praised. The photographer found a notebook that belonged to a war hero who was killed in action and he showed it to the assistant director, who was a comrade-in-arms of the fallen hero. The scene then changed to a camp at the front where the hero was reading his own poems in honour of the Leader to his fellow soldiers, and his heroic death was hinted at. The assistant director and the photographer agreed to trace the hero's long-lost daughter.

In the third act, a fishing village was shown where the deep-sea fishermen were returning from the ocean. Girls and fishermen performed a dance about their happy lives. To the tune of a romantic love song from a well-known Viennese operetta, they sang 'Hoist the Flag for a Rich Catch'. The fishermen were moved to tears on hearing that the Leader had given them and their families a holiday in the Diamond mountains, and a male choir sang 'His Love is Deeper Than the Deepest Ocean'. It was in this village that the hero's daughter had been born and we found out that she was rescued by a soldier.

The fourth act took place in the Diamond Mountains, which, for good effect, had been staged with a multitude of spring flowers against a forest of strong autumn colours. While the young ones danced, the older people sang the praises of the blessed socialist system – a song to honour the children's nurseries that look after one and all from birth, the eleven-year school system and the health service, which saw to it that people were still perky when they were sixty years old. Here, the song had a genuine ring to it and it made a fair point, too, because the North Koreans had undeniably been cared for by a health service that had been non-existent a few decades earlier.

In the fifth act, our heroine had reached Mount Paektusan, which has been Korea's holy mountain since days of yore and had therefore also been allocated a role in revolutionary contexts. The stage setting showed a famous volcanic lake with mists that come and go all the time. In the foreground was a forest with an exhibition of a partisan camp with tents, machine guns in glass cases and so on, all authentic down to the detail of the woman guide with her pointer. Songs were sung about how they vanquished the Japanese and liberated the country and their thoughts reached out to the Leader's birthplace (with a change of scenery). The names of the songs were 'Every Tree and Every Flower Beloved' and 'Nostalgia'.

The sixth act was set in a textile factory. The producers had evidently encountered difficulties when trying to recreate a factory environment with a romantically cheerful staging. The background picture showed fancy lengths of cloth. The dancing girls wore factory clothes but the impression was rather syrupy. As in every act, they sang of the immeasurable joy of the people in Korea's socialist paradise. We discovered that the soldier who saved the hero's daughter now worked in a steel mill.

The backdrop to the seventh act showed a photograph of a steel works belching out smoke and dust – what would in other countries have been a picture of an environmental disaster was then a not uncommon propaganda image indicating that their society had become modern and technologically developed. The picture projected was gradually transformed into a glowing ingot. The dance troupe was delightful with their orange-yellow ingot-coloured outfits, and the steel workers had clean white clothes. Against a background of flaming ingots and overhead travelling cranes, and accompanied by march music, the steel workers sang of their pride at being the vanguard of the country with the blessing of the Leader, and about the Chollima movement (Chollima is a Korean winged horse and the symbol of increased production), and of the road to communism through the revolutions of technology, ideology and culture. The act ended with an antiphon, with verses alternating between the workers and the intellectuals about the economic crisis of the world from which their own country had been spared. It was here that the former soldier who saved the hero's daughter worked, and he told how he handed over the girl to a village in the country that is now a cooperative.

The eighth act took place in that same cooperative, where the peasants, under the care of the fatherly Leader, had yet again reaped a record harvest. The harvest celebrations were in full swing, with everyone dancing and singing on the theme 'The Leader's Theses on Socialist Agriculture Bear Rich Fruit'. An old man told the company that his share that year was as much as 10,000 won (for comparison our interpreter, a qualified embassy employee, had an annual salary of less than 3,000 won) and he did not know what he was going to do with the money as he already had everything – a house, food, a TV set, etc. The former soldier met the heroine's adoptive mother to whom he had once handed over the child, and the journalist was identified as the fallen hero's daughter. The North Koreans had difficulties in depicting feelings between ordinary people. When the rescuer and the girl now met after a quarter of a century, they heartily shook hands with each other and exclaimed 'Comrade journalist!' and 'Comrade shop-manager!' respectively. The heroine was moved to tears on hearing that the Leader had instructed that she was to receive her fallen father's medal for heroism. A solo followed: 'His Deep Love Moves Me to Tears'. The men dried the corners of their eyes and the women cried with emotion as they sang the praises of the Leader. They then decided to travel to Pyongyang where the Leader lives.

The finale was set in Pyongyang where the people were still dancing and praising their good fortune. The heroine swore to be eternally loyal to the Great Leader, to whom the people have a debt of gratitude because he had created the *Juche* paradise in which everybody lives in honour and fortune. Facing towards the backdrop, where an image of the sun (a symbol for the Leader) had now been projected, the whole ensemble joined in the chorus: 'We Shall Remain Faithful to the Great Leader'.

What made the greatest impression on the foreign spectators, regardless of which part of the world they came from or what sort of society they represented, was the fantastic proportions of the cult of the Leader. Veterans had learned to try to replace their spontaneous distaste for this with a curiosity as to how many variations it was possible to discover on the themes of veneration, gratitude and socialist fortune. In that way it was also easier to appreciate the aesthetic value of the performances, and the music and decorative beauty.

It was also notable that the artistic means of expression were not founded on indigenous traditions, but had entirely embraced foreign forms of expression. This could lead to decidedly comical effects, such as coming across well-known tunes from romantic operettas in songs devoted to the fishing industry or the Leader's theses on socialist agriculture. But what was the reason behind the fact that their own cultural heritage was conspicuous by its virtual absence? In Chapter 19, entitled 'Confucianism and communism', I attempt to describe the ingredients of the North Korean ideology: the local cultural heritage lives on in attitudes and in the world of the unconscious, whereas communism, a theoretical construction of Western European provenance imported via the Soviet Union, made its mark on the establishment of the new society. A part of this was the creation of a new popular culture as a means of presenting the new political message, and in that context films, as well as revolutionary operas, had an important role to play. As part of modernization, not only the ideological but also the artistic means of expression were to be imported. As an illustrative example, I could mention that in the musical described above some of the young women wore long trousers of a Western cut, something that nobody then had ever seen a North Korean woman wear in real life – not counting the simple working clothes of peasant women and factory workers. Art and culture were thus used to influence the people to abandon traditions and embrace things new.

A couple of months later, it was time to inaugurate the new Presidential Palace. The great building site beyond the university on the outskirts of the city had long been something of an attraction as it was on such a colossal scale and also evidently brought with it a reworking of the landscape. For a couple of years, myriads of workers were kept busy there in a manner that reminded one of the imaginative illustrations of the building of the Egyptian pyramids. This palace had not been sited in Pyongyang's 'forbidden city', the walled and strictly guarded part of the city where the country's highest organ and the residences of the *nomenklatura* were situated. One day, they suddenly closed off the eight-lane avenue – Pyongyang's widest and smoothest street – that led past the building site and it was evident that the head of state was about to move in. For the sake of the traffic, buildings had been demolished and a rather bumpy parallel street built about a kilometre further away.

The security regulations concerning visits to the palace were rigorous. It was not sufficient that several kilometres of the wide road had been closed off and that access roads were guarded. Pakistan's ambassador, who had been received for an audience there, told of how he had first been obliged to travel to the Foreign Ministry, and there change to another car that had permission to drive right up to the palace. On the occasion of a state visit by Gabon's President Bongo, the customary banquet was arranged in the new palace. The heads of mission, who had been invited, had to gather almost an hour beforehand at the ministry to go on from there in an escorted column to the palace. As was the usual practice, the invitations had been issued as late as the same morning, and at the same time we were ordered to journey immediately out to the welcome ceremony at the airport, where we had to wait five hours.

An impressive number of police and, above all, soldiers in dress uniform guarded the entrance. We drove on to a bridge across a man-made, decorative, water-filled moat and through a newly planted grove of pine trees, where each individual tree was guyed to the ground with ropes. Outside the three-metre-high, wrought iron railings, one could see, at intervals of 100 metres, the backs of armoured guard posts. We drove up on to an elevation and stopped in front of the first and lesser of two buildings, the banqueting hall. We walked up wide steps flanked by saluting officers and entered an outer hall which opened up into a gigantic rotunda with marble columns ten metres high. The floor and walls were also surfaced in marble. The ceilings were covered in stucco decorations. The centre of the hall was taken up with a large fountain in which ornamental jets of water rose and fell in a complicated computer-controlled programme, while different coloured lamps in the water were turned on and off. Dozens of chandeliers, of the type seen in opera houses, lit up the hall. There were a number of aquaria along the walls. We were led to the side into a waiting room with enormous wooden doors, which had been unaesthetically situated far too close to the corner of the square room. In the usual manner, large armchairs were lined up along the walls, but they were by no means sufficient for the number of guests. Looking out through the windows one could see the actual palace some dozens of metres away. In between, armed soldiers stood on guard.

After the long wait that seemed to be unavoidable in all North Korean contexts, we were invited into the banqueting hall. It was on the upper floor, which was reached by a moving staircase. If one looked out from the upper part of the escalator down to the bottom floor, people standing beside the columns looked like pygmies. The banqueting hall was huge, with a stage along one of the short sides and a winter garden down the other. About fifty tables, with room for ten guests each, were spread out in the hall. The tables and chairs were of a decidedly simple construction, but everything else was expensive. There were nine sculpted double doors along each long wall and ten enormous glass chandeliers, each one with eight smaller ones around it – every group must have contained about a hundred lamps. In addition, there were twenty-two small chandeliers between the big ones, as well as dozens of double-bracket lamps on the walls. The ceilings and walls were filled with stucco ornamentation of Hellenic influence. In a gallery an invisible orchestra was playing.

The cost must have been considerable, not least on account of the enormous proportion of imported goods for decoration and functional purposes. After having seen the Mansudae Theatre, mentioned above, we knew what was behind the scenes in the form of electricity substations, control rooms for temperature and humidity, internal and external TV monitoring, etc. The expense must have been on such a scale that it clearly inhibited the country's ability to import investment goods – and pay outstanding debts. The labour requirements must have been equally immoderate. A leader cult, North Korean style, has its own inherent dynamics, which give priority to everything concerned with the leader. Far from daring to try to prevent extravagance, everybody feels forced to attempt to outdo the others when it comes to manifestations of loyalty.

6

JUCHE IDEOLOGY

Among all the countries that acquired independence after the Second World War, North Korea was one of those that had achieved the most with regard to industrialization. While the southern half of the Korean peninsula is well suited to agriculture, the northern half is more barren but with rich mineral deposits. During the Japanese occupation, mining activities and industrialization had been launched on a considerable scale, and this had naturally been concentrated in the northern part. Then, during the Korean war, the country was devastated. Armaments factories and other production went literally underground and was, to a large extent, sited in old mines.

After the war reconstruction was started at a forced rate, for which the communist system was well suited. From the first, the country was incorporated ideologically into the circle of communist countries, but economically it was only integrated to a limited degree. The North Koreans had refused to adopt the role of suppliers of raw material in COMECON's scheme of things; rather they were keen to create an all-round industrial and trading base of their own. The regime in Pyongyang thus started to develop indigenous industry and achieved amazing results in a short time. We were often told charming stories about their successes. One of them described how they had been refused a licence to build Soviet tractors, so they decided to set up a tractor factory without any help. Their methods were simple: take it to bits and copy it. After a couple of months, a prototype had been produced – but it only went backwards! They soon solved that problem, however, and since then have been self-sufficient as regards tractors.

They continued in the same spirit, and eventually produced everything from sewing thread to electric locomotives and lorries. The lorries were clearly copies of the US 'Diamond T' truck, which was even seen in Sweden in the late 1930s, and which was delivered to the Soviet Union in vast numbers during the Second World War. These lorries were everywhere, and many were richly endowed with the red stars on the door, which were awarded for every 10,000 kilometres travelled. With barely concealed pride, the interpreter said that they had turned out to be much more reliable than the new Romanian lorries that had recently been imported. The successes were manifest, and increased their appetite. Advanced technology was best purchased in the West. Why, then, import old-fashioned equipment from the communist countries, which were also seen as having exploited their existing monopoly position by charging excessive prices for their products and paying for North Korean products at less than world market prices? So, in the early 1970s, North Korea embarked upon its massive campaign of purchasing industrial equipment in Western Europe and Japan, in the firm conviction that it could rapidly master the technology.

It was tempting to come to the conclusion that North Korea, within the COMECON sphere, had been the same 'success story' as South Korea was about to become in the Organization for Economic Cooperation and Development (OECD) fold. It had become industrialized thanks to its own efforts, and it was also self-sufficient on the agricultural front. The world press reported student demonstrations and labour riots in South Korea, but such things never occurred in the North. For many developing countries – not least those with anti-Western leanings – North Korea ought thus to be seen as an interesting model and one worthy of imitation. As mentioned above, the propaganda phrase 'the freedom of the free world consists of the freedom to starve' was current at the time. The implication was that the state socialist system evidently seemed to provide a more advantageous development alternative than the path of the market economy. While striving to extend its contacts outside the Eastern bloc, it was natural for North Korea to make use of all these circumstances.

The indisputable successes had filled the North Koreans with a pride that exceeded the bounds of hubris and, in combination with an almost total ignorance of the outside world, resulted in a good degree of superciliousness. In the context of this overestimation of their own abilities, a contributing factor was the unrestrained cult of the leader who had been at the forefront of their industrialization. In the terminology of the time, he was one of the greatest figures that mankind had ever produced. The image of this immeasurably wise leader must thus necessarily include the notion that he was a giant, even as a creator of ideology, whose ideas were becoming increasingly appreciated the world over and, in particular, had caught the imagination of peoples who, like themselves, had shaken off the yoke of colonialism. Consequently, they decided to launch Kim Il Sung's *Juche* ideology as Marxism–Leninism for the developing countries of the time.

Juche ideology meant, quite simply, that a developing country must rely on its own resources in its development. The North Koreans did not strive to spread the dogma to other socialist countries; rather, they used it as bait for the developing countries. No study group was formed anywhere in Africa to read Kim's works, but they were described in detail in the North Korean media, not least in the *Pyongyang Times*, which was published in English. The groups were evidently legion, but they seemed to have a highly marginal influence, if any. To the extent that the North Korean example caught the interest of developing countries at all, it was most likely because North Korea was a practical example of an alternative rapid development process. Its non-capitalist character probably increased its powers of attraction, as did the emphasis upon independence vis-à-vis the great powers. The ideology in itself may have been of particular interest to left-wing extremists, but it was the concrete achievements that, in general, would have carried more weight.

The fact that *Juche* ideology was particularly aimed at the developing countries should not hide the fact that it claimed to be Marxism–Leninism, and indeed that Marxism should be studied with *Juche* as the starting point. The *Juche* ideology was the very basis of Kim Il Sung's efforts to stand out as a prominent ideologist. It was thus logical that he emphasized that not only ideological but also other scientific and theoretical problems must be solved with recourse to *Juche* ideology. Above all, he was against a dogmatic approach, by which he meant a rigid adherence to the views of the 'classics', or even worse, allowing oneself to be influenced to an unacceptable degree by the opinions of others, adopting an attitude of servility vis-à-vis the great powers. By this, Kim meant that the *Juche* ideology was a development of Marxism–Leninism that was of particular relevance to developing countries. The North Korean example showed that it was possible to skip the capitalist stage and go directly from feudalism to socialism. For orthodox European communists, of course, this must have seemed like a foolish hotchpotch of heresy, hubris and ignorance. For representatives of developing countries, educated in Eastern Europe or the Soviet Union, the dividing lines must have been clear.

A necessary condition for Kim Il Sung's behaviour, as both an independent ideologist and a participant in foreign as well as trade politics, was, of course, the antagonism between Moscow and Beijing. On account of this, Moscow was deprived of its decisive influence in Pyongyang, while Beijing adopted a tolerant attitude as long as North Korea's actions did not conflict with Chinese interests. Kim's efforts to release his country from its powerful neighbours' superior influence were successful. 'Our epoch is the epoch of independence', he often said, and this gained spontaneous sympathy and respect in the fold of developing countries, which were at the same time also impressed by the rapid industrialization. But this did not come to mean that *Juche* ideology won support in any broader sense. This was because even a preliminary study of a society steered by *Juche* ideology gave cause to question the degree to which it could serve as a model. It was all too clearly a product of highly specific circumstances. The geographical location (a peninsula with superpowers as neighbours in the north, and totally blocked off in the south), the political situation (a divided nation with a life and death struggle to demonstrate the superiority of each side's system), the human material with its ideological heritage (disciplined, hard-working and for over a thousand years indoctrinated with the hierarchic ideals of Confucianism): all of these were factors that were not known in the same combination anywhere else.

The result could be observed in a thoroughly disciplined, indeed militarized, society in which the citizens were as good as totally relieved of their leisure time and aspects of the distribution of wealth had undoubtedly been taken into consideration in as far as there were no beggars or starving people to be seen, but in which the governing elite lived in its own world and did so in perhaps even more luxury than in other countries in which leader worship and veneration for one's superiors had acquired suffocating proportions. In short, it was a society in which the degree of personal and intellectual freedom had sunk to one of the lowest levels ever reached anywhere, and not least in which the people's self-estimation and attitude of superiority led to their expectant visitors actually finding them condescending and offensive.

When North Korea celebrated the achievement of launching a ship of 20,000 tonnes, it was impossible not to draw a parallel with South Korea, which was in the process of bankrupting Western shipyards by launching ships in the 200,000-tonne class. North Korea was confronted daily with its difficulties in paying its foreign debts, and the East European diplomats claimed that food production in the country was only sufficient for twenty-five daily rations a month. The writing was on the wall, although at the time it could only be seen from up close. Already, by the mid-1970s, there were signs that the race between the economic systems of North and South Korea was about to be won by the South.

Although the target group for the export of *Juche* ideology, i.e. the leaders of the developing countries, might at first spontaneously exhibit a positive reaction, this would quickly be replaced by one of scepticism, which, in turn, became negativism when they found themselves at the receiving end of North Korean criticism. Visitors, Africans in particular, often did not even bother to hide their pronouncedly negative reactions. It was hardly surprising if they concluded that not only was it not possible for them to reproduce the North Korean example, they did not want to follow it, period. So *Juche* ideology never won any international following, with some insignificant exceptions such as verbal support from the heads of state of Benin and Madagascar, and the opening of an Ethiopian Embassy in Pyongyang during Mengistu's years in power. One reason was, without doubt, that the ideology did not emanate from any important centre of power, nor was it associated with material advantage – a few North Korean patrol boats or ship-loads of cement were little match for what Washington or Moscow had to offer.

Of greater import, however, were the repeated experiences of North Korea's imperfect reliability as a working partner. Colleagues from Zaire could tell of North Korean military instructors serving on their side of the frontier who suddenly appeared on the other side of the border serving the Angolans and carrying new passports – whereupon military cooperation was cut short. Syria and Egypt had, now and then, broken off relations with each other, but their embassy officials in Pyongyang were personal friends and could testify that they had both – separately – been assured of complete support on the part of Pyongyang in their conflict with each other.

At the conference of non-aligned states in Colombo in 1976, the North Koreans succeeded in offending and alienating many countries by an importunate and unreasonable attempt at forcing the other participants to accept the historic importance of the Korea question and support North Korea at the imminent UN discussion. An Algerian who had taken part in a bilateral advisory group prior to the UN discussion testified to it being like negotiating with Martians! Nor was Korea's reputation in the Third World improved by the smuggling scandal that occurred in the same year in the Nordic countries, and which is described in this book in Chapter 10.

Above all, developing countries demanded to be treated as equals in their bilateral relations, and their own self-confidence led them to reject totally any idea of subordinating themselves to a self-appointed and obviously megalomaniac chief ideologist on the other side of the earth. They considered that self-confidence, *Juche*, self-reliance – call it what one may – was an invaluable resource, but that it could not replace international cooperation. Or, in the words of the Kenyan minister Tom Mboya some years earlier at a Pan-African conference that threatened to degenerate into an incantatory rite upon the theme of self-reliance, 'I accept the slogan of self-reliance. The man in the bush has always been self-reliant and that is the reason why he is still in the bush.'

A quarter of a century later, we have the final results. The *Juche* ideology led the North Korean people to starvation and destitution.

7

A MEETING OF THE PARLIAMENT

The North Korean parliament – the Supreme People's Assembly (SPA) – conducted sessions twice a year, usually for three days at a time. The Fifth Assembly's seventh session took place on 26–29 April 1977, and foreign embassy personnel were allowed to observe most of the plenary meetings.

The SPA met in what appeared to be a theatre auditorium in the closed area of Pyongyang. In the middle of the stage sat the head of state at a table of his own. Behind, and on each side of, him were the thirty-three members of the SPA's Standing Committee. These were seen to include both vice-presidents and the Administrative Council's premier and deputy premiers. Of the thirty-three, five were generals and one was a woman – the head of state's wife. The three Assembly Speakers, one of whom was also a woman, sat at a smaller table beside the podium. In the auditorium, the Assembly members were seated at the front – 475 of 529 were present, and I estimated the military element to be about one-quarter. Behind these were several thousand guests from all parts of the country, as well as the diplomatic corps. Simultaneous interpretation into Chinese, Russian, English, French and Spanish had been arranged. The SPA could only be called a legislative assembly in the purely formal sense. The main purpose of the members' present was presumably to spread knowledge of the stipulated policies and the wishes of the head of state after they had returned home. This made its mark on the assembled gathering.

Shortly after the auditorium had filled, the head of state entered the stage. A vociferous ovation and loud applause erupted, and this did not end until the head of state gave the final sign for it to stop. Not until he had taken his seat did the rest of the dignitaries enter. The Assembly Speaker opened the session and even in his first sentence mentioned the reunification issue. This was followed by a report on the latest successes both within the country and abroad, with continual reference to the leadership of the head of state. Then a committee chairman was given the floor, and he announced the two items on the agenda, namely the previous and the present years' budgets and land legislation.

The Finance Minister read a detailed report concerning successful branch results, the *Juche* spirit, the struggle against imperialism, reunification and the leadership of the head of state. Regarding the financial accounts for 1976, it was reported that income had amounted to 10.6 billion won (about a third as much in US$), which was 8% higher than the previous year and 0.8% above the plan; expenditure had amounted to 12.3 billion won, an increase of just over 8%, but 1.5% less than planned. He also dealt with local budgets, which had increased by 10% and given a surplus of 3 billion won to the national budget. At the same time, there were, however, administrative districts that had required state subsidies. The year 1977 was declared a 'period of readjustment' before the launching of a new seven-year plan – which a critic might well interpret as meaning that the existing plan was, in fact, being extended by one year – and budgeted income was estimated at 13.7 and expenditure at 13.8 billion won. It was particularly emphasized that the mining sector must achieve a good result in relation to the processing industry, and that the transport sector and food production must be given more attention, as must the technical training of workers. Furthermore, the automation of industry should be speeded up, there must be a more economic use of energy resources and raw materials, and the utilization of capacity must be improved.

It was then the turn of the chairman of the Budget Committee, and his report was almost identical in content. One could perhaps note here tendencies to the occasional carefully worded critical formulation. The first sitting drew to a close with the Assembly Speaker informing the auditorium that all questions and comments concerning the agenda should be submitted in written form. There was no real debate about the budget. Those who spoke usually started by moving that the budget be approved – but many of them forgot to do so. The speeches were entirely about experiences from the speakers' own workplaces. The members who addressed the gathering gave an instructive picture of assembly members' leading positions in society. First was the Minister for Heavy Industry, followed by a deputy regional chairman, a woman head of department at a sugar factory, a head of a section in a machine factory, a woman chairman in an agricultural cooperative, the representative of the Koreans in Japan, a director of a coal mine, another chairman of a cooperative, a chairman of a regional administrative committee, a deputy director in a mining industry, a brigade chief/locomotive driver, a woman director of a teacher-training college, a chairman of a province committee, a fishery director and a woman head of department in a textile factory.

As the speakers churned out their decidedly similar speeches, the message of the year became all the more apparent: Apply innovation in order to increase production and reduce the wear and tear on machinery, economize on raw materials and energy consumption, improve financial management, deliver larger surpluses to the state and concentrate more effort upon local industries. By 'local industries' were meant those that did not require any budget resources, which in reality must have meant that they were not a part of the plan – and if they were to be given priority, it must in the eyes of an outsider mean that this should be at the sacrifice of the plan. There were innumerable references to how the speakers, at their own workplaces, had succeeded with these tasks on account of the Fatherly Leader having inspired them on a visit, through the means of telephone instructions or through his written works. Such references gave regular cause for sustained applause.

The chairman of a regional administrative committee, mentioned previously, had hardly started giving his speech emphasizing the importance of local industry, when he was interrupted by a powerful humming noise in the loudspeaker. Kim Il Sung himself began to speak: 'Everyone must follow the example of this region! It is the best region. There are great benefits to be had by allowing local industry to raise the living standards and give their surplus to the public treasury.' He named regions that ought to better themselves, and went on, 'Large industries should help local industry with both money and surplus material! This region is also best at saving coal. You are using too much coal so that there is not enough for the power stations. You must overfulfil the plan targets! What we lack most, compared with other countries, are services for the people. Where only water is served, you should serve fruit juice too! One thing you can do is produce mineral water. Do not wait for orders from above! Make decisions locally! Mobilize the trade unions! You are not doing so now.'

He held an interrogation with representatives of the provinces, one by one, questioning them about the production of mineral water: 'What? You only have one solitary factory? You all should also manufacture rice from maize! [i.e. press maize flour into rice-like grains]. Then the country could get another 90,000 tonnes of cooking oil into the bargain. How many hectares do you need to increase the production of soya beans? We need 400,000 hectares of new land. Now we are wasting maize by feeding it to pigs and such! The northern Hamhung province has everything, but there are shortages of most things there because you work badly. You must improve! You must give more to the people! There is plenty of fish on the west coast. But you have not organized the catch properly. You only catch large fish, not small ones. Where is the Minister of Fishing Industry? What sort of fish do they like in the northern Hamhung province?'

The minister stood up in his row like a miserable schoolboy, and mumbled an inaudible reply. 'What?' Kim Il Sung retorted, 'But there aren't any left! Ha ha ha!' The entire auditorium cautiously laughed along with him. He continued, 'The transport losses of fish are enormous. Fishing village X is best. They are old soldiers. But you must put engines in your boats so that you can go further out to sea! Now it can take four days to the fishing grounds, and four back again. Put a tractor engine in the boats, that's easy! You must unload quicker and better so that the fish reaches the town population earlier! You have no social spirit. The wives of workers should be mobilized to process fish! Then you can earn more too. These issues must be discussed in the committee meetings this afternoon!' The speaker was then allowed to continue his address, which mainly concerned the solicitude of the Fatherly Leader, the wretched state of affairs in South Korea and the necessity of reunification.

Following this 'discussion', it was time to approve the budget. The Assembly Speaker asked for comments. There were none. Thereupon, the chairman of the Budget Committee read the proposal to approve the financial accounts of 1976 and the budget for 1977. These consisted of richly detailed texts with ideological arguments and reports as regards both results and targets. The components of the budget were gone through at such a speed that it was difficult to follow, particularly so as the principles were unfamiliar – they seemed to have different sorts of accounts for various forms of national income from commercial activities, state enterprises and profit from cooperatives. The proposals were approved without dissent.

The second item on the agenda, 'land legislation', was introduced in a long and virtually unintelligible speech by the chairman of the Legislative Committee. He emphasized that the Leader himself had formulated the law; it was thus the duty of the people to receive it and abide by it. The auditorium applauded after every sentence, which led the foreigners present (most particularly the East Europeans, who considered themselves initiated 'Pyongyangologists') to assume that the issue was somewhat sensitive, but nobody actually knew what the law was about and why it had been presented to the Assembly on this occasion. The speech included a historical exposition that went back to feudal conditions and considered irrigation, climatic problems, tree-planting, the restructuring of nature and the mechanization of agriculture, etc. The eighty or so clauses of the law were then read out, and we could ascertain that they covered most aspects of earth and water, forest and air, wild animals and natural resources and the utilization of these assets. It was, for example, stipulated that it was the task of the government to defend nationalization of all land in the northern half of the Republic, and strive to initiate similar conditions in the whole nation, i.e. including South Korea. The law was approved without dissent.

The method of conducting assembly meetings illustrated not only the authoritarian but also the patriarchal features of the wielding of power. The fatherliness gave the impression of benevolence, of concern for the living standard of the people and their patterns of consumption. Yet, simultaneously, there was never any doubt that the Leader in this way fomented the relentless spirit of competition and performance anxiety that was characteristic of virtually every Korean one came into contact with. One can readily imagine not only 'loss of face' but also the hair-raising fear of social degradation, loss of honour, and perhaps even of family support or of life, that could be the fate of the officials in administration or factories held to be responsible for actual or supposed failures. In order to cope with this threat, those in positions of responsibility had to prove themselves to be extremely loyal and effective – something that could only ultimately be achieved by increased workloads for their large mass of subordinates.

Kim Il Sung's demand that the plan be overfulfilled and for 'local industry', i.e. production outside the plan, deserves further mention. This was a continually recurring theme, and the fixed multiyear plans were often said to have been fulfilled prematurely. But one could tell that it was often a case of achieving some sort of aggregate production target. Although some sectors had not fulfilled the plan, others had exceeded it. As a Westerner, one was obviously completely dependent upon the information supplied by the authorities, and the results were usually announced as percentages, so that any judgement had to be based upon decidedly uncertain statistics. When production targets were said to have been exceeded after an exceptionally short time, then, at least for non-communists, it became apparent that under the existing conditions it must be impossible to follow any sort of established multiyear plan. If the textile sector exceeded its plan, then it must have used more energy than the plan envisaged, and this must of necessity have affected other sectors. If this, in turn, had led to an expansion of the energy sector, then this too must have been at the cost of some other sector. The system of continually demanding that the planned targets be overfulfilled, and that there be production outside the plan, must mean that the plan never served as a guiding rule, but that there was a continual resort to improvisation. The various cog-wheels of the machinery of production, were not encouraged to link with each other in cooperation; rather, the opposite was the case, with each one going as fast as it possibly could. The focus of economic policy on quantitative achievements, each isolated from the other, was perhaps expedient in a development phase, but must be regarded as being one of the major causes of the economic collapse of the 1990s.

8

ABOUT NORTH KOREAN JUSTICE

The chances of obtaining any reliable information about North Korean conditions were extremely slim. My East European colleagues liked to make out that they were well informed, but it was doubtful (to put it mildly) whether they had access to reliable facts. The Chinese and even the Russians were perhaps the exceptions that proved the rule, but they were singularly uninformative. Otherwise, the East Europeans in North Korea were, if anything, just as much at the mercy of accidental contacts and sporadic impressions as Western diplomats often were in the East European communist countries. So our colleagues' value as sources of information depended much upon their staff and even more so upon their observational faculties and their discernment as well as, of course, upon their readiness to share their insights with a Westerner.

An unintentional illustration of their limitations was afforded me on a hunting trip, to which I had been invited by a number of East European ambassadors. The destination lay some thirty or forty kilometres from Pyongyang, and we needed special permission in order to get there and were checked at several police control points en route. The designated area lay in a densely populated agricultural district, so it was not much of a hunt. A Czech had once succeeded in shooting a crane, which had subsequently been stuffed and was exhibited in his study as a trophy. With my Pakistani colleague, I took a long walk across the fields, but there was not a wild animal to be seen. No shots were fired during the hunt, and I had my doubts as to whether the others had even loaded their guns. It turned out that hunting was not the main reason for being there either.

It was winter and there was a bitingly cold wind blowing across the large fields. We gathered together behind a little pump house, which in milder weather supplied the artificial irrigation. The East European drivers lit a wood fire and grilled some spare ribs – imported from Eastern Europe – which we washed down with a considerable amount of vodka. Then appeared the pump house mechanic in his thin working clothes. It was evidently part of the ritual to let him eat his fill, while conversing with him in more or less broken Korean. I then realized that this poor worker represented one of the rare contacts my Eastern colleagues had, perhaps indeed the only one, with the common people – 'the man on the street'. I had made similar efforts to come into contact with 'the man on the street' when I had been stationed in Eastern Europe and was desperately trying to break out of the official isolation.

Another time, I heard the Yugoslavian ambassador ask his Syrian colleague if there were any law courts in North Korea. The Yugoslav had been stationed in Pyongyang for at least four years and the Syrian was the doyen of the diplomatic corps with a six-year stretch, and he had also been stationed in the country for several years previously. Neither knew the answer to that question. The Yugoslav told, too, of his unsuccessful attempt to come into contact with representatives of the North Korean judicial system. When he had established the Yugoslavian Embassy, he had been presented with a rental contract in Korean for signing. He had then got in touch with the Korean Foreign Ministry to ask for assistance in contacting a lawyer – standard international practice – with whom he would be able to go through the translations he also wished to be given. The reaction of the North Koreans was at first evasive and indifferent. When the Yugoslav insisted, it became totally negative: 'Do you doubt the proletarian justice of our socialist state?' All he could do was sign the contract. The Syrian added that on the occasion of an international conference of lawyers in Damascus some years previously North Korea had only managed to send a representative for the Committee for Cultural Exchange with Foreign Countries.

In the absence of proper information, every conceivable type of rumour would circulate among the foreigners in Pyongyang. They ranged from the tale that a member of the domestic staff who had accepted some packets of cigarettes had been thrown into a deep mine to work there forever to reports that periodic purges and 'corrective exile' in the form of heavy labour were so institutionalized that most people, knowing that such a fate was inevitable, took every chance to enjoy the pleasures of life and thus cared little for the moralist imperatives of the Party. Discerning colleagues claimed that on at least one occasion a purged senior Party functionary had been seen working as a building labourer. This, however, seemed to be a rather worthless piece of information, because all officials, except the very highest ranking ones, were obliged to put in one day a week as a manual worker. On one occasion when I had an urgent message to pass on at the highest level possible – which for me as 'chargé d'affaires' turned out to be the Under-Secretary of State – it took several hours and a great deal of effort to mobilize the person in question, because on that particular day he was working on a construction site on the outskirts of Pyongyang.

I read the news bulletin from the North Korean news bureau every day for more than two years and during that time only came across one 'article' with any legal content. In September 1975 it was announced that an amnesty had been granted to criminals on the occasion of the thirtieth anniversary of the Party. There were no details other than that the amnesty would apply immediately, and that jobs would be waiting for the released prisoners. My immediate reflection was that they would hardly have been kept unemployed during their time in prison.

As I said before, facts were in short supply. It was naturally impossible to get hold of the texts of any government acts of law. But, in the 'Constitution of the

Democratic People's Republic of Korea', there was a section about the system of courts of law, which was said to consist of the central court, provincial courts, people's courts and special courts. Judges and lay assessors should be elected by the SPA or by local constituencies, as the case might be, and should have the same mandate period as these. The task given to the courts was, in a few words, to protect socialist society and state property, to ensure that everything and everybody cooperated in the struggle against class enemies and law breakers, but also to make decisions with regard to questions of property.

Kim Il Sung made speeches on every conceivable subject and these have been collected together in a comprehensive number of bound volumes. In a speech in 1958 addressed to a national conference for officials in the legal system his views are made quite clear: the slogan 'All shall be equal in the eyes of the law' was a bourgeois lie, the purpose of which was to suppress the working people and disguise the class character of the laws. The organs of the legal system were a weapon in the service of the functions of the proletarian dictatorship. Any 'citizens' who were opposed to socialism were not to be treated impartially. Judges were not to deform the basic spirit of the law by separating it from politics. Laws were subordinate to politics. It would never be possible to both follow the law and refuse to be governed by the Party. The juridical officials should know that they are Party workers who shall apply the Party's policies in the course of their duties.[a]

I personally experienced the system when, at the beginning of my time there, I attempted to obtain the usual information as to regulations for home transport or local burial of deceased Swedish citizens. I could not obtain any proper information or, rather, the answers were extremely vague. It was my impression that the North Koreans quite simply intended solving any problems as and when they cropped up and in a manner deemed suitable in each particular case. One can certainly not exclude the possibility that this same approach was applied in North Korean legal processes in general. That, at any rate, is the impression made by Kim's speech as described above. Presumably, justice has simply rolled along in the same autocratic tracks during centuries of local despots, Japanese occupiers and the *nomenklatura* of the People's Democracy. And why should it be any different? According to Marxist ideology, existing judicial systems are purely an instrument for the interests of the ruling classes. The very concept of a 'state governed by the rule of law' is absent, and the practice of law is a part of, and subordinate to, politics – and thus becomes, according to our way of looking at things, a question of ideology or indeed faith. Justice at the end of a spear.

a For an account of the human rights situation, see Kim, B.-L., 'Human rights in North Korea', *Korea and World Affairs*, Vol. 3, 1996, 431–50. For example, he quotes a North Korean newspaper article from 24 June 1995, which emphasizes that the concept of 'class' does not allow the extension of civil rights to also include elements hostile to socialism.

9

AUSTRALIAN INTERMEZZO

Any laws about an eight-hour working day and suchlike were conveniently circumvented by 'voluntary' work. Studying the writings of the Great Leader for a couple of hours a day was said to be obligatory. In practice, the population seemed to have four days free per year, namely the Leader's birthday, the anniversaries of the founding of the State and the Party, and 1 May (Labour Day); a fifth was added somewhat later, namely the birthday of the Leader's son. On these days, the city parks were filled with families out walking in their best clothes, partaking in organized leisure activities. Fairgrounds opened up their roundabouts and big dippers and North Koreans could buy ice-cream from street sellers. On such occasions, the embassies too were invited on outings with a picnic outdoors and participation in innocent party games. During the 1 May celebrations in 1975 I was unexpectedly introduced to a newcomer to the diplomatic fold, the Australian chargé d'affaires, who had arrived with his staff the previous day. This was a welcome addition to the small Western contingent, which as a result reached double figures, not counting the children.

In 1972, the Australian Labour Party returned to power after a number of years in opposition. Labour wanted to break with the previous government's policy of not establishing diplomatic relations with Asian communist regimes. Following the rapprochement between the USA and China there were no problems with recognizing Beijing, and it was quickly decided to extend this to Hanoi – the Vietnam War was still going on then. As regards North Korea there was evidently some hesitation, and agreement was not reached with Pyongyang until the summer of 1974. In January 1975, a North Korean Embassy was opened in Canberra, and four months later the Australians were also in place in Pyongyang. These measures seem to have been taken as part of the Australian government's desire to emphasize that it saw itself as being part of the Pacific Ocean region and not just a member of the British Commonwealth.

The Swedish Embassy had been opened by a solitary official, assisted by his wife, and a second official and an assistant did not arrive until six months later. Australia, on the other hand, established a complete embassy from the very start, with five officials, and in general had a very high profile by local standards. For example, its embassy car was one of the fancier models of Mercedes Benz, the only one in the city outside the circle of Party bigwigs. One of the embassy secretaries spoke Korean, having spent several years in South Korea, and this was naturally regarded with suspicion by the authorities. They tried, with the help of subtle Oriental signals, to encourage the newcomers to take things a bit easier; however, the signals were not recognized as such, but regarded simply as the irritating and incomprehensible hassle it was in Western eyes.

The Australians did not pass their driving tests. Negotiations for renting embassy office premises dragged on for month after month, despite there being several buildings empty and waiting in the diplomatic quarter. The Australians then wanted to rent office furniture for their hotel rooms. When this was denied them, they moved the furniture around in the night, while the hotel staff were asleep, switching items between the bedrooms and working rooms to make the area more practical to work in – the Foreign Ministry remonstrated with them over the unsuitability of this. The young women dressed in ordinary, but from a Korean perspective indecently low-cut, summer dresses. When the embassy staff eventually moved into their residential quarters, they celebrated with a party to which all the guests were requested to come dressed as ancient Romans, which resulted in the area being swamped one evening with foreigners wrapped in sheets, a sight that the authorities found disturbing to the highest degree.

Some of the friction was of more substance however, albeit at times of an unexpected nature. The procurement of local currency did not go smoothly, as the bank refused to change money, this being because the North Koreans had missed the switch to the dollar and insisted that Australia still used the pound. The Australians repeatedly lodged complaints about the restrictions on their freedom of movement, and this evidently led to quite heated exchanges. Now and then, the staff took the liberty of venturing, at their own risk, out to a bathing beach or travelling on the underground and buying an ice-cream on the street, which led the Chief of Protocol to emphasize that such behaviour was a serious breach of acceptable conduct. However, it also resulted in the other embassies being invited to organized trips on the underground, which was emptied of Koreans for these occasions. Furthermore, on one of his visits from Beijing, where he was stationed, the Australian ambassador (a sinologist) forwarded requests that must have made the Koreans extremely suspicious – for example to visit prisons and courts of law. Both he and his staff often pointed out the need to intensify efforts to achieve a better negotiating climate between the two Korean states and tried to get the North Koreans to relax their rigid positions a little. Friction between the Australian Embassy and the authorities was commonplace and manifest.

I was nevertheless amazed when the interpreter rushed in one day at the beginning of November 1975 and excitedly reported that the Australians had been instructed to leave the country immediately. A circular originating from the Foreign Ministry confirmed that the Australian Embassy was no longer necessary and that the staff was not permitted to remain. The reason given was that they had repeatedly taken unfriendly steps, engaged in subversive activity and publicly insulted and disrupted the social order of the state with their mendacious propaganda. It was further claimed that the Australian government had prevented the North Korean Embassy in Canberra from conducting its business.

I understand that the North Korean Foreign Ministry had first demanded that the Australians leave the following day, but after hard argument had relented and extended the deadline to forty-eight hours. The Australians then worked day and night to pack their things and send as much as possible by train to Beijing. The North Koreans' willingness to cooperate was virtually non-existent. They supplied a lorry but nobody to help, and at the railway customs office the Australians had to carry in all their cases and boxes themselves, adding up to a hundred or so items. Also, a customs declaration was required for every single item. A third of the Pyongyang diplomatic corps and their families – West Europeans, Asians, Egyptians and Yugoslavs – interrupted their ordinary business and helped with the packing and then waved the Australians off at the railway station. There was no local removals firm, and when we moved out almost two years later we had to do all the packing ourselves too.

As a representative of the country with the closest relations to Australia, I was asked to take care of the packing and transport or sale of any remaining goods and then close the embassy. The North Koreans were very interested in purchasing the fancy Mercedes for local currency. But I had it freighted to Beijing by train. On 30 October 1975, the North Koreans had closed their embassy in Canberra and left the country, only informing the authorities there by letter, which had not arrived until after they had departed. According to my Australian colleague, there had been three differences of opinion in Canberra.

First, because of the highly restricted freedom of movement imposed on foreigners in North Korea, the Australians had required that the North Korean Embassy staff give advance notice to the Foreign Ministry of their travelling plans. It was thus not a restriction on their freedom of movement, as such, but the North Koreans had never abided by this regulation and this had led to several comments. Evidently, the North Koreans did not expect reciprocity; they expected to be treated as a Most Favoured Nation. Second, the embassy had published the usual propaganda advertisements in the Australian press, which had led to the South Koreans doing the same thing. Both parties had then been requested to cease these campaigns against each other. (In the mid-1970s it was common to see full-page advertisements in the Western press with a picture of the Great Leader and a compact mass of propaganda text, which was totally wasted on a Western public, but which could be reproduced as quotes from the US papers in the North Korean press.) Third, the North Koreans had distributed leaflets, upon which the South Koreans had started doing so too. On this occasion, too, both parties had been asked to stop. One did not need to have had much experience of the self-righteous and propaganda-minded North Koreans to realize that these measures must have been seen as preventing one of the most important functions of the embassy.

But local friction in Canberra and Pyongyang would hardly suffice as an explanation for the drastic act of closing the embassies – although this view was espoused by a number of colleagues in Pyongyang. Most of us, however, tended towards the opinion that the North Korean mode of action had been motivated by the Australian standpoint on the Korean question in the UN, and that the North Koreans, on account of unfortunate circumstances, made an erroneous decision.

On the Australian side, they had namely made it clear that they intended voting for the resolution proposed by South Korea and against that of North Korea. On the North Korean side, it had been stressed that a vote against their resolution would lead to fateful consequences in the relationship between the two countries. Australia changed its decision to one of abstaining from the vote on the North Korean resolution, but this change came on the actual voting day – and by that time, the North Korean embassy personnel had evidently already boarded the plane to leave Australia. According to this interpretation, North Korea had decided to react to the Australian 'no' vote by literally closing its embassy in Canberra at a moment's notice, only to discover immediately that Australia had not actually voted as expected. But the mistake had already been made, and to save face they had to see it through to the end, i.e. expel the Australian Embassy. Diplomatic relations were not, however, broken off, but naturally became completely frozen. The value of the vote in the UN is best illustrated by the fact that both the contradictory resolutions were approved by a majority.

As time went by and I gathered together and digested impressions over a long period of daily contact and negotiations with the North Koreans, I started to reconsider my estimation of the reasons behind the decision to kick the Australians out. From the Swedish Foreign Ministry I received instructions on several occasions to enquire about North Korean attitudes to the general Korea question. But, as far as this issue was concerned, it turned out to be virtually impossible to get any chance to discuss the matter with representatives of the Foreign Ministry. Requests for meetings were regularly subjected to diversionary tactics and 'forgotten'. Attempts on my part to raise the issue in other circumstances simply resulted in evasive answers or the usual lectures about American imperialism and the South Korean puppet government. Such a consistent reception could, in the end, only be interpreted as a clear sign that the North Koreans actively avoided discussing the issue.

With regard to the Australians, the Labour government's 'new' Asian orientation included distinct attempts to be helpful in the Korea question, helpful, that is, in the Western sense of bridging differences and facilitating contacts. Foreign Minister Willesee was eager to meet representatives for both Koreas and present compromise proposals and mediate in order to bring about a lessening of tension on the peninsula and in the region in general. Everything indicates that this implied a collision course with North Korean interests. They were already quite clear about their principles for solving the Korea problem, and were only interested in loyal and unqualified support from other states. They did not want any foreign influence on the course of events on the Korean peninsula, and consistently ignored every attempt at interference and mediation. Australia's importune interest was thus unwelcome, and when it did not abate all that the North Koreans could do was avoid it by cutting off all contacts.

10

THE SMUGGLING CRISIS

Members of the higher echelons in Pyongyang believed that they had every reason to look back upon the year 1975 with satisfaction, not least because with the help of friendly nations in the UN – North Korea was not a member itself – a resolution had been passed on the Korea question by the General Assembly. As I have said, it bothered them little that South Korea, too, had succeeded in getting a resolution passed on the same subject, in the same forum, and with a better majority. They looked forward with confidence to being able to move their position even further forward during 1976.

However, 1976 proved instead to be a somewhat trying year. At the meeting of the non-aligned states in Colombo, the North Koreans took it for granted that they would receive broad support, and of course well-deserved admiration and approbation for their status as a militant pioneer in the anti-imperialist struggle. They insisted upon tough wording and standpoints and refused to compromise. As a result, not only did the support not materialize, but they became so isolated that it proved impossible to present a new draft resolution for the UN. Without doubt, a contributing factor in all this was a serious incident in Panmunjom in which two US soldiers were beaten to death and North Korea raised both its voice and its military readiness. The non-aligned nations were not impressed; rather they were frightened by Pyongyang's warlike signals.

And in the autumn of 1976, as the icing on the cake, all the North Korean embassies in Scandinavia were involved in a smuggling scandal, which was widely reported in the world press. There were indications that the scandal even stretched as far as Switzerland, East Germany and Poland, although this was not extensively publicized. The crisis was particularly damaging because it was not possible to evade the issue by blaming controversial political questions. The searchlight was aimed directly at the country's integrity in international contexts and the crisis was made worse by virtue of having taken place in the Scandinavian countries, those very same countries that had made an effort to develop good relations with the Third World and could not be suspected of engaging in conspiracies aimed at discrediting North Korea. On the contrary, Scandinavian countries accounted for most of the Western countries that allowed the establishment of North Korean embassies in their capitals.

Evidently, the police in the Scandinavian countries had observed for some time that the North Korean embassies used their diplomatic tax exemption to sell alcohol and cigarettes on the black market. This had reached such proportions that several restaurants informed the police of the goods they had been offered. The authorities in the four countries agreed to a joint action that would put an end to the racket and avoid sensational publicity. However, it emerged that in Copenhagen drugs were also involved, and this led to the police going in immediately, making publicity unavoidable.

During the weekend of 16–17 October 1976, the radio news first reported that embassy personnel had been expelled from Copenhagen, and similar reports soon followed from Oslo. A day or so later, the Swedish Foreign Ministry confirmed my suspicions that similar activities had taken place in Stockholm. The press were soon on to the story, of course, but the Swedish authorities were keen to avoid unnecessary drama, not least for the sake of their personnel stationed in North Korea. I was granted the authorization to evacuate family members and, in an emergency, all the other staff to Beijing. I was further informed that it had been impossible to conduct meaningful discussions with the North Korean Embassy personnel in Stockholm so that negotiations would necessarily have to take place in Pyongyang.

In the following days, every morning and evening I was summoned to negotiations at the Foreign Ministry, where we eventually sorted out a solution to the dispute. These intensive talks gave an exceedingly valuable and interesting insight into the local psyche and negotiating methods and are thus deserving of a rather detailed account. Above all, they revealed the Koreans' monumental lack of any awareness of the world around them and of standard diplomatic practice. The North Koreans quite simply did not have the necessary qualifications to be able to estimate accurately the consequences of their actions, which naturally led to a considerable degree of vacillation in the decision-making process and a real need of guidance, something which they did their best to hide. It should be emphasized that the discussions were – invariably – conducted without the raising of voices, even though the North Koreans' choice of words could sometimes seem decidedly brusque to a Westerner. I soon came to realize that variations in the 'negotiating climate' were expressed with the help of subtle Oriental hints which may well be the norm in East Asian contexts but which a Westerner could easily fail to detect.

The simplest and perhaps most palpable examples consisted of the long, drawn-out, tiring and, for Westerners, rather meaningless assertions of friendship and mutual appreciation, the likes of which I had grown accustomed to as they were a regular ingredient of the preamble to all meetings in all contexts. I now came to understand that they were an extremely important element of the negotiating process. By-passing them was something that could not be excused by being in a hurry or by a desire to get down to the nitty-gritty straight away. No, the niceties about friendship and the well-being of family members – even though we met several times a day – conveyed an overexplicit signal that the negotiations were in a serious crisis and were in danger of breaking down.

Such instances demonstrated one of the reasons for North Korea's reputation as being rather eccentric among nations. The negotiators' inadequate knowledge of their partners' values and codes of conduct meant that the discussions could easily go off at a tangent without the participants really understanding why, thus leading to a mutual misinterpretation of malevolent intent. Representatives of a superior and successful West had long been highly ethnocentric in their attitudes, forcing a knowledge of the West's own ways upon the world, and likewise forcing the world to adapt to its methods and values. In bygone days, Oriental rulers, such as the Emperor of China and the Ottoman Sultan, had to the very last understood that a fundamental inequality was self-evident – they refused to enter into agreements with other countries on an equal basis and they would only dictate conditions. Foreign emissaries were not seen as representatives of sovereign states; rather, their arrival was seen as a sign of respect and submission. In many ways, the North Koreans still lived in that world of old values, something that visitors could easily forget on seeing their improbable success in rapidly industrializing and urbanizing what had been a Third World country in the space of twenty years.

Questions of rank were important. My own rank was that of counsellor, but in the absence of the ambassador (who seldom left Beijing) my position would be that of chargé d'affaires, i.e. acting head of diplomatic mission, and in that capacity I was never received on a ministerial level. Chargés d'affaires with the rank of minister plenipotentiary usually got to see deputy ministers, and counsellors like me were usually referred to assistant ministers, who might well be compared with heads of department in a Western administration. So I particularly noted that my opposite number in the negotiations was presented as a deputy minister, which could reasonably be interpreted both as a courtesy and as a sign of the importance attached to the discussions. At crucial moments in the course of the negotiations, he often politely left the room for a few minutes as if for a visit to the lavatory – but I soon realized that he was receiving instructions from a superior who, as far as can be judged, was listening in on our conversation from an adjoining room.

The deputy minister was assisted by a couple of officials, one of them a stenographer, as well as, I should perhaps add, by our embassy interpreter, who had, of course, been lent out to us by the ministry. During the car journeys between the embassy and the ministry, I sat and thought aloud in his company and generally aired my reactions and enquired as to his views. This was probably the most important element in the entire negotiations, because he was thus enabled to supplement the formal discussions by later explaining my viewpoints and methods of reasoning to his own side. For the duration of the negotiations, I hardly caught a glimpse of him, and I presume he spent most of the time engaged in the internal discussions. I myself was alone, as the embassy's other two officials were obliged to devote all their time to deciphering reports and instructions – with the technology of the time, this was a dreadfully time-consuming and intellectually demanding task.

Meanwhile, my wife was fetching suitcases from the storeroom and packing both our private belongings and the office equipment so that the North Koreans would be in no doubt that we were preparing to evacuate the embassy. The ways of leaving the country were, however, restricted. Because of earthquakes in China, the railway was closed and there were only two flights a week to Beijing and one to Moscow. Alternatively, one could choose the week-long train journey on the Trans-Siberian railway through the Soviet Union but, from experience, we knew that such a journey required planning and preparation in the form of provisions and cooking equipment, particularly if one travelled with a baby.

The previous day, the deputy minister had started the first sitting by regretting the sudden decisions in Copenhagen and Oslo to expel North Korean Embassy staff without prior consultations. If any illegal activities had taken place, he declared, those guilty would naturally be strictly punished. Judging from press reports, he went on, it was now the turn of Stockholm, and if we were to behave in the same manner it would give the impression of a joint Nordic action against the People's Republic, which would have serious repercussions upon our relations. He expressed particular concern over the position of their ambassador, pointing out that, were he to be expelled, it would be tantamount to a breaking off of diplomatic relations. I gained the distinct impression that the North Korean side were keen to find a way to save face, particularly as regards the ambassador.

The following morning I was summoned to new discussions. This time the deputy minister sharpened his choice of words considerably, but the pitch of his voice was still as calm as before. He denied that the North Korean officials in Stockholm, and particularly the ambassador, had been guilty of any illegal acts at all, and stated that if they, nevertheless, were expelled, then similar action would be taken against the Swedish Embassy in Pyongyang. I replied that the Swedish judicial system did not take orders from the government. For the North Koreans this would most likely have been an incomprehensible state of affairs, which they probably did not believe, just as little as they (after the large industrial exhibition) believed that I lacked the authority to give orders to Swedish businessmen. Under the circumstances, I went on, it was out of the question to consider any other outcome but that Swedish justice would run its course, and there would be no exception from the rule that any embassy official caught doing something like this would be obliged to leave the country. Finally, I pointed out that the deputy minister's categorical statements gave little cause for hope as to a neat way of settling our differences. Upon which, I put pen and paper back in my pocket and prepared to leave.

But the deputy minister showed no sign of ending our meeting; he remained seated and stared straight ahead. I thus took the chance to explain something that I had noticed the North Koreans had not seemed to understand, namely that the measures that were applied by the Swedish authorities were directed only at the guilty officials personally and not at the embassy or at all the embassy staff. To this I added that Pyongyang would surely be most anxious to receive as little adverse publicity as possible, so the North Koreans had everything to win by recalling the officials concerned back to Pyongyang before any expulsion order could be issued. As regards the ambassador himself, I continued, it would be quite natural in a situation such as this to recall him for consultations. The deputy minister was interested, and asked a number of questions that revealed his above-mentioned ignorance of international relations. He particularly wanted confirmation that an expulsion order could be avoided if the officials concerned had already left and that this, above all, would apply to the ambassador.

Upon my return to the embassy, I kept the interpreter on for a more thorough conversation – just the two of us. He was a talented and well-qualified official who had been stationed in East Berlin as embassy secretary. And, above all, after one and a half year's cooperation, I knew him and could tell if and how he understood what I had said. And so it was possible to go into detail and explain things in quite another way than with the deputy minister. When I was with the latter, I was never really certain whether or not he had understood me, a circumstance that was made even worse by his pretending to have a thorough knowledge of the world outside and its social mores.

With the help of the interpreter, it was thus possible to supply information on how similar cases had been solved on other occasions. I impressed upon him that any action taken was directed only towards individuals and not towards the embassy or North Korea itself. I went into detail on the independent standing of the judiciary in Sweden and the role of the free press, and I stressed how unreasonable it was that only Sweden – which alone had acceded to the North Korean request for consultations – should be singled out for reciprocal measures. As an example of North Korean vacillation, I can cite the interpreter's reaction to my information that recalling an ambassador did not involve lowering the level of diplomatic relations but that they could immediately send off a new ambassador. 'Is *that* the case?' he said, 'Can I tell them that at the Foreign Ministry?

Later the same evening, it became obvious that the roundabout route via the interpreter was a success. The deputy minister explained that the North Korean side would be prepared to recall their ambassador to give his report if they were afforded guarantees that the Swedish authorities would do their utmost to limit unfavourable publicity. Above all, they demanded an assurance that the ambassador, following his departure, would not be pronounced officially guilty by Sweden. The deputy minister was visibly tense. While his words were being translated he fixed me with a worried stare with his mouth half-open, trying to read every reaction.

In accordance with these guidelines, the final solution was eventually reached. On the third day, foreign news broadcasts announced that all the North Korean Embassy staff in Helsinki had been expelled. Of Sweden, it was said that police investigations were going on. This made it possible for me, during the frequent bouts of negotiation, to emphasize the danger of delay. I was, however, careful to ascertain the exact wording of the undertaking given by the Swedish side in order to prevent the North Koreans subsequently presenting their own interpretation of its meaning. The gist of it was that – on condition the ambassador left Sweden before the weekend – the Swedes would limit themselves to noting, in a press release, that the ambassador had left the country on a certain day. Even then, it was not all plain sailing. First, the ambassador tried to delay his departure by several days. He then gave notice of his intention of leaving, together with staff that had not been involved in the smuggling, but leaving two guilty accomplices behind. I informed the interpreter that all of the agreed plan for a calm settlement of the episode would be at risk. In both cases the ambassador was supplied with the necessary information to make a better decision, and all those involved left Sweden within the allotted time.

It had not been necessary to expel anybody and the publicity had consequently been moderate. That they had not managed to achieve this in the other Nordic countries can only have been because of the impossibility, due to pressure of time, of negotiating with North Korean Embassy staff locally. The embassy staff was completely hamstrung by rigid rules and regulations and, in practice, were restricted to passing on messages from home. They did not understand how their host countries worked, and probably did not dare negotiate or even inform their own Foreign Ministry of the arguments against them, afraid of being regarded as not totally loyal. Any negotiation worth its name would have to take place in Pyongyang, where those in power did not actually take part but were at least indirectly accessible.

It is another matter entirely that I later came to suspect that the Swedish authorities might, in their hearts, have welcomed a failure on my part to bring the negotiations to a successful conclusion. Without anyone having to take the blame they would then have been able to rid themselves of embassies, in both Stockholm and Pyongyang, that had shown themselves primarily to be a source of problems that were difficult to solve, unpredictable and time-consuming. It was not for nothing that even by the end of the twentieth century, the only Western embassy in Pyongyang was the Swedish one.

The crisis should thus have come to an end but, bearing in mind the monumental self-righteousness of the North Koreans and the signs that during the negotiations they had carefully avoided any recognition of guilt, at any rate vis-à-vis Sweden, I predicted that it would resurface and the North Koreans would have the last word. And a few days later I was indeed summoned yet again to the deputy minister.

A sinister atmosphere was immediately created by virtue of the total absence of all the usual conversational niceties as to health, friendship and cooperation. In their place, he reminded me directly of the Swedish assurance of the previous week and then read aloud some texts that were said to have been published by the Swedish Foreign Ministry. He claimed that these were full of unseemly and unfounded slander, and were in glaring contrast to the approved agreement. Pyongyang categorically rejected these newly published documents and regretted this treachery on the part of Sweden. I should immediately point out that the deputy minister's tone was quite normal, which, in the light of the climate in Pyongyang, was more significant than the content of the message. As regards the choice of words, one should also note that, by local standards it should be seen as relatively normal – any less aggressive phraseology would, rather, have been seen as a sign of compliance. Particularly worthy of note is the fact that not a single word of threat was directed towards the Swedish Embassy. They evidently considered that some sort of balance had now been re-established and both parties had consequently saved face. I was therefore content to reply that we, on the Swedish side, had, if anything, more than fulfilled our commitment as we had not expelled, or even named, any North Korean official.

A week or so later I was yet again summoned to the Foreign Ministry, this time to the head of the European section. The conversation was preceded by calming asseverations of good wishes and cooperation. He then proceeded to ask for my help with a problem that had arisen in Stockholm. A signplate had been screwed on to the entrance of the North Korean Embassy, on which was written a message for visitors to the 'Wine & Spirits Cooperative' asking them to go to another address because the shop was no longer in business. The embassy personnel were unpleasantly affected by this and, above all, feared for their safety. I found it hard to keep a straight face in the light of this prank, which had probably been the work of students from the nearby Royal Institute of Technology.

The smuggling episode aroused considerable interest among the other embassies in Pyongyang. From all of the embassies, including most of the communist ones, with the exception of those of the Soviet Union, Romania, Cuba and Cambodia, we received a visit from either the head of mission, or some linguistically able official, to obtain information. Even the Vietnamese came. In every instance, it was clear that they were not hiding their critical attitude to North Korea, which thus can be said to have enjoyed even less credibility than Sweden among communist countries. Regardless of whether they represented a country from the East, West or South, it did not seem to have occurred to any of them to question the news from Scandinavia to the slightest degree, nor did they doubt the justification of the accusations against the North Korean Embassy officials. Rather, the opposite was the case, in that they did not hide their opinion that the officials had obviously been acting on instructions from home. The Eastern Europeans in particular, could barely suppress their joy at North Korea being given a real lesson – and that they had not had to do it.

Another, doubly remarkable circumstance was that the Chinese ambassador made his return visit, according to diplomatic protocol, to me during the crisis week. This is worth noting because, first, the Chinese ambassador would not normally make a return visit to a chargé d'affaires and, second, it had been one and a half years since I had visited him. In Oriental contexts, this must be seen as a subtle pointer to which party in the dispute the influential China favoured. In addition, he had with him his own English-speaking interpreter. On the occasions I had visited him, we had communicated with double interpretation via Korean through my German-speaking interpreter and his Korean-speaking one.

Some days prior to the commencement of the smuggling crisis we had invited most of the French-speaking heads of mission to dinner – the Yugoslav, the Syrian, who was also the doyen of the diplomatic corps, the Vietnamese, the Cambodian and the Algerian. The dinner took place a few days after the resolution of the crisis and, as luck would have it, happened to coincide with a large 'banquet' to which the Nigerian Beijing ambassador had invited the Foreign Ministry and the heads of mission on the occasion of his visit to Pyongyang to hand over his letters of credit. The invitations were handed out by the Korean protocol section quite late on the very same day, as was their wont, so we were not afforded the possibility of adjusting our programme. Under the circumstances, about a quarter of the heads of mission in Pyongyang found cause to decline the Nigerian invitation in order to come to us. The doyen deemed it necessary to absent himself for half an hour or so to travel to the banquet and apologize to the Nigerian, on which errand he was accompanied by the Cambodian.

When the guests had departed, the Yugoslavian couple stayed on for a little while. Ambassador Vucic's face lit up with a broad smile: 'You don't know what you've managed to stir up! This was really excellent! A situation in which the representatives of North Korea's best friends are at the Swedish Embassy although they could easily have found an excuse – in the form of the Nigerian invitation – not to have come if they had so wished. But they wished the opposite! You can rest assured that the North Koreans have made particular note of it!' Vucic also told me that during the previous week he had been able to meet the member of the politburo responsible for foreign policy (who was more centrally placed than the Foreign Minister, who was only a member of the Administrative Council). They had discussed the matter at length, and Vucic had tried to convince him that, in the face of world opinion, North Korea had nothing to gain by worsening its relations with Sweden.

11

THE ROAD TO
THE SMUGGLING POLICY

How could the North Korean authorities even get involved in something so doomed to failure as making their embassies self-sufficient by earning money through smuggling? It must require a very special sort of public spirit.

It was not possible to really understand how the North Koreans thought about things. However, I can describe everyday experiences in order to give a picture of how they seemed to think. So far, virtually every chapter has been intended to show particular expressions of their unusual public spirit, and in the sections on ideology and their concept of reality I attempt to analyse the philosophy that governed their thoughts and actions.

There were a number of characteristics that separated North Korea from the rest of the world – in different ways depending on whether the country in question was East Asian, communist or had a market economy – and these became gradually all the clearer to me as being conditions for, or ingredients in, their behaviour and patterns of thought: a long period of isolation, an artificially extended state of war, hyper-nationalism and xenophobia, self-righteousness and an overestimation of their own abilities, a hysterical attitude towards achieving results, shortsightedness, uniformity, indoctrination and blind slave-like discipline. Introversion was also an important ingredient. They took from outside what they thought they needed, but were careful not to include critical appraisal, moderating viewpoints and expressions of doubt, or even ordinary common sense.

Isolation is a historical fact. For centuries, Korea had been even more closed than Japan. It opened up later, unwillingly, and was subject to less influence than Japan ever was before the Japanese occupation again closed the country. After the Second World War, Korea immediately acquired its new guise and its new isolation. The conceptions the people had of the rest of the world were limited by what their masters conveyed to them – and the knowledge of their masters was both imperfect and negative. North Korea considered itself to be at war with the USA, with which a temporary truce held. Internal and external security was adapted to the demands of war with an ever-present military and an autocratic secret service. It is hard to imagine a more totalitarian state. The entire population was permanently mobilized as soldiers, either with weapons or with working tools.

Nationalism and xenophobia could well be seen as the inevitable results of

69

their historical experiences and the self-assumed state of war, which aimed for reunification. The country had been a Chinese vassal, a bone of contention fought over by superior neighbours, and then occupied by Japan, after which it considered itself a primary target of US imperialism. The authorities distrusted their powerful communist allies too, for they had allowed the state to reach the very verge of destruction during the Korean War, and the Soviet Union, in particular, on account of its parsimonious assistance and egoistical trading policy. They respected China, but not the rest of the world.

Not only was ignorance of the world around them rife, but the North Koreans seemed to cultivate attitudes of pure delusion. How could one otherwise explain the reaction of the interpreter to the way my wife looked after our son? When the boy arrived in Pyongyang, he was only two months old and was obviously the object of all imaginable and natural motherly love. But one day the interpreter confided to me that he had been deeply impressed by the genuine human love (*Menschenliebe*) that he witnessed daily in the relationship between mother and son and which was entirely what would be observed in his own country. This comment reveals the character of what he had been taught about human relations in the rest of the world.

Centuries of dependency and submission created a need for Koreans to assert themselves, and it was under the influence of the feeling of being alone in a hostile world that the *Juche* idea was developed, a do-it-yourself ideology that knew no bounds. They boldly set about industrializing the country and, without doubt, achieved great things. Being continuously indoctrinated the population could not fail to be aware that every town was newly built, that the country had become self-sufficient with regard to food supplies, that education and health care for all had been introduced, the countryside had been electrified and almost everything from ships to clothes could be manufactured – and all this purely with their own resources. The selection of goods produced was exhibited at the permanent industrial exhibition at which both the indigenous population and foreign visitors were given object lessons on the capabilities of the North Korean people. In the 1970s, the standard of living in North Korea was probably higher and more equally distributed than in South Korea. They were so impressed by their own successes that it seemed logical to call their country a 'paradise'.

But they went even further. The captains of ships at sea operated on sick members of their crew, inspired by the thoughts of Kim Il Sung. Only Korean feats were celebrated, no others, so that the people believed that both the defeat of Japan in 1945 and the victory in the Korean War were solely the work of their forefathers – as was purported in the museums of war and revolution. Kim Il Sung's *Juche* idea was portrayed as a more advanced social ideology than socialism/communism, and it was propagated as an export item that was gratefully received by the peoples of the world. The faith of Koreans in their own ability seemed to lack all bounds, and this lay behind the sudden and large-scale import of high technology. They took it for granted that they would rapidly reach the level of the most advanced nations – and ignored the fact that they had only themselves to compare with.

The rapid modernization required a work input on an unparalleled scale. As mentioned above, the whole population was mobilized in production and the only days off allowed were a handful of political holidays – evenings and weekends were devoted to 'voluntary' efforts. The Eastern Europeans claimed that the 'plan economy' was not worth its name, as every project was planned separately and, for example, the construction of new industries was not coordinated with increased energy production, a circumstance that was confirmed by the sight of imported capital goods from Scandinavia rusting away outdoors because they could not be used in production. This fragmentation consolidated the impression that the North Koreans were always preoccupied with storming the first rampart. To this could be added the Algerian's observation, on the occasion of the cooperation on the UN resolution, that it was impossible to prepare plans for various alternatives because the North Koreans insisted on deciding only about the most immediate measure. In other words, if the first target was not achieved, they had no alternative strategy in reserve so they had to improvise.

The blind, slave-like discipline and the uniformity just beggar description. It was not only work brigades and school children that marched on the streets. When the people were to gather together for a spontaneous celebration on the occasion of a state visit, those from each work place arrived in platoon formation at the designated site. 'Uniformly coloured' and 'monolithic' were prestige words. When talking with Koreans it was noticeable that they never seemed to question anything they had been taught. Ideas that had not been presented by their superiors just did not exist. There were no alternatives to their own, approved line. Arguments were not rejected, they were ignored.

These attitudes never ceased to amaze. A Swedish drilling engineer described his experiences with an example, the gist of which (somewhat simplified) concerned a central power generating unit which supplied, say, twelve horsepower and could thus power three four-horsepower or four three-horsepower drilling machines. But his work team insisted on exceeding the plan, by connecting four four-horsepower drills. His attempts at explaining that there was only twelve horsepower available were simply ignored. He had to let them get on with it and learn by experience. A French research consultant told of a similar experience within a theoretical subject; in desperation, he finally gave up with the sarcastic comment 'Congratulations, you have just discovered a new law of nature!'

The self-assumed role of lead state in the struggle against imperialism provided the foundations for a self-righteousness that demanded unswerving loyalty from all 'progressive' forces. The establishment of diplomatic relations was interpreted as a sign that the country in question had seen the light, and North Korea thus expected loyal and active support. During the debt repayment negotiations, they not only put forward (in all seriousness) their expectations of generous conditions because of Korea's state of war, but even suggested that it was our moral duty to shoulder a part of the burden. On a trip for foreigners to an agricultural cooperative we were greeted with the following words: 'As chairman of the guards' cooperative of the second rank "The White Stone" I bid you welcome and express our gratitude for your support in the struggle against the US imperialism.' This elitist spirit of avant-gardism permeated the entire population.

In November 1976 the South Korean press published an interview with a North Korean defector. According to the defector, the North Korean regime, to alleviate the growing shortage of foreign currency, had formed special 'work companies' in every town and district with the aim or earning foreign currency. Each company consisted of forty or fifty persons aged 30–40. They were to grow peppermint, ginseng, medicinal herbs and mushrooms under the auspices of a newly established purchasing centre for foreign currency. Add to this Kim Il Sung's order to the people, described in Chapter 7, to devote themselves to local production outside the plan, and you begin to obtain a clearer picture of the expected work input, and the hysterical attitude towards achieving results.

Colleagues warned us that the sewing section of the shop for foreigners regularly 'used' more material than was actually required for the curtains, clothes or whatever that had been ordered. At first we took no notice of such warnings, as we assumed the social control by North Koreans would make it impossible to own foreign goods – the cloth was mostly privately imported from China, which produced cheaper and better goods. But we soon came to realize that there was indeed substance in these allegations. In addition, a variety of items disappeared from our own supplies, such as ballpoint pens, window putty and nails, and even objects that could be used as models to copy, such as door handles and corridor lamps. Other embassies reported similar experiences. After the smuggling crisis, we came to the conclusion that it was not a case of private petty theft, but rather that every Korean had been instructed to contribute to the 'national housekeeping' as best he or she could.

During my conversations with the embassy interpreter, I gradually built up a picture of how the North Koreans regarded the world around them. As mentioned above, the interpreter had been stationed at the embassy in East Berlin, and from there had evidently made a number of excursions to the West, including Sweden. Indirectly and unintentionally, he came to reveal the deep scorn he felt for these societies, which were characterized by a lack of discipline and determination. He saw sloppiness everywhere, in the clumsy border controls, in the crowds of people that obviously did not make work a priority, in the confusing traffic, in the lack of a police and military presence on the streets, and much besides – all things that, for us, are indicative of a civilized and democratic society. The terrorist attack and the blowing up of the West German Embassy in Stockholm seemed to him almost to be a hopeful sign of the times and a natural phase in the anti-imperialist struggle – and it was also significant that the sloppy state had been unable to prevent such actions. He did not touch upon questions of living standards, because like all communists he compared capitalism's existing production capacity with the future promise of socialism.

All this is not intended as a description of a North Korean national character, but rather as an illustration of the environment, the system and the indoctrination that bred the smuggling embassy officials. The reasons for the smuggling crisis are no stranger than the fact that when the officials moved abroad they took with them, from their home country, a frame of reference of conditioned behaviour. They were evidently a 'special force' for foreign currency and were convinced they were smarter than the host countries' authorities.

This particular form of social spirit was genuinely North Korean in the sense that they had formulated their own categorical imperative that was not generally applicable and was only for North Koreans.

12

BETWEEN BEIJING AND MOSCOW

The non-communist foreigners in Pyongyang speculated over North Korea's relationship with Beijing and Moscow. To which sphere of influence did the country actually belong? And was it inching one way or the other? They examined the frequency of state visits in various directions and studied communiqués and news bulletins to find support for one view or the other. There was every reason to be sceptical about this form of 'Pyongyangology', particularly as it had a tendency to reflect only the incidents of the day and took little notice of more long-term contexts.

In East Asia especially, one should be careful not to underestimate the power of tradition and historical experience. Korea had lived in a sort of coexistence together with China for centuries, admittedly as a vassal, yet with its own king and its own institutions. As China became weaker during the nineteenth century, Korea was forced into fateful contacts with the rest of the world, which culminated in the Japanese occupation and later in the division of the country. The first appearance of Russia on the Korean stage lasted until the Russian–Japanese War of 1905. When the Russians returned in 1945, China had not yet recovered from its state of weakness and was more than ever preoccupied with internal struggles. Thus, North Korea came into being entirely under the protection of the Soviet Union.

It seems to be virtually impossible to separate myth from reality as regards Kim Il Sung's activities before 1945. The most likely version is that he cooperated with the Chinese communists up until about 1941, and then with the Soviet Union, where he spent much of the Second World War. He was born in 1912, moulded in guerilla struggles together with the Chinese, and was educated by the Russians, with whom he experienced crucial years and in whose wake he returned to Korea in 1945. He ought thus to have gained a thorough knowledge and experience of both China and the Soviet Union. It would have been natural for there to have been a certain tension between East Asian tradition and Soviet ideology. Circumstances dictated, however, that the Soviet-inspired fraction gained the upper hand in the Korean Communist Party.

North Korea must have learnt ineradicable lessons from the Korean War. When the country was threatened with annihilation in the autumn of 1950, it was Chinese troops that saved it. A decisive factor in that context must surely have been that the authorities in Beijing would not have been able to tolerate the idea of great foreign powers controlling North Korea – unlike the situation in Hong Kong and Taiwan. The Russians, however, were wary of direct involvement, and confined themselves to delivering essential supplies. Chinese sources have claimed that all Soviet supplies, even of armaments, had to be paid for. Similar claims have emanated from North Korea, but these were less certain. The Chinese contributions to the rebuilding of North Korea were thereafter given on more generous terms than the Soviet Russian ones.

Above all, trading relations with China appear to have been characterized by equality, whereas the Soviet Union is said to have used its position in a way that was unfavourable to North Korea. In addition, Moscow applied pressure to incorporate North Korea into the communist world's economic system (COMECON) as a supplier of raw materials. But to achieve a balance in its trade and industry and avoid being economically integrated into the Soviet Union, North Korea kept its distance from COMECON as far as was possible. Soviet counter-measures took the form of suspending aid, and this experience led to the development of the *Juche* ideology. Since the 1960s the North Koreans have publicly complained of the Soviet Union delivering goods and charging above world market prices while supplying themselves with North Korean raw materials and paying below the world market price.

Such quarrels do not seem to have occurred in the country's relations with China. In general, the Chinese seem to have treated the Koreans with considerably more tact than the Russians and other Eastern Europeans. When it came to communist doctrines, both Russians and Chinese were very ready to condemn every deviation from their own views as heresy, or at least to ridicule them. During the Cultural Revolution there was some youthful criticism of 'the fat revisionist' Kim Il Sung but, on the whole, the Chinese seem to have been both discreet and loyal with regard to North Korea.

The superior attitude of the Eastern Europeans was in contrast to this. Their representatives in Pyongyang did little to conceal the fact that they regarded the Korean contribution to Marxism as being at an adolescent level. In addition to this, one can naturally assume that they were genuinely shocked by the pretentiousness that Marxism/Leninism should be studied from the starting point of Kim Il Sung's *Juche* ideology. Furthermore, the leader cult must have aroused unpleasant recollections of the Stalin era. They seemed more inclined to deny the affinity of the social systems and could even take offence at the way the North Korean workers were being exploited.

It was difficult to gain a clear picture of the North Korean leadership's actual standpoint on the Sino-Soviet conflict. This was a dispute that had obvious advantages for North Korea, as well as disadvantages. On the one hand, the front against imperialism had been split, which made it more difficult for North Korea to get help in eliminating what it saw as the major obstacle to reunification, namely the US troops in South Korea. The thesis of peaceful coexistence, introduced by Stalin's successors, was entirely against Pyongyang's interests, which seemed to accord entirely with Mao Zedong's unrelenting adherence to world revolution. The North Korean reaction to the Soviet retreat during the Cuba crisis was therefore negative. But North Korea's dependence on both China and the Soviet Union led it also to oppose Beijing's increasingly fierce anti-Soviet diatribes while the Vietnam War was still being waged.

In contrast, Kim Il Sung continually warned against adopting an attitude of servility towards the great powers and emphasized that the North Koreans were now undergoing a period of independence. This attitude seemed so genuine that it was hard to imagine anything other than that he welcomed the room for manoeuvring that the split offered. It should be noted that the verbal diatribes against the influence of great powers seem, like so much else, to have been inspired by old communist Chinese models. At the same time, from the point of view of Pyongyang, it would have been entirely reasonable even to count China among the great powers. In the wake of the normalization of the relationship between China and the USA, North Korea became even more isolated in its anti-imperialist extremism, and it tried to alleviate that isolation by using the *Juche* ideology as bait for developing countries.

Although the Sino-Soviet discord afforded North Korea room for manoeuvre that it had not previously known, the COMECON experience (mentioned earlier) showed that there was a risk of jeopardizing its own development programme if it was to find itself on a collision course with an important donor of technological aid. Even though the North Koreans felt a greater affinity with China – to use a common local expression, they were as close to each other 'as lips and teeth' – they were technologically dependent on the Soviet Union. But the new room for manoeuvring could be used to broaden their contacts, and release themselves from a far too one-sided relationship. The problems with the Soviet Union were reason enough for this – to which one could add the insight that they no longer had any cause to barter their valuable minerals on poor terms in exchange for obsolete Soviet machines while the Russians were themselves acquiring better technology from the West. This new economic orientation was complemented in the foreign policy sphere with a wide-ranging offensive to broaden their contacts and diplomatic relations with the whole world.

As the intensification of the economic contacts with the West was intended to reduce North Korea's dependence on the Soviet bloc, it was undoubtedly regarded with pleasure in Beijing. Meanwhile, one can safely assume that Moscow, for the same reason, would hardly welcome the development, although it would mean that it would be relieved of loss-making and thankless projects on the North Korean market. But it soon transpired that North Korea was not at all ready to enter the world market, as demonstrated by the heavy debts it incurred from the purchase of capital goods, goods that subsequently could not be utilized in profitable production. The result was an economic setback on such a scale that it had repercussions on the policy of non-alignment. New economic contacts could not be developed to replace the old pattern. The Soviet Union had the satisfaction of seeing how the capitalist world got its fingers burned in its attempt to penetrate North Korea, and how Pyongyang was forced to submit and yet again foster trade with the Soviet bloc – and this time from a considerably weakened negotiating position vis-à-vis Moscow.

As will be revealed in the chapter on North Korean ideology (Chapter 18), there can be little doubt that the North Koreans had a much more relaxed attitude to China than to the Soviet Union. Developments following the Korean War can, for the reasons described above, only have strengthened this tendency. For the Koreans, isolated as they had been since time immemorial, China represented the known world that exerted an immeasurable influence, both culturally and politically. Their dealings with the Chinese had established a practice, and the Chinese understood the Koreans far better than did the deviant Japanese or Russians, neither of whom really tried. The Koreans had indeed developed their own self-esteem, but this incorporated a respectful acknowledgement of China as a sort of frame of reference.

The answer to the question at the beginning of this chapter concerning the comparison of North Korea's relationships with Beijing and Moscow, is thus quite clear – Beijing's influence was, without doubt, greater than Moscow's. In practice, opposite tendencies could naturally occur, but these were limited to short periods. In addition, the Sino-Soviet discord afforded North Korea the unique opportunity of room for manoeuvring, which no longer exist. Following the dissolution of the Soviet Union, Russia reverted (in Korean eyes) to its former role as one of the great foreign powers. But China is China, as ever.

13

THE REUNIFICATION ISSUE

An assessment of the situation in 1977

It would be no exaggeration to say that the question of Korea's reunification was always brought up in every context. In the head of state's principal speeches, in discussions and conversations with officials on all levels, and even on visits to agricultural cooperatives, the question cropped up. However, it would not be correct to say one discussed it with the Koreans – one listened to the same exposition time and time again.

There were many who felt obliged to raise the issue with the North Koreans and explore what could be done to lessen the tension on the Korean peninsula. As has been described in Chapter 9, the Australian Foreign Minister made determined attempts – which most probably contributed to the North Koreans decision to order the Australian Embassy staff to leave the country. Prime Minister Bhutto of Pakistan offered his services on an official visit – but nothing came of it. The Algerians, who had helped North Korea to present a draft resolution in the UN, confirmed that it was hopeless trying to analyse problems with the North Koreans: 'One can never discuss tactical negotiating alternatives in relation to the probable course of events, but only deal with the very next measure – it is like talking to Martians!'.

Sweden's interest in the Korea question was brought about by membership of the NNSC (Neutral Nations Supervisory Commission) in Panmunjom, which was set up after the Korean War. This led to my often being sent instructions from home to ascertain North Korean viewpoints in general, and when this turned out to be difficult, or even impossible, to raise some detail such as the effect of a UN resolution on the NNSC or on North Korean principles and how these might concern the NNSC. As a rule, I was not given any chance to discuss things, but occasionally it could not be avoided, such as the times I was summoned to the ministry to listen to a lecture about the situation in South Korea. In addition to the usual standard lecture, one was sometimes told that a particular question would be dealt with when it became topical. It seems that the Koreans nevertheless understood, to a degree, that Sweden's freedom of action was, in practice, influenced by its membership of the NNSC. And Pyongyang did not want to risk the continued existence of that committee, presumably on account of it being the only forum in which they had direct contact with the USA.

The various statements that were churned out on cue could gradually be put together rather like a jigsaw puzzle, to form a complete picture. One such statement was that the NNSC's purpose was to control the import of weapons and the observance of the armistice agreement, while the reunification question was a matter for the Koreans themselves to deal with. Another came from the head of state at a banquet in honour of North Vietnam during the almost delirious celebrations that erupted in Pyongyang when the USA evacuated Saigon. He then congratulated Hanoi on achieving the *peaceful* reunification of Vietnam. As this reunification was the result of several decades of war, I found the wording revealing. It could only mean that North Vietnam, by winning the war, had created the necessary conditions for a peaceful reunification. If applied to the situation in Korea, then the North Korean attitudes became more understandable. For example, Pyongyang insisted upon negotiating directly with the South Korean people and refused to have any contact with the government in Seoul. By, in some way or other – not excluding force of arms – removing that government conditions would undeniably have been created for a similarly 'peaceful' reunification in Korea too.

An account of the North Korean understanding of the situation on the peninsula, and of how reunification was to be achieved, was given on the occasion of a visit in the spring of 1976 by a high-ranking official from the Swedish Foreign Ministry, who sought an audience with the North Korean Foreign Minister. I realized that the audience had been granted when, at about nine o'clock in the evening, a doctor and nurse suddenly arrived at the embassy and told us we were to be given a basic medical examination. Shortly after their arrival, we were informed by telephone that we were expected to present ourselves at the Foreign Ministry just before midnight. The Foreign Minister was assisted by a deputy foreign minister, who presented the following account of the situation on the Korean peninsula:

The main problem consisted of the US policy of aggression, which was far older than the Korean War. Ever since their Declaration of Independence in 1776, said the deputy minister, the USA had been aggressive. The Japanese occupation of Korea at the beginning of the twentieth century had been with the secret approval of the USA, and in 1945 the USA finally attempted to carry out its aggressive intentions towards Korea. With the collapse of Japan, people's committees were formed spontaneously throughout Korea. But, without the Koreans' consent, the US troops suddenly occupied South Korea and dissolved the people's committees. In 1948, he went on, the USA wrote election laws and proclaimed an election in South Korea; the South Koreans did not do it themselves. On the day of the election, the US troops killed half a million people. As the governments in Seoul had, since then, been entirely dependent upon the USA, South Korea was not an independent nation. The North Koreans had themselves organized elections simultaneously in both the North and the South. In the North, participation was 99%, in the South only 75% (by implication, in the underground elections they had arranged). Therefore, the Democratic People's Republic of Korea represented all the people of Korea.

The Korean War itself was not mentioned in this presentation, but, as is well known, Pyongyang has always claimed that it was triggered by an attack from the South. With regard to the present situation, the deputy minister pointed out that the USA was in a deep economic crisis and was trying to solve this by waging war. In South Korea, the USA had the role of a colonial power as it wanted a supplier of raw materials and a strategic military base to – in the first instance – conquer the whole of Korea. Via South Korea, it already controlled Japan, and prevented it from developing in a progressive direction. From its base in Korea, the USA intended to control China and the Soviet Union.

North Korea's mission, above all else, the deputy minister went on, was to bring about reunification. Their guidelines in this task were the three principles of independence, peace and democracy (by the last they meant that different social systems were not an obstacle). Nobody could have any objections to these principles, not even South Korea, and they were also named in the joint communiqué of 1972. But South Korea had immediately breached those principles: they had violated independence by requesting the stationing of foreign troops; they had violated peace by increasing their armaments and introducing atomic weapons; and they had violated democracy by refusing to live under the same heavens as the communists – how could one possibly reunify Korea if one refused to recognize the existence of communists?

And what is more, he continued, in South Korea they spoke of a two-Korea solution. Under these circumstances, those on the North Korean side considered it pointless to continue negotiations, but they were naturally prepared to restart them on the basis of the three principles outlined above. North Korea's will to maintain peace was well documented. The risk of war consisted of an attack from the South.

The most immediate actions for the realization of reunification would be, in the opinion of the Deputy Minister, the dissolution of the UN military command and the withdrawal of the US troops. This would thereby create a beneficial climate for North–South discussions. It would also mean that the armistice agreement would cease to apply, and could be replaced by a peace treaty. Because the armistice agreement had been signed by the UN command and not by South Korea, this meant that South Korea was not party to the agreement. Because the UN command was dominated by the USA, North Korea and the USA were the real parties in the agreement and these two should negotiate a peace treaty. A comment to the effect that the Chinese volunteers, too, had signed the armistice agreement was rejected on the grounds that they had long since left the country and had no intention of taking part.

The Foreign Minister himself mentioned the debate in the UN General Assembly in 1975 and expressed his satisfaction with the success that North Korea had won by virtue of the pro-North Korean draft proposal having been approved. (This was seen by the North Koreans as implying that the USA had been enjoined to remove its troops from South Korea. A pro-South Korean draft resolution had also been approved, as described above, and with better voting figures, but this was regarded in Pyongyang as 'non-existent'.) In this context, he wished to voice a degree of gratitude for Sweden's sympathy but added that, 'In all honesty, Sweden did not behave well in the UN. You do not understand the kernel of the problem!'

It was with a certain bitter-sweet satisfaction that I regarded my colleague, and superior, who had travelled to Pyongyang. There could now hardly be any doubt of my reports being realistic and by no means as full of fancy as some people seemed to have assumed. And all our questions and observations following this presentation of the Korea problem were patiently and long-windedly rejected by the Foreign Minister while he emphasized that the Swedish side did not realize the facts of the situation. All that he said served only to confirm that we had made a correct interpretation of the North Korean standpoints.

The Foreign Minister's criticism of the Swedish performance in the UN naturally demanded a clear response, particularly as it could be connected to North Korean statements to the effect that all those who did not support North Korea were 'US stooges'. But the Foreign Minister reacted to our response by laughing, a very common gesture of embarrassment among Koreans, but one that was usually understood by foreigners as an expression of contempt.

However, could one hope that this embarrassment might be interpreted as an embryonic insight that their previous tactics of verbal brawling struck out at opponents and partial sympathizers alike, and all too randomly, and thus damaged their own cause? It was by then already clear that China and the Soviet bloc were only prepared to give verbal support, and that when it came to action they would avoid strengthening North Korea's potential for war. Nor did these allies become more positively inclined upon being informed that the centre of world revolution had moved to Pyongyang. North Korea had then turned to the non-aligned group in which it enjoyed a degree of sympathy among all the 'anti-imperialists', but there, too, it transpired that potential supporters were alienated by the North Koreans' slogans and their choice of wording in general. Yugoslavia refused to help by being a joint proposer again, and consequently Pyongyang had little choice but to cancel its attempts to put forward a new resolution at the UN General Assembly in 1976.

The extent to which the North Korean standpoints were just totally unrealistic becomes even more evident if one catalogues them so that they are shown in conjunction with summary descriptions of the actual historical events behind them. For example, regarding the division of Korea, they ignored the fact that it was the result of agreements between Japan's conquerors in the Second World War. Instead, the entire blame was laid upon the USA, which had occupied South Korea, while nothing was said about the Soviet Union, which had occupied North Korea and set up the Kim Il Sung government. The North Korean people had been led to believe that it was the Koreans themselves – i.e. the communist underground movement – that had driven out the Japanese.

They also claimed that in 1948 elections had been held in the whole of Korea, with those in the South being held 'underground'. Consequently, the government in Seoul was a puppet government with no right to represent the country or its people. The government in Pyongyang was the only rightful representative of the whole of Korea.

The North Koreans believed that the USA and the UN were one and the same with regard to commitment in the Korean War. The armistice agreement was signed by the UN, North Korea and the Chinese volunteers, but they claimed that negotiations over its replacement by a peace agreement could only be undertaken by the 'true parties' to the armistice agreement, by which they meant, of course, the USA and North Korea. South Korea had no right to participate, and there was no need for the Chinese volunteers to be represented. Their own population was under the mistaken impression that the Korean War was caused by a US attack that North Korea had repelled on its own. They demanded that the UN command be dissolved and that there be an unconditional withdrawal of the US troops from South Korea in order to create a beneficial climate for North–South negotiations. In this context, they rejected any discussion about a balance between North and South Korea with the argument that it was not possible to speak of a military balance in one and the same country.

They ignored the fact that the UN General Assembly had passed two contradictory resolutions on the Korea question in the autumn of 1975, and they demanded that the resolution (singular! – i.e. the pro-North Korean one) should be implemented.

Although North Korea wanted to negotiate solely with the USA about a peace agreement, it nevertheless considered reunification to be a purely internal Korean issue, which was to be solved without interference from outside. At the same time as they prided themselves upon their egalitarian society – in which there was no distinction between government authorities, parties or organizations – they suggested that the North's political parties and other organizations should negotiate with their equivalents in the South, with the exception that South Korean authorities were not to participate, other than on conditions that they abandoned their two-Korea policy, refrained from anti-communism, stopped suppressing democrats and patriots, and gave up all mention of the threat from the North and the war policy that this created.

To an outsider, it was patently obvious that the North Korean tactics worked against their stated aims. Facts are interpreted differently by different interested parties, and it is thus pointless for any one party in a negotiation to consider that they have a monopoly over what is right and wrong. It is a matter of coming to a negotiated agreement, and if one is not strong enough to dictate the conditions, then the best results can only be achieved through goodwill. 'En diplomatie il ne s'agit pas d'avoir raison, il s'agit de plaire' (Diplomacy is not about being right, it is about pleasing). Thus, the negotiator's personality can play a decisive role. It is hardly necessary to say that, in this respect, the North Korean negotiators were their own worst enemies. Nor was their negotiating position improved by the country's enormous expenditure on arms or the revelations about the secret tunnelling under the demarcation line – tunnels that were big enough to allow the passage of lorries.

With this background in mind, from the very first the North Koreans adopted a strictly negative attitude to the proposal put forward, now and then, to convene a special Korea conference. A major conference could indeed be used as a simple propaganda exercise, at which communist and non-aligned states could content themselves with verbal support – as at the UN. But there was an inherent risk that it might lead on to a limited conference for those parties most directly concerned, such as both Koreas, the Soviet Union, China, the USA and Japan.

It was apparent that in such a limited group the major communist powers could hardly be counted on to support Pyongyang. The unarticulated 'rules of the game' of the Cold War would not tolerate any border adjustments that favoured the communist side without there also being a considerable worsening of the political climate. So the interest of the rest of the world, especially of the communist part, in retaining the existing power balance on the Korean peninsula would be exposed without mercy. A North Korean attempt to change this would force all participants to show their cards in a way that would reveal the fullness of Pyongyang's isolation. Moscow and Beijing could hardly be considered prepared to sacrifice the policy of détente and their closer relations to Washington to devote their efforts towards solving their mutual problem and, if it came to the worst, being forced to take sides and support or desert Pyongyang; the USA was keen to maintain its credibility in Asia; and everybody feared that Japan would feel called upon to re-arm, with unpredictable consequences not only for the situation in the Far East but for world politics in general. In order not to draw attention to its actual isolation, Pyongyang must thus oppose any form of Korea conference.

Over the years, the North Koreans learned from their experiences. When, after an absence of over ten years, I returned to Pyongyang at the end of the 1980s I was struck by the degree to which the propaganda had been demilitarized. Nursery children no longer shot at targets representing US soldiers, and in the mass performances the Korean War was illustrated not with uniformed soldiers but with dancers dressed in white, bearing sticks instead of rifles.

But the reunification issue did not come any closer to a solution during the decade I was absent, nor in the decade that followed. It must be concluded that the North Korean position in the reunification question was simply not negotiable. Korea would be united after the US troops had been withdrawn, and the Seoul government's influence had been undermined.

North Korea's stubbornness in following its policy, with the methods and arguments described above, was seen by the whole world as unrealistic, and for those observers most closely involved it seemed to be a deliberate 'sham battle'. But in Pyongyang they evidently judged the situation by other yardsticks. Neutral mediators seemed to be regarded as harmful and, as such, were to be kept away from any involvement and influence, because that could only serve to extend the life of the Seoul regime. As described in the chapter on ideology (Chapter 19), the people were inoculated with a solid Confucian–communist ideology and thus convinced that it represented both a just form of government and a development in accordance with scientific laws. The way into the cul-de-sac was already mapped out.

14

BACK TO PYONGYANG

In the autumn of 1988, the Democratic People's Republic of Korea was to celebrate its fortieth anniversary, and dignitaries from all over the world were invited to take part in the festivities. The Swedish parliamentary elections at the same time gave all the Swedish politicians a natural (and presumably welcome) reason to decline. Somebody then got the bright idea of entrusting me – who had been the first man there – with the task of representing Sweden as 'Ambassadeur en mission spéciale'.

The ordinary chargé d'affaires had recently been transferred to Abu Dhabi and Minister Kiesow – with several years' experience from Pyongyang – had been 'borrowed' from his posting in Tokyo for a month only, and was forced to return there. Consequently, after the anniversary I was asked to staff the embassy for a week or two while a new chargé d'affaires or a proper temporary officer was recruited. To recruit staff for service in Pyongyang was, however, usually an uphill job … and of course I remained there for a couple of months.

My impression from the 1970s was that North Korea had shown a better rate of development than South Korea in the first quarter of a century after liberation but had already begun to stagnate. Even then one could predict that the economic race would be won by South Korea. The year 1976 had illustrated what sort of cul-de-sac the country had manoeuvred itself into. In particular, the breakdown of economic relations with the West could not fail to lead to serious economic consequences, not least through forcing Pyongyang back to an increased dependence upon the Eastern European communist states. By virtue of its arrogant attempts to muster international support at the conference of non-aligned states the DPRK had ended up being isolated in international politics, and this meant that the Korean question could not be pursued further at the UN because its former allies refused to accede to North Korea's conditions. It was quite obvious that they would, of necessity, have to change course, but it was doubtful if the North Korean leaders were capable of realizing this, or indeed willing to do so.

The years I spent in North Korea left an indelible impression, and my interest in the country's fate had never faded. I had regularly read the special journals available. From them, and from all the conversations over the years with my successors in Pyongyang, it was abundantly clear that everything was still trundling along in the same old tracks. This was, of course, hardly surprising, given the petrified structure of North Korean society. A couple of embassies had closed, namely those of Gabon and Zaire; however, a few new ones had been added, including Ethiopia and Nicaragua, which were newcomers to the socialist camp, and Iran, which was in the middle of the war with Iraq and was understood to have exchanged oil for North Korean military material. This, in turn, had led Iraq to close its embassy. The UNDP had established an office too and this had a Swedish chief, which meant welcome company for me.

The Korean question had not advanced, but they were still talking, now and then, about having talks. Direct negotiations with South Korea were – as ever – unthinkable as they would imply that the regime's picture of South Korea as a USA puppet would have been declared null and void. As a symbol of South Korea's improved international reputation, Seoul had been chosen to host the Olympic Games, which had naturally been regarded with ill ease in Pyongyang. It was seen as particularly disturbing that several of their former allies among the communist states were evidently not intending to comply with the North's request that they boycott the games. The North Koreans' schizophrenic outlook had, if anything, been accentuated – they saw themselves as living in an aggressive world that bullied them while, at the same time, considering themselves to be an ideological centre, celebrated the world over on account of Kim Il Sung's *Juche* idea.

And they were still lagging behind economically. According to international statistics, the per capita income in the 1950s had been twice that of South Korea – now, thirty years later, the situation was the opposite, 965 US$ against 1,954 US$. Under the influence of glasnost and perestroika, the Eastern European satellite states had begun to complain openly about North Korea's way of managing its trading relations, and they promptly curtailed deliveries as soon as contracted commitments were not fulfilled. There had also been signs of internal opposition in the form of posters, but this could not be confirmed. The Albanians, of all people, had called North Korea an unbelievably closed society. And even the previously so withdrawn Chinese knowingly shook their heads and wanted a more flexible economic policy. Koreans lived on both sides of the Korean–Chinese border, which was evidently open for the local population, and there it was obvious that the North Koreans' once higher standard of living had become the opposite.

This miserable economic development would seem to be the result of the usual wrong priorities and the disorganization caused by the continued efforts to increase production by demanding the manufacture of goods in addition to the fixed plan. Kim Il Sung had launched a campaign for increased agricultural production by ordering the draining of 300,000 hectares of coastal land for rice growing. This could only be done by denying planned production the necessary resources (in the form of transport capacity and labour) to such a degree that it must naturally affect the fulfilling of the plan. As well as which, the desalination process had not worked as had been hoped – one can but wonder whether it was based on scientific or ideological grounds – so that the greater part of the programme had come to a standstill.

Priority was also given to rebuilding the centre of Pyongyang – there was to be a gigantic triumphal arch, a *Juche* tower, a hotel of 100 storeys, and, not least, an enormous athletes' village in the vain hope of attracting some parts of the Olympic Games from Seoul. In addition, a start was made on the construction of a motorway from the Chinese border all the way down to South Korea. All these laid claim to resources that would have been more profitably used in keeping industry going and for the acquisition of new means of production. Ignorance of economic issues, scorn for science and proven experience and a stubborn adherence to a superstitious ideology all staked out the course towards the breakdown that was to become a reality some ten years further down the road. But the most obvious difference was considered to be that the privileges of the *nomenklatura* had become more evident. Well-dressed officials, with their chauffeur-driven cars, were seen with foreign guests at the hotel restaurants. Thus many of the outer signs of equality, still cherished in the 1970s, had been abandoned. As the rest of the population had only experienced slight improvements in their standard of living, the social divide could be seen in a more undisguised fashion.

The number of flight connections to Pyongyang had not increased over the years. In September 1988 I first took a flight to Beijing. It was like a completely different city. The simple dignity and helpfulness that had made such an impression a dozen years previously, all that was gone. Then, one of the hotel staff would come running with a pair of worn-out socks, discarded in the waste bin, in the belief that they had been forgotten. When we had dropped a thermos full of hot water for baby food in the hotel lobby, a porter had immediately come to sweep up the broken glass and then run out to buy a new thermos and fill it with hot water in the kitchen. Then, the prices had been modest, indeed strikingly so – if one had a glass of Chinese brandy in the bar after dinner it cost about one new penny sterling and there was no question of a tip. Then, the staff in the three antique shops were highly educated, elderly gentlemen in blue dungarees, who (in good English) explained to the foreigners about the works of art and helped them to choose.

Now we stayed in a hotel that was entirely Western style, with cafeterias and long bars and fast-food stalls. Now everything had been commercialized so that it was unrecognizable and there was no more talk of gratuitous helpfulness or skilful advice and reliable prices. For anyone who had got to know China in the old orthodox times, the country seemed to have lost its soul. But, at the same time, the increased economic activity was evident as was the improved standard of living.

The airport at Pyongyang was full of travellers who were going to take part in the festivities, all of whom were received officially – there were still no taxis. I was taken directly to the empty Swedish Embassy where I installed myself. The extension, that I myself had once planned, with the offices and the main residence on two adjoining plots, was already looking its age and had become a trifle shabby. But it nevertheless conveyed a decidedly pleasant impression now that the gardens had become established. But then again, the little set-up now seemed desolately large as it was manned by a single official, at best accompanied and assisted by his wife.

The premises proved useful when Ambassador Skala, newly appointed to Beijing, came to present his credentials. He was accompanied by his wife, as well as an official, and there was plenty of room for all. In an impressively short time, we were granted an audience with the president. We motored many miles north to a tourist area with a newly built luxury hotel in Myohyang, which had been inaccessible in my day. Kim Il Sung seemed to be prepared for the Swedish side to bring up North Korea's outstanding debts. After a monologue of some minutes, he cut the seance short before any discussion of anything could even start. This was an illustration as good as any that they wanted diplomatic relations – but on their own terms.

The journey to Myohyang at least gave us the opportunity to enjoy some mountain walks in the breathtakingly beautiful and dramatic landscape with hilltops formed like minarets, sometimes crowned with a temple, and deep, forested ravines. There was an old Buddhist monastery, converted into a museum, which contained hundreds of carved log-ends with woodcuts for printing, more than 500 years old. Besides it, in a large building, all the presents that the Great Leader had received from an admiring world were exhibited. If I remember rightly, there were about 65,000 objects in all, ranging from railway wagons and cars to the Swedish decorative glass pieces that I had presented a decade earlier on various state occasions. The most famous object was a stuffed alligator, standing on its hind legs and holding a tray with a carafe and glass in its front paws.

When the visitors from Beijing had gone on their way, it became undeniably rather lonely in Pyongyang. Admittedly, the Eastern Europeans had become much more accessible and were evidently prepared to accept the consequences of South Korea becoming all the more recognized. The only exception appeared to be the East German, who – one may assume – had special views on the problems affecting divided countries. Apart from that, it seemed to me that the diplomats in Pyongyang were considerably more despondent and passive than in my day; they seemed to have given up and were uninterested and bored. This reflected North Korea's worsening reputation and diminishing role in world politics. In the 1970s things were different; we could certainly laugh at the government, but we still had a grudging respect for the people despite everything. By the end of the 1980s the death knells had already started ringing for the communist system, and the stubborn perseverance of Korea only served to mark it out as a certain loser. As a diplomatic posting, Pyongyang had always been one of the most difficult, but now it had also become lacking in content and really rather pointless, which, of course, affected the diplomats there. It was typical of my time there in the 1970s that we tried to see the humorous side of things – now nobody seemed to care.

There were exceptions. The Polish and Yugoslav ambassadors were not career diplomats but cultural writers, for whom a dying society was, if anything, exceptionally absorbing. They both told me, in a somewhat resigned fashion, that Kim Il Sung's major anniversary speech had included a section with criticism of the bureaucracy, which had been reported in the Polish and Yugoslavian press with the comment that perestroika had now at last spread to North Korea. As a result of this, both ambassadors were summoned to the Foreign Ministry where they were seriously reprimanded for this unprecedented lapse. It was demanded that their governments should ensure that the newspapers concerned should print retractions and apologies, because the People's Republic had no need of either perestroika or any such 'winds of change'. The ambassadors were duty bound to forward these demands to their superiors at home with explanatory comments. But their own ministries reacted quite ungraciously and remonstrated with them about the unsuitability and the insincerity of making fun of their host country in this way.

The situation was very familiar to me. Each and every attempt at describing the values and reasoning that characterized the North Korean negotiators met with undisguised distrust back home in Sweden. In some way it seemed also to be regarded as if I was making fun of the very profession of diplomacy, and this was not approved of by influential elder colleagues at home who had never lived outside Europe or the North Atlantic area. For communist ambassadors, the situation was probably made even worse because they could be suspected of joking about the political system. For the officials who were actually out there, such experiences were usually only amusing the first few times, becoming purely macabre as time went by.

Pyongyang would again manage to demonstrate that they were not interested in mediation on the Korean question but wanted to deal with it themselves. Directly after the Swedish elections, the Swedish Foreign Minister set off on an official visit to a number of East Asian countries, including Japan and South Korea. He had then kept a few days in reserve for a possible visit to Pyongyang before going on to Thailand. The connecting flights with North Korea were still characterized by time-consuming detours and, in order to follow his schedule, he wished to travel directly from Seoul by road to Pyongyang via Panmunjom.

This set in motion what, for me, was a round of negotiations just as Kafkaesque as those I had suffered twelve years previously on the occasion of the smuggling crisis. For the North Koreans, a visit by a Western Foreign Minister was naturally extremely welcome. But it soon became quite clear that they were still guided by an all-embracing negative attitude to anything that could be interpreted as meaning that Pyongyang was prepared to shift ground on the Korean question and allow some form of foreign intervention. In the end, it turned out that not only was it totally unthinkable to allow someone to arrive via the proposed route but also to receive a Foreign Minister in Pyongyang if he had already visited Seoul on the same journey. It was evidently thought that such a combination could not avoid being interpreted by the outside world as interference in the Korean question. My argument, that the Swedish officers in Panmunjom regularly travelled across the line and that the same right could – without prejudicial effect – be accorded the person who appointed them, was rejected without explanation.

The North Koreans thereby showed that they had decided to ward off the visit but in such a way that it was the Swedes who made the decision to cancel it. The negotiations thus started with a request for elucidation, discussions about flight connections and time schedules and, not least, postponed or cancelled meetings to gain time. In negotiations of this type, little attention should be paid to the content of what was said and the form in which it was presented. Instead, it was important to concentrate one's efforts upon trying to gather the intention behind the words. When this gradually became clearer, I set my mind on not allowing the Swedish side to be provoked into shouldering the blame for a cancelled visit. The continually postponed meetings and the vague or barely decipherable arguments from the North Korean side could only serve the purpose of making us feel that we were being treated in a degrading manner so that we would break off the discussion.

One of the methods adopted was the local speciality of downgrading the level, i.e. the rank, of their negotiator to the lowest possible in the hope that the opposing party, finding himself in a situation unworthy of his dignity as a representative of his country, should leave the room. However, I continued to ventilate such possibilities as special flights and other suggestions to show goodwill and a desire to reach agreement to the very last. After about ten days, on the afternoon of the last possible day of arrival and having done their utmost to avoid negative formulations, the North Koreans were finally obliged to play their hand and actually spell out the fact that it was not suitable to receive a minister at that particular time. Nor was it suitable a week later, i.e. after the journey to Thailand, or that someone else from the minister's group came in his place. They were, however, at the same time exceedingly anxious to maintain a pleasant atmosphere and detained me and my companion for an extra quarter of an hour with personal and friendly small talk.

A course of events such as that described above is well suited to the experiment of trying to describe how differently it must have been experienced from the perspectives of Stockholm and Pyongyang. This can best be done by writing a Swedish and a likely Korean version:

From a Swedish standpoint everything would be simple and straightforward. A decision would be made that the Foreign Minister, during his East Asia trip, should, if possible, visit Pyongyang too. The new ambassador in Beijing would be instructed to try to present his credentials in North Korea beforehand. The acting head of mission, coincidentally still *in situ* in Pyongyang would be instructed to remain at his post until further notice to prepare a visit. Stockholm would approve his request to temporarily reinforce the embassy with an embassy secretary from Moscow, who just happened to be in Pyongyang on a (so he believed) short tourist visit. After which, negotiations would be entered into as to a suitable date for the visit. These negotiations would not lead anywhere on account of a lack of interest on Pyongyang's part.

How then might this have looked in the eyes of the suspicious, as well as hierarchically and conspiratorially inclined, North Koreans? They could well have seen it as a carefully planned attempt from the Swedish side to introduce some new and unknown element into the Korean question. They may well have had a picture like the following before them: when Counsellor Naessén had completed his tour of duty in Pyongyang in August, he was replaced for one month by an official with a higher rank Minister Kiesow, who was the second-in-command at the embassy in Tokyo and who had previously served several years in Pyongyang. He, in turn, was replaced in September by an official of even slightly higher rank, an ambassador who had also served several years in North Korea. The telegram traffic to and from the Swedish Embassy increased considerably. Then Stockholm requested that the new ambassador in Beijing should present his credentials at short notice. Additionally the Swedish Embassy enquired whether the North Korean Foreign Minister would be in the country during the coming weeks. After which all the Swedish diplomats in Pyongyang travelled to Panmunjom to meet with the Swedish ambassador to the Republic of Korea. Having returned to Pyongyang they immediately informed the authorities of the proposal that the Swedish Foreign Minister should come on a visit the following week and that it was his intention to travel overland from South Korea. Meanwhile, a Swedish embassy secretary had arrived from Moscow on a putative tourist visit, which was immediately transformed into his being incorporated into the embassy staff for the period of the ministerial visit in question. Such a course of events could not be a matter of mere chance; therefore, it would be advisable not to take any risks. This was confirmed by virtue of the fact that when the visit was cancelled, all the Swedish personnel departed within a few days and left the embassy unmanned.

This description is somewhat simplified and dramatized. But on the whole, it can well be imagined to reflect what the North Koreans thought they had established. What were the Swedes' intentions? Why did two former heads of mission return at this particular time to Pyongyang? Why was the proposal for the Minister's visit to Pyongyang only presented with one week's notice? Was it in some way connected with the ongoing consideration of the Korean question at the UN? Did this interference by the Swedish Embassies in Tokyo and Moscow mean that both Japan and the Soviet Union were involved? Could one ignore the fact that Sweden was the only country that had people stationed in Pyongyang, Panmunjom and Seoul, and had put into effect the repugnant idea of 'cross-recognition', i.e. that the international community should recognize the existence of two Koreas? It would doubtless have been impossible to convince them that the successive escalation of events was not intentional but entirely a matter of chance.

The only lasting result of the episode was that embassy secretary Semneby enriched the Swedish vocabulary with the verb 'att pyongyanga' – i.e. 'to pyongyang' – as a foreign service equivalent of the seafarers' 'shanghai'.

15

CARNIVAL IN PYONGYANG

It was claimed that about 350 foreign delegations attended the ceremony to celebrate the fortieth jubilee of the North Korean Republic. By delegation was meant anything from heads of state, with entourage, to solitary representatives of study groups (studying the works of Kim Il Sung) from the African bush. The programme consisted of a commemorative gathering, some theatre performances, the people's celebratory march-past and a jubilee banquet. The festivities demonstrated, above all, that the Republic untiringly continued to advance along the one and only path. The cult of the leader had acquired even greater proportions and the desire to impress foreign visitors had been allotted even more resources.

It began somewhat blandly with a visit to the permanent industrial exhibition. This was like the old routine for anyone who had several times been dragged round the enormous 1970s' 'Three Revolutions' Exhibition, which displayed everything from sewing thread to locomotive engines, and in which all the chairs and benches upon which the Great Leader had rested on his round tour had been honoured with protective coverings and roped-off sections. The greatest interest was this time aroused by two motor cars of the 'Pyongyang' marque, which was a very fancy model and, with the exception of the design of the radiator and a strange soft-glossy spray finish, was a spitting image of the Mercedes Benz 190. Were these prototype models? Did they ever start up series production? Or – heretic thought – were they simply slightly modified German originals?

On 8 September, all the guests gathered in a comparatively small room in the Party headquarters. We were squashed together in several rows along the walls, while the Great Leader, his son and his entourage walked round and shook those hands that were stretched forth from the throng, with the interpreters announcing who we were. Later, we all entered and took our places on the podium in the large assembly hall, where thousands of Party members clapped their hands and cheered loudly. A large proportion were military men, including several hundred generals, who were richly decorated, as were many of the civilian participants. During the Leader's speech, members of the audience regularly stood up and gave voice to their approval. As was usual in ceremonial contexts, the ovations were accompanied by the clinking of medals.

In the evening a large gala performance was held in the army club's great theatre, during which 5,000 participants presented *Song of Paradise* – the Paradise being, as we know, their own country. The show was grandiose, overwhelming. Off stage, on each side of the stalls, stood choirs of about 500 persons each. For some items their number was doubled. On stage, myriads of artistes performed in beautiful costumes in continually changing song, dance and music numbers. There were innumerable musicians in the orchestra pit, and the conductor kept the whole ensemble together without a score. The lyrics of the songs were projected on to the wall beside the stage in four languages, and there you could wonder at the epithets fêting the Leader, the saviour of the nation, the sun of mankind, the eternally generous, the benevolent, the admired, the beloved, the venerated and so on … for about two hours.

Many first-time visitors met with difficulties when trying to evaluate the performance because they were repelled by the exaggerations. But we 'who had been through it all before' could enjoy the magnificence and the beauty and, not least, expertly analyse the variation and the elements of renewal in the panegyrics. We could only verify that both the above qualities were conspicuous by their absence – words lost their value, superlatives became flat and emotional storms stereotyped, and special effects became futile when any freshness and spontaneity had become so completely pushed aside by the deliberate repetition.

The culmination of the jubilee took place the next morning before the tribune of honour on the great square, which was filled with people in rectangular formations – 50,000 or perhaps more like 100,000 – with large, plastic flowers in different colours in their hands so that the square would change colour from red to pink to yellow, to portraying the jubilee message in contrasting coloured letters. In front of the tribune were two military music corps – the only military element – consisting of about 1,000 men altogether, which played in turn for the almost two-hour march-past, during which one million people paraded by in rectangular formations of fifty columns about one hundred deep and all keeping perfect time. Every type of citizen was represented: brigades of cooks, mine workers, students, farmers, fishermen, music corps, children, and massed standards. There were large, rolling podiums with – besides, of course, statues and pictures of the Great Leader – models of multistorey buildings, athletics arenas, ships, operating theatres, factories and harvest festivals. A cohort of women pioneers beat time with drums, another group played the clarinet, a third had red banners, which were waved in complicated patterns, a fourth, a fifth … To lighten things up a little, they had included, here and there, regiments of beautiful, young dancing girls in romantic tulle veils, battalions of fairytale princesses in pastel shades swinging parasols, flower arrangements, fans, tambourines. Colossal. Gigantesque. Perfect direction and perfect execution.

In the afternoon, everyone was gathered together for a dance and gymnastics programme at a stadium. The grandstand on the opposite, long side was, as was customary, full of schoolchildren with their large blocks of different coloured pages before them. By turning the pages, they could form different images that covered the whole of the long side – pictures of the leader, of slogans, landscapes, factories, indeed even moving pictures of, say, a tractor trundling across a field. By 1988 it was an exhibition of peacetime activities, whereas in the 1970s it had shown how American planes were shot down and exploded in the air. On the field in front, thousands of young people performed gymnastic dances which illustrated the forty-year history of the Republic. As usual, it was all executed to perfection. But I found myself calculating how many millions of working days had been spent on preparations for the jubilee.

In the evening there was a banquet at the presidential palace. Just before the entrance the police stopped my car, the only one among all the cars with flags, and we had to wait a while as the driver palavered with a police chief who had been summoned before we could proceed. In the banqueting hall, the chandeliers lit up more than a hundred tables and a thousand seated guests. There was food and drink in abundance, but it was served at a very rapid pace. Sometimes only half the table was served; sometimes the plate was removed while one was still eating and one was left with only a knife and fork. After less than an hour, it was indicated that it was time to break up and everyone left to look for their cars, which took an endless amount of time as several hundred were parked tightly packed outside the palace. Behind my car was one bearing the flag of Mali, and its representative, who was the member of parliament for Nioro de Sahel, and had attended my presentation as Sweden's ambassador in Bamako, joyfully embraced me in his arms and kissed me – did he spontaneously regard me as a representative for a civilization that he understood?

The cars eventually started to get under way, and rolled out through the exit and on to the six-lane motorway, where all the lanes had been made one-way for the return journey. Once we were on the road, all the drivers seemed to be affected by some sort of intoxication and, as at the start of a motor race, the whole width of the road was filled with furiously accelerating limousines, with roaring engines, trying to get past each other. The journey took us back past the tribune of honour by the great square, where a hundred thousand or so people with burning torches performed a figurative march exercise in regimental block formation. Above all this, the skies were illuminated by a fantastic pyrotechnic display. I cannot deny that it was beautiful, but my ability to absorb any more impressions had run dry.

During the following weeks, sections of the festivities were broadcast on TV every evening. One could even see close-ups of the individuals in the large march-past, men and women of all ages, pioneers and children. Their faces reflected moods: young men with determined stony faces, fairytale princesses with make-up, smiling pleasantly, and 'ordinary people', moved by one of the solemn moments of their lives, crying through emotion or with eyes staring in hysterical ecstasy. In fact, one could enjoy Korean TV quite well without knowing the language. The news bulletins, speeches and panel discussions were, of course, unintelligible but were, no doubt, completely predictable as to their content. Otherwise, one of the channels usually screened a feature film about how the evil designs of the occupiers and imperialists came to nought, or about heroic deeds in working life; the other channel showed programmes with every imaginable aspect of the Great Leader's life, now and previously, and his visits to industries and farms as an illustration of the Republic's development and the people's joy. The honour of work was proclaimed in its varying aspects, on wheatfields, in the tractor factory, in the modern power stations' bare control rooms, in the glowing inferno of foundry and forge – these all being positive symbols for development in the worst spirit of *Magnitogorsk*. In the background, a trembling voice ranted on while people who had been able to meet their Leader cried with emotion and in reverence. A report from an election voting station should not be omitted. Two colonels entered the station and walked up to the ballot-box. They bowed in front of the portrait of the Leader and his son, then pushed their voting slips into the box with both hands before bowing again. But then North Korea was the only country I know of that was not satisfied with 99% election wins – there the result was regularly 100%.

A 200-day campaign had been launched for the fortieth jubilee so that the extra effort and working input would facilitate the completion of the preparations and achieve better production results. Shortly after the jubilee, a conference of heroes was held, involving war veterans, Party cadres and successful workers. The conference recommended a new 200-day campaign in preparation for the 1989 International Youth Festival, which was to take place in the capital. So it was immediately time for the people to muster all their strength for yet another, albeit more modest, carnival in Pyongyang.

16

1988 – A YEAR OF AFFLICTIONS

On returning to Pyongyang after an absence of more than a decade, I was immediately struck by some new impressions. The people, and particularly the women, were considerably better dressed. Variations in cut and pattern were manifest and left plenty of scope for personal preference. People were much more relaxed; they looked at foreigners and could smile at them, indeed even flirt a little. Young couples could be seen strolling through the city. At the theatres things often seemed rather chaotic as more people were admitted without tickets or occupied better seats than they were entitled to – both of which would have been unthinkable in the 1970s. And, of course, it gave me some patriotic satisfaction to notice Volvo cars still on the road while competitors of a similar vintage had virtually disappeared from the street scene.

Similarly, the warlike attitudes had been considerably toned down. One did not see quite as many uniforms in the city, even though more could be seen there than anywhere else. Among the million people in block formation who had marched past in step during the celebrations, there were hardly any uniforms. At the large gymnastics and dance performance, which portrayed the Republic's history, in the 1976 version a uniformed band of riflemen poured back and forth in mock battle while the background illustrations described how American planes were shot to pieces. In the 1988 version, the participants wore overalls and had white staffs instead of weapons.

Previously, foreigners were not allowed to buy things in ordinary shops but were obliged to use the diplomats' shop and the hotels' dollar shops. In 1988, there were several special currency shops that anybody could use, not with ordinary won, of course, but with special black won notes, which could be purchased with non-convertible currencies such as the rouble, or red won, which were obtainable for hard currency. These shops were crowded with Koreans, who evidently had access to currency. The trade was not exactly lively, and most of the customers probably belonged to the *nomenklatura*, but I was told that, for example, agricultural cooperatives that exported and were paid in hard currency could use some of the profit for their members' private needs. The prices, however, had been set so high that the people would be given a pedagogically correct picture of the price levels in the capitalist world.

But otherwise, most things were the same. The cult of personality, which even before was excessive, had as good as acquired the form of a state religion. The expansion of the capital city was on an enormous scale, and the monuments more numerous than ever. Self-centredness seemed, if possible, to have increased and now was clearly a key to the interpretation of the Republic's economic and political path. In his major speech on the occasion of the jubilee, Kim Il Sung pointed out that the DPRK had built up an exceptional socialist economic system. To an outsider, it looked like a closed economic system, as near as one could come to the theoretical models of the economics textbooks, and apparently it intended to stay that way. Through *Juche* (self-reliance) they would arrive at *Chajusong* (independence). It was from this starting point that one had to judge the Republic's economic policy and foreign trade. The latter was on the whole an 'extramural' category that which did not fit within the model and which they therefore did their best to ignore.

It is fair to remember that a great deal had actually been achieved. In thirty-five years, a relatively underdeveloped country, one which had been bombed to destruction too, had practically lifted itself by its hair and been transformed into a nation that seemed to have all the outer attributes of a modern industrial state. At the enormous industrial exhibition they still displayed a boundless assortment of achievements, an admirable feat, even if much of it obviously consisted of copies, for example of Atlas Copco tools or Mercedes cars. The clearest example of achievement was all the building and construction, especially in the capital. In 1953 Pyongyang had been flattened, but by 1975 it could already be described as being like an enormous 1950s' sprawling, European city suburb, and they had not rested there. Now they were busily completing a new housing area with thirty-storey buildings along a six-kilometre motorway. The façades displayed an attractive richness of variety, but about the insides, the water and heating it was impossible to get any information – and did they have enough energy for the lifts? Close by was the large athletics village, which had been built for the Olympic events that they vainly hoped would be sited there instead of in Seoul. This contained about a dozen large sports halls, each one devoted to a particular sport, and whose architect had been inspired by the paraphernalia concerned such as a badminton net, a cut-open football. Work had been started on both the housing area and the athletics village only two years previously.

In recent years, the Koreans had also constructed a large triumphal arch, which spanned a five-lane road in the city centre, and a colossal *Juche* tower, built to honour the leader's seventieth birthday and therefore built with as many stones as the number of days he had lived. Judging by the TV programmes, they were constructing triumphal arches and towers all over the country. I could not help but reflect that, although there were bulldozers and cranes, it was plain for all to see that a considerable portion of the work was carried out using manual labour. Similar gigantic and forever ongoing projects were just as much a feature of the industrial and agricultural sectors.

The fortieth jubilee was a typical illustration of the economic policies. Besides the direct costs, the work input was gigantic. As described above, one million people marched past their leader and his son and in the evening hundreds of thousands performed a figurative march exercise with burning torches. From my own military service, I remember how long it took to prepare for the funeral of King Gustav V at which we had to march in step in columns of a modest eight soldiers abreast. Here, the one million Koreans had to march in step in fifty parallel columns. One can only guess that the preparations for the various parts had required tens of millions of working days! It is clear that they ignored all known principles for the allocation of resources, comparative advantages and international division of work. If international trade played an integrated role in the economy, the working force could, with advantage, have been directed to export industries. However, foreign trade was not guided by the principles named above but – apart from the consumption of the *nomenklatura* – served, as the industrial exhibition bore witness to, the purposes of transferring technology, which, in turn, was used to consolidate *Juche* and *Chajusong*.

However, even in that respect, the North Koreans sawed off the branch they were sitting on. In the spirit of self-reliance, they imported only those components that they thought necessary and then added to them with copied parts of their own manufacture. To a large degree this was successful, and it explained the Republic's rapid development, but when it came to more complicated production processes they were not successful in starting up the units or systems and running them properly. The extravagant investments did not result in production, and the debts remained.

What tended to confound the foreign observer most was that the North Koreans did *not* seem to learn from repeated experiences, but stubbornly persisted. It appeared to be built into the essence of *Juche* ideology that self-reliance exceeded ability, and this developed into a vicious circle of its very own. To be able to understand the psychological mechanisms, one had to return to the background of the North Korean leadership, the country's isolation and the fact that Kim Il Sung was entirely a product of the Eastern environment as opposed to, say, Chou Enlai or Ho Chi Minh with their Western education. Kim Il Sung could see the results of the fantastic development the country had undergone under his leadership, and he lacked the capability in his old age to realize that the methods hitherto applied had reached the limits of their viability.

North Korea's achievements were undoubtedly awe-inspiring. Yet it was also possible to compare them with what South Korea had achieved. Among the state socialist countries, North Korea stood out as being as successful as South Korea among the market economies. In that way, North Korea became an unwilling illustration of its system's more limited economic possibilities and its dependence upon forced measures. It thus became abundantly clear that the DPRK had steered right into a cul-de-sac.

Kim Il Sung was approaching 80, which meant that the question of his successor had become the most important political issue on the home front. This had aroused particular interest because something seemingly remarkable had taken place in that he had proposed his own son as heir to the throne. I say seemingly because it showed that North Korea represented old-fashioned Asian despotism just as much as communist dictatorship. There was no way that one could form an opinion on the spot of the possible complications of the question of the succession. Of the three continuous revolutions – the ideological, the technical and the cultural – Kim Jong Il had evidently had the responsibility for the last and he had been noticeably involved in the building projects. But on the whole, he was unknown. He totally lacked his father's charisma and was not a born leader. He did not meet any foreigners and had not been abroad, except perhaps to China and the Soviet Union, where his father had tried to 'anchor' his position. But there was all the more speculation, particularly by Eastern Europeans who, for ideological reasons, instinctively revolted against the very idea of a communist hereditary kingdom. Real and presumed purges and reorganizations in the party hierarchy and the armed forces were explained by stands taken for and against the crown prince. But there were no hard facts.

From the Eastern Europeans, there were only indignant huffs and speculations reflecting their hopes that the Party, in due order, would elect a worthy successor. The Chinese kept quiet and smiled – China demanded a reliable regime in Pyongyang but seemed tolerant when it came down to detail. So it was more fruitful to talk to the representatives from the Third World, above all the Indian, who had some understanding of the dynastic legitimacy of Asian societies. These commentators were more open to the change of generations that the son represented. The fortieth jubilee illustrated to excess the way in which the nation was totally absorbed in Kim Il Sung's earlier exploits – the guerrilla struggle, the civil war, the reconstruction work – and in which the rest of the aged leadership also tended to glory. Kim Jong Il was, rather, the person who had stood for the softer style described above – more beautiful clothes, friendlier attitudes, demilitarization and the limited opening up of the private economic sphere.

The principal foreign policy objective remained, as ever, reunification. The North Koreans were still categorically opposed to a solution based on the German example, a recognition that there could be two Korean nations. Instead, they proposed the formation of a confederation in which both parts could retain their different social systems. Ever since the Korean War, they had maintained that the primary obstacle in the path of reunification was the US troops in South Korea, which gave essential support to the puppet government in Seoul. It would, of course, be naive to believe that Kim Il Sung could contemplate a reunification based on the principles of the market economy; rather, he considered himself to have a 'heavenly mandate' to lead the entire Korean people. The historical and ideological justification that lay behind these claims is dealt with in more detail in Chapter 19. However, to put it briefly, he presumably regarded himself both as an advocate of the (according to Marxist ideology) predetermined socialist future and as the 'son of heaven' with the legitimate right to rule over all of Korea. The rivalry between North and South Korea was thus not restricted to a conventional fight for power, but the outcome would show who enjoyed the 'mandate of heaven' and who had been banished to the dustbin of history.

With this background in mind, South Korea's continually growing advantage boded ill. It was regarded as a serious loss of face that the socialist brothers, with China and the Soviet Union in the forefront, had not shown solidarity with Pyongyang but accepted that the Olympic Games be sited in Seoul. When Hungary and South Korea as good as established diplomatic relations, the bitterness acquired eloquent expression and North Korea tried to threaten and frighten the other Eastern Europeans so they would not do the same.

Even more fateful was an initiative on the part of Gorbachev in Krasnoyarsk, in which he proposed an East Asian regional meeting with both Koreas as participants and (even worse) tempted South Korea with being able to participate in the development of Siberia. The plain truth was this: North Korea was not only of no interest as a collaborator, rather, it was seen as a liability with its demands for ideological solidarity on top of its bad record of debt repayments and its importunate delivery requirements. The Chinese were, of course, subtler and more pragmatic. Their trading arrangements with South Korea had already acquired considerable proportions without them having made a great fuss – this also reflected the North Koreans' more humble attitude towards China.

17

THE EQUATIONS
OF REUNIFICATION

An assessment of the situation in 1988

At the end of the 1980s the state socialist system found itself in an obvious crisis, but it was not yet apparent that it was rushing headlong towards its dissolution, and that within a couple of years it would really still be applied only in North Korea. The economic collapse, and its repercussions in a number of sectors of society, that affected North Korea in the mid-1990s was naturally hastened by the fact that what was called 'the socialist camp' had ceased to exist. Despite the disdain it felt, the communist bloc had found itself compelled to keep North Korea afloat in order to save socialism's face before the world of the market economy.

When the bloc disintegrated, *Juche* and *Chajusong* (self-reliance and independence) were put to the ultimate test – which they failed. One could, of course, read the writing on the wall as early as 1988 – but no one realized it would happen so quickly, or that North Korea was as vulnerable as it subsequently proved to be. What were the repercussions that this development would have for the reunification question?

The North Koreans of 1988 must have been living in a world that was becoming all the more incomprehensible to them. If one likens the world to a project for building a house, they were standing with the plans in their hand but were bewildered by the appearance of the house as it took shape: it did not look as it should. With their communist-schooled minds, they knew that state socialism was the economically and morally superior system that had the future before it, and they saw proof of it every day in the modern society that had taken shape round about them during the last few decades. Furthermore, their upbringing included a malicious portrait of other social forms, the accuracy of which they had never questioned. With their Confucian instinct, they further felt that power justly belonged in the hands of the person who was morally superior and who would govern well. How then should they interpret the latest signals from the rest of the world? Why had the other socialist countries abandoned their centrally planned economy and why were they also so eager to open contacts with the morally inferior regime in South Korea?

From a Western point of view – and probably also Eastern European and Chinese – the Koreans lived a sort of communal barracks life. Work, food, clothes and lodgings were assigned to them. Their wages were more like pocket money, which also affected the availability of goods – there were no ordinary shops in the sense that we know them. Work discipline was rigorous, free time minimal and massive work input for the common good was almost like a religious ritual. The only existing source of information for decades had taught generations of citizens that they lived in the earthly paradise; every evening on TV starry-eyed artistes sang, as if transfigured, about how happy everyone was in the People's Republic. The rest of the world was unknown or unappreciated. Under such conditions, how could the societies of the North and South merge? To what extent would structural, economical, political and ideological factors on both sides come to bear? This was, after all, a people that was proud of having retained its identity and unity for more than one thousand years in the face of pressure from two vastly superior neighbours; this was a country that was divided as late as 1945 as a result of foreign intervention.

For Pyongyang, there had always been only one self-evident view on the reunification question. They had never queried their own communist system's superiority to South Korea's, in their eyes, feudal, old-fashioned and capitalist-oriented society, which could only survive with the support of US imperialism. Add to that Kim Il Sung's claim to be a leader of the same calibre as the great leaders in the history of the world, a leader who was called to save the entire Korean people, and one can see why the North Koreans believed that South Korea would fall like a ripe fruit if only the US troops were removed.

South Korea's enormous boom was either denied or attributed to imperialist help; it was certainly not credited to the country's own efforts. The position was continually being undermined, and the recent successes for Seoul – the Olympics, trading relations with China, the Soviet Union and Eastern European states, Gorbachev's proposal in Krasnoyarsk in September 1988 for an East Asian regional meeting with both Koreas – must have made it all the more obvious to the leadership in Pyongyang. South Korea's development had admittedly been under way for at least ten years, but it had suddenly accelerated to such an extent that the *nomenklatura* were now obliged to adopt defensive positions. The question of the succession was also involved. Kim Il Sung was seventy-six years old and wanted to hand over power to his son. This had evidently met with internal opposition, but in the current situation the country could not afford a power struggle that could only weaken the leadership's claim to a monopoly of legitimacy. In Pyongyang, members of the government did not allow themselves to be influenced but continued with their established policies, with reunification as their main priority. But they were prepared to reveal how this should be accomplished just as little as before. The old metaphor was still valid – North Korea's journey could no more change direction than a train on tracks without points.

What, then, did the problem look like from Seoul's horizon? The South Koreans had little cause to doubt that the market economy alternative would prevail. Time was on their side, and they were going to win the tug-of-war. But how should they subsequently deal with the northern part of the country? North Korea was rich in natural resources, and thus had potential, but its production apparatus was not competitive. It would, therefore, not be able to survive, and how, then, were the millions of workers and their families to support themselves? One could not reasonably expect that the cooperative peasants in the barren North would find markets for their products in competition with the more fertile South. How should all the personnel in the armed forces be integrated – would they not rapidly be transformed into hordes of rootless people without work? Would the North's drilled workers, in any case, be able to adjust harmoniously to a market economy, or would they simply be proletarianized? And how, in that case, would these new proletarians react – impoverished, unemployed and with no chance of betterment, for many of these outcasts there would be no other outlet than to coalesce into an enormous fermenting party of discontent, which, in the worst case, would yearn for the safe, old days when they had work, accommodation, food and clothes. Thus, in the case of reunification under the leadership of the South, South Korea would acquire the role of scapegoat for the third of the joint population that would have problems supporting themselves. Would the developing, but still fragile, (South) Korean democracy survive such a social situation?

This scenario was, of course, unrealistic in the sense that reunification was not, in fact, an immediate prospect. But it illustrated the temporal aspects of reunification. Even ignoring all the political complications, on economic grounds alone the entire industrial and commercial structure of North Korea would be forced to go through a time-consuming perestroika before one could even start thinking in terms of concrete reunification measures.

An 'unforeseeable development' could not be ruled out either, and this did not refer to war, because even the North Koreans must surely realize that they would lose a war without allies. The question was, rather, how to evaluate the strength of the North Korean economy in its isolation. The problems with foreign trade were well known but they seemed to stand on their own when one looked at the domestic economy, which evidently managed to produce food (albeit an absolute minimum), clothes, shelter, education and health care in a manner that seemed unaffected by economic fluctuations. But the outer world's knowledge of what was really happening in North Korea was limited. Was North Korea strong enough to avoid sliding down into the same manifest supply crisis in which Romania found itself?

Even if life in North Korea seemed about as inhuman as life in an anthill, it could not be denied that the system had hitherto ensured that basic material needs were satisfied by way of 'drawing the bow' (i.e. work input) almost to breaking-point. But if the bow were, in fact, to break, if basic supplies were no longer forthcoming, this would lead – even among broader sections of the population – to doubts over the leadership's ability and thus its very legitimacy. Any suspicion of, or insight into, an initial or permanent crisis that would have to challenge the indoctrination of a lifetime might be able to open minds in both the governing *nomenklatura* and the broad masses. In such a situation the adjustment process would begin before reunification, thereby preventing South Korea being landed with the role of scapegoat for any supply problems. On the contrary, the economic system of the South would appear both more legitimate and tempting. In conclusion, for the South it could not but be risky to try to hasten the reunification process.

In all scenarios, one would also have to take into account the powerful position of the security services. It was they that would have the most to lose from a change of system, and it is the case that these services have been responsible for the continued existence of many totalitarian regimes well past the point at which they had lost the confidence of the citizens. In the case of North Korea, everything indicated that the security services held an exceptionally powerful position.

One thing was quite certain, no changes could be expected as long as Kim Il Sung sat at the helm. In the autumn of his life, he could not be expected to reconsider his life's work and his world view, particularly as he must have assumed that his choice of path up until then had been successful. Considering its starting point, North Korea could easily stand comparison with most underdeveloped countries. Its limitations lay more in the fact that its methods were not generally applicable. The reason for this was illustrated by the map of the world in the Friendship Museum, where lamps lit the countries that the Great Leader had visited – outside the communist bloc, only Mauritania and Algeria were lit up. North Korea considered itself called upon to assume the position of leader among nations whose culture it neither knew nor respected.

Impressed by the softer attitudes that had undoubtedly become discernible in Pyongyang, and which were associated with Kim Jong Il's influence, one could perhaps hope that a change of generation would gradually lead to a more flexible policy. But the claims of the Leader's son seemed to be controversial, particularly among the military and, above all, he did not give any impression of being the sort of decisive leader figure that would be absolutely essential to push through a change of course. Furthermore, his knowledge of the outside world seemed to be just as limited as that of his father. Was it not conceivable that the security services would assume real power and use him as a puppet figure? And was it even possible to reform the system with the old guard still in power? This last question was answered some years later by the developments in Eastern Europe.

Finally, one also had to consider the influence that traditional East Asian values might be expected to have upon the attitude of the North Korean people to revolutionary social changes, in the end to a change of regime. Such speculations were based upon the circumstances described in Chapter 19. To go into these now would be premature because in 1988 the regime in Pyongyang still had the situation under control, but during the 1990s North Korea was hit by a supply crisis that was even worse than that in Romania and which made the need for social changes even more pressing.

18

THE IDEOLOGICAL ISSUE

Khrushchev expressed the conviction that socialism would be victorious because the citizens of underdeveloped countries would, deep down, be convinced of the system's superiority. On the contrary, however, the state socialist recipes showed themselves to be catastrophic from the point of view of both the supply of basic needs and the general well-being of the economy. The underdeveloped countries found much more tempting models in the South-East Asian 'tigers', indeed even in China.

The system's shortcomings had long been manifest but the critics were, nevertheless, on the whole, surprised that the breakdown occurred as soon as it did. The collapse was so total that one researcher (with words that have been misinterpreted) spoke of the end of history. History does not, of course, come to an end, but there was no longer any competition for the market economy system, and thus the conditions for the Cold War no longer existed. History had been off on a detour and could now gradually find its way back to its old tracks.

The breakdown meant that the countries affected found themselves in a state of more or less pronounced economic chaos. As mentioned in Part II, Marx and Engels, in connection with the revolution of the Paris Commune, had noted that the working class was incapable of simply taking over the capitalist machinery of state for its own purposes. The reverse was now being seen in Eastern Europe in that private enterprise was incapable of simply taking over a socialized employment and supply system. But the North Koreans, more or less the only ones still following the old system, felt more than any other people 'in their stomachs' the abyss to which the state socialist system had driven them.

Why did the state socialist economies collapse? If one is content with a general answer, it will have to be a platitude: their system, based on Marxist ideology, lost the contest against the market economy. Why could the system not be reformed? Why did it go so far that the machinery just seized up? These types of questions have to be reformulated to deal with the content of the ideology, which meant that for half a century a superpower let itself slowly, but irrevocably, be led towards a self-inflicted collapse, without losing a war or being plunged into revolution or civil conflict. The same applies, *mutatis mutandis*, for North Korea, and there is the additional question of why they kept on going as if nothing had happened instead of following along in the socialist camp's general ideological break-up. They ought, at least, to have been able to learn from the Chinese and entrust the Party with the task of leading and supervising the economic restructuring. Below, I shall examine the basic tenets of Marxism and some of the milestones in the history of its development in order to shed some light on the issue. Was there something wrong with the ideological presumptions? Or was the implementation flawed? Does the ideology contain elements that lead to fateful economic choices? All of these questions will be answered in the affirmative.

The European socialist countries belonged to that European cultural tradition that produced Marxism. China, North Korea and Vietnam, on the other hand, belonged in the possibly even more distinct east Asian civilization that had been imbued with the heritage of Confucian thinking. Greatly simplified, one could regard Confucianism as ethics developed into a philosophy of government. Confucius (K'ung-fu-tzu), who lived in the sixth century BC, from the starting point of the traditional heritage of ideas and the endless and cruel wars of the Chinese small nations, developed his concern with learning how to create happy and contented societies through good government. And good government could only be achieved if the country was ruled by eminent (in the sense of morally superior) individuals who thereby served as models for the broad mass of the people. In this respect, Confucianism is elitist and hierarchical. But it also celebrates the idea of equality by emphasizing that every individual is capable of moral improvement – and should be given the possibility of achieving the same – which would lead to a position of authority. As an ideology, it is primarily concerned more with human advancement than with scientific, technological and material development.

Confucianism has played an absolutely crucial role in Chinese tradition and society and has spread to neighbouring countries such as Korea, Vietnam and Japan. Societies influenced by Confucianism have been characterized by an extreme social discipline in coordination and a hierarchical power structure, which has created states that have been able to survive unparalleled upheavals without losing their civilized nature. An instructive example is at hand in the form of Japan's development from an isolated feudal state to one of the world's most prominent industrial nations. One should also note that the Confucian heritage was the one distinguishing factor that was shared by the countries that took the lead in the modernization process that gave them the name 'the Asian tigers' – Taiwan, Hong Kong, Singapore and South Korea. Making allowances for the gigantic dimensions of their development problems, one could also justifiably include China in that circle. And, as has been noted elsewhere in this book, one cannot deny that North Korea in its day served as the state socialist camp's prize example of rapid industrialization, in the same way that South Korea was upheld as an example to the OECD nations. For these modernization processes to take place it was necessary that these societies accepted the demands of science for unconditional review of Confucian thinking and, in that respect, social discipline had a decisive role to play if the re-orientation of the economy was to succeed.

After the Second World War, China, North Korea and (North) Vietnam embraced Marxism, which contained an opening for the influence and social role of science within its framework, but this was not unconditional. This ideology seemed, at first sight, to have completely taken over. But the continued development of China and Vietnam provided evidence of these countries' continually increasing readiness to liberate themselves from the fetters of state socialist ideology in favour of more unconditional choices. North Korea alone remained stubbornly opposed to any reconsideration of state socialism. It is therefore important to try to establish what aspects of the local, as well as the imported, intellectual baggage were crucial in forming the particular North Korean line.

To a foreign observer it was evident that the North Koreans were imbued with traditional East Asian habits, thinking and conception of the world, namely being disciplined and hard-working as well as respecting hierarchy and authority. This must be considered as a natural consequence of the people's history of living in isolation. However, it was also obvious that they regarded themselves as having left that stage behind and now, having become genuinely modern, they were living in the age of scientific socialism. They had taken the deliberate step of distancing themselves from traditional thinking and Chinese civilizational influences in order to modernize by embracing the Russian brand of communism, which was believed to be more modern than Western capitalism. But the East Asian inheritance was ingrained to such a degree that it was taken for granted that it belonged to the common traits of humanity. When trying to understand their conception of the world and ways of reasoning it became more and more obvious that their instincts were East Asian but their minds were communist schooled, a combination that produced a state of mind and conception of the world not found anywhere else. Because of their isolation, and lured by a boundless nationalism, they interpreted the two intellectual heritages – Confucianism and communism - in a way that was highly distasteful for Chinese and Russians alike. As shall be seen in what follows, both had good reason to suspect North Korean ideology of propagating a communism that does not aim at replacing capitalism and a Confucianism that aims at replacing Confucius.

To begin with, a selection of the basic elements of Marx and Engels' doctrines shall be presented, followed by a description of how they fared when applied by Lenin and Stalin to a political programme for shaping and developing the Soviet Union. The presentation is both brief and selective, and any reader requiring more details on the ingredients of some key issues, or references to the sources, is referred to Part II of this book with its more detailed – but far from exhaustive – accounts of some of the more important doctrines, as well as comments on their often obvious lack of applicability in real life. The description in this chapter is intended only to give an idea of the instruction received by Kim Il Sung during his years in the Soviet Union, which must have constituted his only higher education. Consequently, it represents the political and ideological basis used by Kim for the formation of the Democratic People's Republic of Korea. Later, Kim coined his *Juche* ideology under the pretence of representing the ultimate Marxism in the same way that the pretensions of the *Koran* represent ultimate monotheism. *Juche*'s relation to (and deviations from) both Marx's original writings and Soviet-Russian and Chinese ideology and practice will be discussed in the following chapters. It is perhaps unnecessary to stress that this ideology enjoyed the privilege of being *the* uncontestable truth, in which the adherents believed as strongly as any fundamentalist member of any other extremist religious sect, being prepared both to die and to kill in its service.

It must, above all, be emphasized that Marx formulated a conception of history, not a political programme. The development of human societies was, in his view, bound by a 'law of society' as inescapable as any law of nature. The history of mankind has proceeded, according to the dialectic principle, through three stages:

1 The thesis: the original state of nature before man formed proper societies.
2 The antithesis: the formation of societies characterized by state power and antagonisms between classes.
3 The synthesis: the future stateless and classless society.

Existing societies have always been characterized by class struggles between the 'haves' and the 'have-nots' – between the owners of land, cattle, machinery, etc., who establish state power in order to protect their ownership, and all others, who must sell their capacity to work, their muscle power. There have been different class societies: in antiquity society was characterized by slavery, which was followed by feudalism, which was followed, in turn, by capitalism. The present period is that of capitalism, which will be replaced by socialism, which, in its turn, will lay the foundations of the future state- and classless society, the synthesis, according to the principle of historical development. The future classless society will be ruled directly by the people and, as an inevitable consequence, state power will not serve any purpose and accordingly wither away.[1]

This is not a political programme – it is an ascertainment of an inescapable historical fact. It means that everyone who acknowledges this fact is progressive while those who do not accept it are reactionary and will be dumped in the dustbin of history. Where North and South Korea belong is obvious.

The present capitalist society is doomed because its economic organization with private ownership of the means of production, such as factories, machinery etc., is not efficient enough to give the growing population, and especially the working class – the proletariat – a decent standard of living. The capitalist mode of production leads to the concentration of wealth in fewer and fewer hands while 'the capitalist utilization of machinery' results in the impoverishment of a superfluous population of jobless workers. Therefore, the proletariat will rise and, by means of violent revolution, conquer state power and as the new ruling class –

112

the dictatorship of the proletariat – appropriate the means of production with the aim of socializing them.

This 'theory of impoverishment' is based on 'the labour theory of value', which contains 'the law of the falling tendency of the rate of profit'. This theory – more or less the keystone of Marx's ideology – can be summarized as follows:

1 The value of a product is determined by the hours of work a worker has spent in producing it.
2 The employer's surplus, his profit, thus consists of the extortion of unpaid work from the workers, in practice that part of the price of a product which exceeds the wages of the workers.
3 As all profit has its basis in the extortion of unpaid labour from workers, the introduction of machinery with its concomitant savings in labour costs (which equals 'the capitalist use of machinery') means that the capitalist removes the source of his profit (because the means of production – e.g. machinery – consists of work that has already been paid for and which thereby ceases to be a productive power that generates profit).[2]

The point of Marx's labour theory of value was to explain why owners of means of production, i.e. capitalists, are not entitled to any share of the production that the workers produce with these means of production. When this share takes a cooperative form it apparently does not give rise to ideological misgivings – but, as is well known, state ownership is not necessarily the same as cooperatives. Furthermore, the share can also be expressed as a requirement to yield interest on the cost of acquiring the machinery – but this is not acceptable because, according to the ideology, the consequence of demanding a yield of interest equals exploitation of the workers, which, with historic necessity, leads to the socialist revolution. According to the labour theory of value, investment costs obviously do not affect the value of a product in capitalist society but are profitable under cooperative forms of production. This exception, however, contains the admission that the theory is not universally valid and consequently cannot be respected as a 'law'.

It is difficult to see all the inter-related theories and doctrines as compatible with reality. The labour theory of value and the law of the falling rate of profit aim at prohibiting the yield of interest. As such, they do not constitute economic 'laws' but are based on morally motivated articles of faith, which can be found in the Old Testament and in the *Koran*. The consequences of applying this theory, the gist of which is that only muscle power produces profit, inevitably leads to the prohibition of making comparative calculations of profitability, in which due regard is paid to all costs, namely labour, machinery, energy, transport and environment. The consequences can easily be seen, for instance, in the poor maintenance of buildings and machinery in communist countries and in the opaque allocation of resources in North Korea.[3]

Marx and Engels had devoted themselves to studying the conditions for when and where the revolution would occur but had never taken part in one. It is, however, obvious that a socialist revolution was expected only to occur in its historical context, i.e. in advanced capitalist states. Lenin, in contrast, was, above all, a practical revolutionary with a clear end in sight. He let the end dictate the means and, as he lived in a comparatively underdeveloped country, adapted the theories accordingly.

A good example is the question of the peasants. For Marx, the role of the peasants in society constituted a problem because in Western Europe they were anti-revolutionary landowners without being capitalists. In Russia, the number of workers was insignificant compared with the number of peasants, who had been emancipated from serfdom as late as 1861. Conditions were different, and it was in Marx's interest to regard the peasants as a rural proletariat with a contribution to make to the revolution. It was, however, true that the historically necessary capitalist development promoted the development of large-scale production – foreboding socialist structures – while the peasants wanted small, individual plots. Sound tactics meant that the peasants should be used against the landowners in the revolution, only to be abolished later because large-scale production was an integral part of the construction of socialism.

Similar tactics were applied during the revolution in 1905. In Lenin's vocabulary, it was a bourgeois revolution intended to topple the Czar and give state power to the capitalists. He believed that the Bolsheviks should join forces with the bourgeoisie, but as soon as possible after the revolution had been completed the cooperation should be cut off, the former comrades-in-arms should be abandoned and the struggle for socialism begin. He pursued these policies during the First World War by adamantly opposing the war and insisting that defeating Czarism was the quickest way to revolution.

Revolution came in February 1917 and the Czar abdicated. But it was a bourgeois revolution, and Lenin's goal was a socialist one. The Great Socialist October Revolution, which was launched a couple of months later, was not a revolution, it was a *coup d'état* that brought Lenin to power. In order to prevent a counter-revolution, all forms of opposition had to be crushed. The old society had to be annihilated. The methods used were terrorism and impoverishment. When every individual depends on the state for his daily food rations, he has to conform or die – thus, the totalitarian state has achieved its goal.

The economic policy of the Soviet Union during the years 1918–21 has been called 'war communism'. The state took over all means of production and distribution, decreed that work was obligatory and controlled the work of every citizen, and even attempted to abolish money by requisitioning, for instance, farm products by payment in kind. Galloping inflation served to finance the Revolution and undermine capitalism.[4] The results were catastrophic. Production declined and products were of lower quality, famine ravaged the towns as the peasants preferred to leave their land uncultivated than deliver goods without being paid. Opposition grew, and in 1921 the Kronstadt sailors rebelled; the same sailors who had once helped Lenin to power now demanded new elections with a secret ballot, free agitation and freedom of speech, of the press and of assembly.

The rebellion was thoroughly crushed but led Lenin to reconsider the economic policy. The result was NEP, the 'New Economic Policy'. Private enterprise was accepted within certain limits, but heavy industry and the transport sector were kept in the hands of the state. Forced labour ceased, the value of money was stabilized, a normal tax system was introduced, and requisitioning from the peasants ceased and they could dispose of their surplus production, after tax, as they saw fit. In the following years, the economy slowly improved. Lenin did not try to disguise his retreat, but admitted that they had gone too far and had been forced to make concessions. But the objective, about which there was to be no doubt, was that NEP Russia would, in due course, be transformed into a socialist Russia.

Lenin died at the beginning of 1924. His epitaph can be summarized by the verdict that he transformed Marx's conception of history into a political programme. Making ideology the irrefutable principle and source of inspiration, the foundations were laid for the monumental degree of discrepancy of words and deeds that became the special characteristic of the Soviet Union. Putting the political action programme on the throne meant treachery against the basic thesis of Marxist ideology, that of the inevitable development of society in accordance with the materialistic concept of history. This showed that the causes of the Russian Revolution are to be found in Russia's own history and revolutionary traditions, and cannot be understood with the help of a social theory with such a defective base in reality as Marxism. As in most other revolutions, the Russian one, too, was characterized by it being a means for a small group to acquire the political, and thereby the economic, power.

After Lenin's death, a struggle for power ensued, ending in Stalin's victory, first consolidated in 1929. The main features of Stalin's epoch were the violent collectivization of agriculture that cost millions of peasants their lives, the five-year plans for industrialization, the purges and the cult of personality. Stalin was no ideologue, and Marxism was, to a growing extent, restricted to playing the role of servant to the actual, or desired, development. Ideology was used to eliminate Stalin's rivals for power. Trotsky criticized the concessions to 'peasant-capitalism' and was branded as a left-wing deviator. His counterpart was the right-wing deviator and leading theoretician Bucharin, who was accused of having an incorrect, un-Marxist 'theory of the *kulaks* (land-owning peasants) growing into socialism'. Trotsky was assassinated in exile and Bucharin executed in the purges. The death penalty had been introduced 1932 for the theft of state and collective property and later, also, for discussing strike action. The wage system became highly differentiated.

The conformity of these policies to the original ideological concepts was, to say the least, dubious. A leading principle of Marxism was the inevitability of capitalism being replaced by socialism because of the historical logic of economic development and the belief that it would take place in all capitalist countries.

Furthermore, the proletariat would overcome state power and introduce socialism, a development that would lead to the proletariat exercising power; after it had consolidated its power, communism would follow and be characterized by the absence of state power. But, in reality, revolution had taken place only in Russia, which Lenin had tried to explain by declaring that it was the weakest link of capitalism. Trotsky's alleged deviations also included the fact that he insisted upon spreading revolution by force – the so-called 'theory of the permanent revolution' – while Stalin preferred more cautious tactics. In any case, the fact remained that the Soviet Union incarnated an ideological deviation, that of socialism in *one* country. In this context, Stalin made his contribution to Marxist–Leninist ideology, i.e. by declaring that by introducing communism it would, as long as there existed inimical capitalist neighbours, still be necessary to retain the state in order to protect the communist society against foreign aggression, i.e. he launched the theory of communism in *one* country (as opposed to throughout the world). In this way, Stalin declared the authority of the state to be permanent in the Soviet Union, which in fact meant a declaration of bankruptcy of the official ideology in its entirety. This amounts to an ideological contradiction and a conceptual absurdity, as it implies that the communist society could be a class state – which it cannot be, as communism, by definition, equals the future stateless and classless society. But Stalin's view prevailed because all opponents were executed. It should be observed that Kim Yong Il in 1982 echoed Stalin's view of communism in *one* country or some regions.[5]

After the Second World War the Soviet Union annexed or installed puppet regimes in a number of Eastern European states. This extension from socialism in *one* country to a socialist bloc was in no way a confirmation of the Marxist concept of the development of history but purely a result of revived Russian armed imperialism.

Stalin died in 1953, transmitting an empire to his successors. The very word 'empire' indicates subjugation of foreign peoples, but Stalin's empire exerted a reckless totalitarian power not only over foreign peoples but also over the Russians. His successors were determined to soften the rule, but only to a degree that jeopardized neither their own positions of power nor that of the Soviet Union in world politics. The clearest change of policy consisted in the introduction of collective leadership with different leaders for the Communist Party, government, military and secret police. Already under Malenkov's leadership there were signs of a change of economic policies in the direction of greater production of consumer goods. But the softer policy had its risks, as evidenced by workers' demonstrations in East Germany, which had to be suppressed by tanks. Malenkov was pushed aside by Khrushchev but not executed. In 1956, Khrushchev launched a full-scale attack on Stalin at the Party congress, accusing him of having organized the great purges, of having had a disastrous influence on military operations during the War, and of megalomania and paranoia. The increase in freedom, however, seems to have been restricted to higher ranking Party members while the masses were governed as before. The pressure for more freedom led to a workers' rebellion in

Poland, and in Hungary in 1956 even the Party was involved in trying to use de-Stalinization to liberate themselves from the Russian grip. Order was restored with violence, and the process was repeated in Czechoslovakia in 1968. The new leaders never questioned the inevitability of the ultimate victory of socialism over capitalism and, in order to promote the spread of world revolution, Moscow intervened militarily in several places in the Third World (Angola, Cuba, Ethiopia, Mozambique) and engaged in a proper war of aggression in Afghanistan – none of these countries has yet recovered from the interference.

As an element in the de-Stalinization process a need arose for a comprehensive study of the 'proper' and original ideology. A group of Soviet academics put together a handbook entitled *Outlines of Marxism–Leninism*, which can thus be regarded as officially sanctioned. Comparing its contents with the ideological keynotes given above, the concord is remarkable.[6] There is, however, one apparent exception: the labour theory of value is described primarily in the same way as in Marx's *Capital* but with the exception of the law of the falling rate of profit, which is conspicuous by its absence. An attempt is, however, made to keep the labour theory of value as intact as possible by adjusting the theory of impoverishment, regarding which the handbook emphatically denies that there is a continuous worsening of the living conditions of the workers under capitalism. However, it allows that the relative position of the working class is worsened, i.e. its share of the national income decreases. And it is maintained that when the means of production participate in the production process they do not create any new value, whereas labour power participating in production creates a surplus value. Could it be so, that former conditions in Russia contributed to the survival of this attitude? (The wealth of the landowning aristocracy in Russia was based not upon the value of property, of land, but on the number of serfs tied to the land.[a])

A problem that must have become all the more pressing for the Soviet leaders could be called the end of ideology. Of course, living standards rose, albeit slowly, but the promises of the ideology that the Soviet Union would overtake the West in terms of wealth and freedom remained empty, and it became all the more obvious that they could not be fulfilled. During the last decades of its existence, the Soviet Union increasingly came to resemble a traditional dictatorship in which ideological motivation was replaced by petrified ritual. The hierarchical system produced elderly leaders who were unable to free themselves from the economic and political conditions of the Stalin epoch. It was not until Gorbachev that a leader came to power who was from the generation that was born after the Revolution. He realized that the system demanded change but evidently believed in the possibility of limited and gradual reforms. But even his hesitant steps towards reform were enough to set powers in motion that quickly toppled the system.

---

a See N. Gogol, who in *Dead Souls* tells the story of a businessman who trades in deceased serfs.

The reason for the system's failure is presumably, to a not inconsiderable degree, to be found in the way the fundamental labour theory of value stipulated that it is only the labour input that creates value. State socialist economic thinking was thereby fettered with obsessions, the practical consequences of which were that economic growth was created more through greater allocation of labour-related resources than through efficiency measures. In the absence of the well-researched market economy methods of measuring cost-efficiency, the state socialist system thus led to waste and the ruthless exploitation of resources – not least of the environment – because it lacked, and even denied the existence of, an applicable yardstick. On top of this, the totalitarian, centralized decision-making form of administration rendered it impossible to reform and improve the system.

The system simply ground to a halt, and virtually every communist country embarked upon an arduous and trying transition to a market economy. The conspicuous exception was North Korea, which as recently as 1988 still indignantly denied the need for perestroika and has continued since then to persevere along the same, old road. The development of the Eastern European countries showed that the reforms were hard earned. But, by not following their example, Kim Il Sung and his successor led North Korea not only to economic collapse but also to famine.

19

CONFUCIANISM AND COMMUNISM
An attempt at orientation in North Korean ideology

If Western writers are to be believed, the thirty-three-year-old Kim Il Sung was virtually unknown to the Korean people when he returned to his home country in the company of the Red Army of the Soviet Union in October 1945. Some even claim that Kim Il Sung was not his real name but one that he had taken from a famous fighter in the resistance against the Japanese occupiers.[1] Nevertheless, the *Pyongyang Times* wrote of the enormous expectations with which 'the greatest leader that our people have known for the last several thousand years' was greeted by the massed crowds on his homecoming. He was described as 'the incomparable patriot, national hero, the ever victorious, brilliant field-commander with a will of iron' and as 'the country's Great Sun that swept away the dark clouds of national suffering'. His greeting to the people 'was also a blessing to Korea's Mother Earth' and: 'He was a man equipped with such exceptional powers that popular legend told of how he mowed down the enemy like withered leaves in the autumn just by looking at them, and could make dead branches come into blossom by smiling at them.'

These quotes clearly show that the official North Korean ideology has had other sources of inspiration besides Marxism–Leninism. It also contains strong elements of the East Asian heritage of ideas and a good dose of nationalism. The dominating impression is that North Korean communism combines theories taken from Confucianism's hierarchical worldview and Soviet Russian industrialization ideology of Stalinist vintage, blended to form a unity, the specific Korean characteristics of which they are keen to point out.

Korean nationalism on both sides of the armistice line is well documented. It is also remarkable that, while the Koreans over the last few centuries have embraced an immeasurable influence of Chinese intellectual baggage, they have retained their culinary habits, the women's special clothing and their living conditions – thus Koreans sit and sleep on the floor, not at a table or in bed. This distinctive Korean character can be traced through hundreds of years and is emphasized by the fact that Korea's self-imposed isolation from the rest of the world – with the exception of China – was more rigorous and lasted longer than that of Japan.

There had been communists in Korea since the 1920s, but they were never able to acquire any influence during the effective Japanese occupation. Nor were they ever able to unite because of factional struggles, a constant characteristic of domestic Korean politics. These circumstances may have contributed to the monumental scale of the cult of personality in North Korea, where experiences of tolerance towards dissidents had been only negative. It should also be emphasized that many Vietnamese and Chinese communist leaders had acquired experience of the world through education and work in Europe. The worldview of their North Korean equivalents was, however, restricted to experiences from China and, to a certain extent, the Soviet Union. The only reasonable opportunity Kim Il Sung could have had to broaden his worldview and receive a theoretical education would have been during the poorly documented Second World War years he spent in the Soviet Union. Apart from his early guerilla years, his education was thus marked by the Russia of the Stalin era, and the quotes above remind us also of the panegyric exaggerations of the Stalin cult.

Nevertheless, communism in Korea ought not to be lifted out of the East Asian environment in which it had developed and which was imbued with Chinese cultural tradition. The influence of Chinese thinking can be illustrated, in such a way as to leave no room for doubt, by South Korea's flag, with its symbols taken from ancient Chinese mysticism. This ascendancy has been not only symbolic but also deep-flowing; Confucianism is so deeply embedded in Korean society that an expert on the region – Reischauer[2] – has claimed that Korea became more purely Confucian than China itself.

Of the Confucian influences, there are three in particular that should be noted: first, the insistence upon rulers having ethical standards; second, the egalitarian (in principle, if not always in practice) examination system as a basis for employment and advancement; and, third, the principles for relations between people – between ruler and subject, between father and son, man and wife, older and younger brother, and between friends. With the possible exception of the last one, they are all clearly hierarchical and connected with authority.

However, people do not always practise what they preach. Confucian and communist imperatives might well lead a secure life as a part of public consciousness without them necessarily seeming to decide an individual's actions. In this respect, it is easy to find parallels in the West. The parable of the needle's eye has prevented few Christians from striving for riches. The presence of Eminences, Lord Bishops and Right Reverends hardly fits in with the message of the gospels, and which Christian thinks of Jesus as His Holiness or the Right Reverend? But just as one can hardly ignore Christianity when studying expressions of Western thinking, one cannot avoid taking Confucianism into account in the case of Korea.

The ethical element, the opinion that good government is built upon behaviour worthy of imitation, and that the basis for leadership is knowledge and ethics, would seem to lead to the inevitable suppression of free opinion. This means that the political system is seen as a reflection of a universal moral order. Because one cannot then distinguish between politics and ethics, differing political views become, by definition, unethical. Loyal and legitimate opposition cannot therefore exist.

The question of how the transfer of power, like the dynastic changes in China, can be incorporated into this philosophy is solved by the ruler's authority being based upon the 'mandate of heaven'. With the growing weakness of the Emperor's ability to rule and with his moral authority withering away, oppositional elements and rebel movements arose, and the person who won then showed himself, through his very victory, as the possessor of the heavenly mandate. And, as it is quite unthinkable for the common man to rebel against the will of heaven, society as a whole swings 'from unity to unity'.

The example of the mandate of heaven cannot be applied unequivocally in the case of Korea, but this reservation should not be taken as an opportunity to question the principle's fundamental relevance. Historically speaking, Korea was a sort of autonomous Chinese vassal state, and the Korean King ruled not with a heavenly mandate, but with the approval of the Emperor of China. The King's standing was therefore not as absolute as that of the Chinese Emperor, and he could thus be criticized. Korea's dependence upon Beijing meant that Koreans could not change their ruler. As a result, during the last 500 years they failed to undergo the revitalization processes that the dynastic changes meant for China. Korea's weak royal power also led to the hereditary aristocracy acquiring a strong position, which was, however, characterized by eternal factional fighting, and this was both bitter and bloody on account of the confusion of politics and ethics.

The educational and examination system was based upon Confucius' emphasis that knowledge and ethical qualities were the qualifications for leading positions; they were not hereditary. The system was in principle, though not in practice, decidedly egalitarian. It should be noted that the aim of education was not training in practical or administrative skills but rather at the formation of morally outstanding personalities by the study of classical works. However, in comparison with China, developments in Korea took a different path and the examination system never came to function as it was intended. Most villages in Korea did indeed have their own schools as a part of the system but, in practice, the higher exams were reserved for children from the upper classes. Members of privileged families could even be awarded official posts directly and take care of the exams afterwards. In this way, a rigid class system was created and retained in Korea, a system that was irreconcilable with the Confucian ideal of equality. Korean society thus stagnated in a totally different way from Chinese society, and this reinforced the impediments to revitalization.

The communist assumption of power did not bring about a revitalization but upheld the traditional stagnation. Society was, so to speak, turned upside down. All leading positions were seized by the revolutionary guerillas, who favoured subjects with a proven proletarian background and their descendants. Intellectuals and other members of the former ruling classes and their descendants were confined to collective farm work, or other toilsome occupations, with no hope of being able to improve their lot. It was certainly difficult for a poor man to advance in the time of the monarchy – and for the descendant of a class enemy in the Democratic People's Republic it was out of the question. The old leadership was replaced by a new one, which had neither the insight nor the ambition needed to change the traditional unequal structure of the society.

The hierarchical relationship between people is based upon the importance of knowledge and ethics as a foundation for high office, and in Korean society, with its aristocratic character, this seems to have been accentuated while at the same time being distorted. The extent to which these attitudes have made their mark, even in North Korea, was clearly to be seen in the manner in which superiors treated their inferiors, and men treated women, and how this was regarded as self-evident by those it affected.

Communism was imported ready-made into Korea. An ideology that had been created in, and for, Western industrial countries was to be applied in a stagnant East Asian agrarian society. This naturally led to a considerable shift of emphasis. The Japanese occupation had brought about the beginnings of a working class but had not assisted in the emergence of domestic capitalism, and consequently there was no basis for a classic class struggle. After the dreadful destruction of the Korean War, almost everything had to be built up from scratch, and the North Koreans took the opportunity to omit the capitalist stage and go directly from feudalism to socialism. The large landowners had been eliminated by a land reform shortly before liberation, and the class struggle was therefore interpreted to mean the transformation of the peasants into a working class. The method chosen was to herd them together into large state farms or cooperatives.

The nationalist element made itself felt during the purges of pro-Russian and pro-Chinese Party factions. These demanded comprehensive measures, bearing in mind that Korean communism, as a result of the Japanese occupation, had primarily been a movement in exile. Further, North Korea refused to let itself be assigned special functions within COMECON's socialist division of work because it wanted to develop a multifaceted industrial sector of its own. As a base for this more independent policy, the North Koreans introduced their *Juche* ideology of self-reliance, which was eventually defined as independence in politics, self-reliance in the economy, and self-defence to protect national sovereignty. *Juche* got more lift as a result of the Chinese–Russian conflict, in which North Korea was careful not to take sides but rather extended the boundaries of its own freedom of action. Thus, the *Juche* ideology came into being in order to serve concrete Korean interests, but over time it came to acquire a much more distinct character of general applicability.

We can assume this to be connected to the cult of personality. As this became all the more dominating, its practitioners came to realize that the North Korean backyard had become too small for a leader with aspirations to universality. The *Juche* ideology was proclaimed as Marxism–Leninism for the developing countries of the day. The nationalist tone was emphasized by the Leader's expectations that

122

the study of Marxism should have *Juche* ideology as its starting point. As a result, ideological contacts with the other communist countries became virtually impossible.

The proportions of the cult of personality beggar description. The Leader's portrait was displayed almost everywhere. In the main square in Pyongyang hung two smaller pictures of Marx and Lenin opposite a larger one of Kim Il Sung. With the exception of the Leader himself and his son, every adult Korean wore a brooch containing a portrait of the Leader pinned to his or her outer garment at heart level. One could not buy these; rather, they were a token that could almost be likened to a Western wedding ring.

Even in nursery school, the Leader's subjects learned about the history of his life, and foreigners could hardly avoid learning it because of the pictures that illustrated various episodes – leaving his childhood home, as a guerrilla leader, the wife who defended him from bullets with her own body, his return to the Fatherland, as a war leader, among children, and as a teacher among peasants and factory workers. This was an iconography that could only be compared with – and unquestionably seemed to have been inspired by – the Christian one of the life of Jesus.

The Leader's birthplace – the humble hut of a poor gatekeeper – had been turned into a national monument and a place of pilgrimage. Visiting groups were herded round between the building, the heap of stones where the children had played 'ships' and always chosen him to be captain, the patch of sand where they had wrestled and he had always won because he used not only his muscles but also his mind, the look-out by the river where his father had shown him where his ancestors had sunk a US warship, etc. Mecca of the Moslems is closed to unbelievers and Christians hardly expect people of other faiths to fall on their knees before the Holy Manger. But foreign dignitaries were taken to Mayondae and expected to bow their uncovered heads. In museums they displayed, in hall after hall, the microphones, telephones, telescopes, chairs and clothes that Kim Il Sung had used on various occasions. If, when opening a library, he had happened to rest upon a chair, it was draped in white and roped off. Inscriptions were chiselled into rock faces to honour the Leader, the letters so large that an adult could stand up in them.

The communist veneer could not hide the fact that North Korean society was permeated by traditional belief. Indeed, so bound were Koreans by tradition that the specifically Korean variants always came out on top.

Against a background of the 'mandate of heaven', the cult of personality – if not all its trappings – was natural. This also helps to explain why it seemed to be accepted without reservation, and why people did not question that even the South Koreans were expected to subordinate themselves if given the opportunity. Further, the presentation of Kim Il Sung's son as successor was logical. At the same time, it is tempting to see both a national and a hierarchical element in the way in which all of Kim Il Sung's ancestors were made out to be eminent revolutionaries. What was this, other than an insistence upon aristocratic breeding of a suitable sort?

In this context, grooming of the leader's son, Kim Jong Il, began in the mid-1970s by his being mentioned increasingly frequently – he was called 'the Centre of the Party' – and by his being placed beside his father on the monumental paintings. We noticed that at this time the pictures of the son seemed to change, and we attributed this to the rumours that Kim Il Sung had two sons, the elder one from an earlier marriage. Had the elder one been forced to renounce his rights as first-born in favour of his brother? In the local climate this remained speculation, not least because it was of no importance for the course of events.[3]

The ethical element, the ruler's example and the view that the basis of leadership is knowledge and moral stature was always present. In North Korea, this was strengthened by the Stalinist type of communism, which, by definition, declared the Leader's policy to be the correct one vis-à-vis all sorts of right and left deviations, and resulted in a moral–political monopoly that was absolute. The 'beloved and revered Leader' was a teacher in all areas and a model in all respects. Every workplace referred to his guidance – in children's nurseries, factories, museums and farming cooperatives one was shown notices detailing how many times he had given instructions on the spot or by telephone. The Leader's monopoly of moral example excluded dissentient opinions and made opposition impossible. Consequently, there was no place for even that tiny percentage of dissent that was allowed in Eastern European elections under communist rule. In North Korea it was an absolute requirement that both election participation and the number of 'yes' votes should be 100%.

It is also from the starting point of this moral monopoly that we have to understand Pyongyang's perception of the regime in Seoul. This was regarded as immoral, which makes any further discussion unnecessary. The idea that one should be able to judge similar actions by the northern and the southern sides by the same criteria, and every attempt to mediate between the two, was (precisely on account of this starting point) seen as immoral and a sign of aggressive intent.

The Chinese examination system crowned an education that did not cover particular skills, but only classical works. This reflected their intention not to train professionals but to educate administrators with a high level of morality. In North Korea, an egalitarian school system provided eleven years of obligatory schooling that was preceded by an equally obligatory nursery education from very early infancy. Higher education seemed to concentrate mainly on technical subjects in order to aid industrialization. The ethical aspects were dealt with through an intensive and obligatory study of the New Master's written works. It was the duty of every subject to spend two hours each day on supervised reading of the Leader's works.[4] Tradition served as a model as regards form too. Every newspaper article and official speech quoted the Leader's statements with the invocation, 'Kim Il Sung has taught us …' – in the same way that Confucian scholars over the millennia have written, 'The Master has said …'. In this way, the mandate of heaven and the moral monopoly fused with the cult of personality, but it did not stop there. The figure of Kim Il Sung developed into Confucius' equal and successor – or perhaps his superior.

North Korean society must surely be one of the most hierarchical and elitist in the world. This did not limit itself to the boundless cult of personality; rather, the lack of any sign of equality was, despite all the cosmetic vocabulary, striking at all levels. When visited by not only the Leader but other dignitaries, workers stood cap in hand. Family bonds between the leading men and women of the state seemed to be more of a rule than an exception.

The socialist form of address 'comrade' was originally introduced to emphasize the equality of all men, but in Korea two words are used. One (*damú*) is used for subordinates and equals and the other (*dongshí*) for superiors – thus making a mockery of the whole idea. Officials had quite obviously been allocated official cars according to rank, and the largest of these had tinted windows, and on some roads they were driven in the centre lane reserved for official use. Army personnel, police officers, railway officials and other categories of officials had large badges of rank of Russian type, and the generals, at any rate, had parade uniforms and were as highly decorated as their Soviet Russian counterparts. But in the processions on national holidays, one could see that tokens of distinction had been handed out in abundance.

The position of women had undeniably improved since liberation, but their attitudes were still decidedly obsequious. As a rule they had menial functions and moved discreetly at the edges of rooms behind the men's backs so as not to disturb them. They were well coiffured and were not against using make-up, and they often wore traditional dresses of beautiful silk.

The cut and the quality of a person's clothes and the possession of an overcoat and leather shoes reflected social standing. The embassies' locally employed personnel were to be given emoluments in kind in the form of clothes, which, according to regulations, followed a sliding scale parallel to their wages – only the interpreter, with his intellectual job, was entitled to an overcoat.

Summing up, one could say that the Confucian emphasis upon loyalty to one's family, father and Emperor had been transferred to the people, the party and the Leader in North Korea.

By the mid-1970s, during Mao Zedong's final years and the sinister influence of the 'Gang of Four', the two cities of Beijing and Pyongyang gave spectacularly different impressions. Compared with Beijing's rather shabby environment and its bustling crowds of lively, curious, blue-clad people, Pyongyang was quite a contrast and seemed more like an Eastern European urban scene with deserted streets and a reserved, perhaps almost hostile, population mainly dressed in a European style. Whereas Chinese women were unpretentious and wore unisex clothes, Korean women put their hair up and wore skirts and court shoes. The impressions of the differences were strengthened after each visit, and it felt more and more as though they were deeply ingrained.

Chinese people in shops and hotels were friendly and helpful, had a natural dignity and a candid attitude and seemed to feel at ease with themselves – perhaps secure in the knowledge that they were Chinese. North Koreans deliberately kept themselves apart from foreigners, collectively as well as singly, did not let them into shops and could hardly be accused of being helpful. The impression one received was that they were concealing an inner insecurity and desperately trying to show that they were self-contained – perhaps an expression of generations of experience of forced docility.

It is worth repeating that for a long time China was the only 'outside world' that the Koreans knew. As a logical consequence of this, many North Korean phenomena were based on Chinese examples. The Kim Il Sung brooch would seem to have been inspired by the now-forgotten Mao brooch. Further, the big industrialization programme was originally meant not to take place at the cost of being self-sufficient with regard to food. Mao's faith in 'the Great Leap Forward' would appear to be the model for both the 'Chollima' movement and the campaign to capture the Red Banner of the Three Revolutions. On the other hand, the Cultural Revolution, with its hostility towards authority, did not find any sympathy with the North Korean Leader.

This brings us to the way in which China was characterized by revitalizing dynastic changes, and that this had no counterpart in Korea. In Mao's China, the development went in waves back and forth and, above all, the Chinese showed themselves, time after time, capable of reconsidering decisions after they had found to have negative consequences. In sharp contrast to this was North Korea's clear tendency to persevere; when it came to changing course or reconsidering bad decisions, they had obvious difficulties, or were perhaps simply incapable of doing so. For example, Beijing soon abandoned the backyard industry project initiated as part of 'the Great Leap Forward'. The North Korean leadership had also embraced the idea and demanded major efforts in the form of local production in addition to nationalized industry and agriculture. However, this policy was never reviewed; rather, it continued to be compulsory for the population to produce something extra, regardless of the comprehensive national economic planning.

The sudden changes in Mao's policies would suggest that he realized the importance of periodic revitalization and considered this to be necessary, even while he himself was at the helm. His successors showed the same insight and, indeed, went so far that they have as good as broken with Mao's principles. That is not the case in North Korea, where Kim Jong Il continued in his father's footsteps right up until the time the nation was unable to feed its own population and he was forced reluctantly to seek aid from outside. His respect for local traditions should also be noted. Kim Jong Il waited more than three years before he took over his father's position as the General Secretary of the Party, 'apparently reflecting the traditional period of respect shown by a Korean son on his father's death'.[5] On the occasion of the fiftieth anniversary of the DPRK in September 1998, he chose to make his position as chairman of the National Security Council into the highest office of state. Thus, he did not make himself president; instead, the deceased Kim Il Sung was declared 'President for Eternity'. One can but ask whether this is just an expression of filial reverence, or should it be interpreted as indicating that Kim Il Sung was to be regarded as a figure on a level with Confucius? Whatever the case, any understanding of the need for revitalization is conspicuous by its absence.

In part, these attitudes can perhaps be explained by reference to Korea's rigidity as it has manifested itself over the course of history. But it is more a question of looking for an explanation in the difference between the Chinese and the Korean communist leaders' objectives. Particularly with the Cultural Revolution, Mao showed that he was interested in more than purely material progress; apparently he wanted a sort of permanently 're-born' revolution that, even at the cost of lasting poverty, would prevent the emergence of new privileged layers or classes – presumably with the exception of the helmsman, Mao, himself as arbitrator.

The cultural influence from China was particularly noticeable at a subconscious level, as a historical prerequisite and a sort of starting point. It was the Soviet Union's influence, however, that seems to have dominated the politically aware, communist construction of society with its distinct character of Stalinist industrialization ideology. This consisted in both an insincere commitment to increased material equality and the impressive achievement of having industrialized the country during the first twenty years after the Korean War and raised the population's living standards. But, just as with the Soviet Union, there was no deeper interest in the qualitative aspects of equality. The growth of the *nomenklatura* and its privileges revealed the construction of a cynical class society in which ideology served the interests of those wielding power. The economic policy proved successful in the build-up stage but led first to stagnation and then to decline. When this was combined with an inability to change course, it was a steep downhill slide to a predictable collapse.

The differences in attitudes and in aims and methods and choices would seem to reflect differences in Chinese and Korean mentality. By pure chance I happened to be in Beijing when Mao Zedong died, and when Chou Enlai died, too. The reactions of the Chinese people – the man on the street and staff in hotels and shops – provided food for thought. On Mao's death, everyone in China behaved with decidedly solemn dignity. When Chou died, both women and men cried silently yet openly. Mao and Chou were respected, revered and loved as men. Kim Il Sung, on the other hand, was declared immortal.

When Mao's successors observed their communist neighbours – the Soviet Union and North Korea – they must have come to the conclusion that neither of them had succeeded in building up either an equal or economically prosperous society. Both these neighbours were clearly a long way down the cul-de-sac, something that China had to avoid whatever it cost. At an early stage, the pragmatic Chinese decided to go off in another direction.

20

KIM IL SUNG'S MARXISM

The original form of Marxist ideology and its one hundred-year history have been accorded a relatively large amount of space in the previous chapters. The purpose of this has been to describe the economic and political frames of reference that governed the building of Kim Il Sung's North Korea. Professional, or convinced, interpreters of communism may perhaps consider the description all too succinct and selective, but this has to be weighed against the reader's patience. For example, for someone wishing to gain a basic understanding of early Christianity, it is sufficient to be given a somewhat limited description of the principles in the dispute as to whether the Son was of the same or similar essence as the Father. For those concerned at the time it was a matter of life and death, in the same way that – during the twentieth century – it was for communists to be branded as deviators to the right or left. Like other communist dictators, Kim Il Sung, stipulated the one and only faith, i.e. the Party line, and that line will be briefly described as deduced from his writings and speeches as well as his policy in practice.

Kim Il Sung's endeavours to stand out as a prominent ideological figure not only in communist contexts, but even more so in the underdeveloped countries, were based upon the *Juche* ideology. It was thus logical that in his comments on the problems concerning the transition period to socialism and on the dictatorship of the proletariat he emphasized that these – as other scientific and theoretical problems – must be solved from the starting point of *Juche*. Above all, he objected to dogmatic attitudes, by which he meant a rigid adherence to the views of the classics, or by letting oneself be influenced to an unacceptable degree by the opinions of others and thus be steered by servility towards the great powers.

According to Kim, Marx based his analysis upon the situation in developed capitalist countries, in which rural areas, as well as the towns, had been subject to a complete capitalist transformation, and there were thus both industrial and agricultural workers, but not really any peasants. Marx assumed that there were no class differences between the working and the peasant classes and that, consequently, there were only two classes, capitalists and workers. What is more, he lived in the pre-monopolistic capitalist epoch and thus believed that the revolution would be victorious relatively soon.

Lenin however, according to Kim, lived in a backward capitalist country, with existing class differences between workers and peasants, and thus considered that the transitional period to socialism would be relatively long. In order to bring about the socialist society, Lenin, too, had pointed out the necessity of eliminating the differences between workers and peasants.

Against this background, Kim stipulated that it was a right-wing deviation to believe that the transitional period would only last until socialism became victorious, and a left-wing deviation to claim that it would last until communism had been established. He did, however, emphasize that the definitions of the classics had been correct from the starting point of the historical conditions pertaining in their time. But, as far as Korea was concerned, it was essential to start from the *Juche* ideology and realize that in North Korea they had carried out the socialist revolution in a backward, colonized agricultural country. (It was implied that the destruction of the Korean War had meant that they had been forced to rebuild society from scratch and, in that situation, had taken the opportunity to carry out the socialist revolution.) The country had not passed through the capitalist epoch, so the forces of production were backward, and the difference between the working class and the peasants remained after the socialist revolution.

However, it was by no means necessary to first let society go through a capitalist phase. With the working class in power, this stage could be passed under a socialist regime. In such circumstances, developing the forces of production and building a classless society took a relatively long time. The perfect socialist society was not established until the peasants had been turned into members of the working class, which would come about through the mechanization of agriculture, the use of fertilizers and irrigation, and by introducing an eight-hour working day.

In summary, this meant that, according to Kim, the transitional period lasted some time after the socialist revolution, until such time as the middle layers of society had been won over, the difference between the working class and the peasants had been eliminated and the classless society had been constructed. Because North Korea had stepped directly from feudalism to socialism, it could not show any class struggle between workers and capitalists. The meaning of class struggle was, in North Korea, characterized by turning the peasants into members of the working class.

In addition, Kim noted that, because the transitional period had taken the form of a society without exploitation, then it was a socialist society. He further stated that, as long as capitalism remained in the world, the state could not wither away in a particular country or region that had achieved communism, but instead the dictatorship of the proletariat must be retained. These views, he ended, did not mean a revision of Marxism–Leninism but were a creative application in the light of new historical conditions and in the actual situation in which North Korea found itself. In this way, dogmatism and servility towards great powers were resisted and the purity of Marxism–Leninism was retained.

When reading Kim Il Sung's description of the views of Marx, one cannot refrain from asking whether his analysis of the conditions in Europe in the mid-nineteenth century was based on fact, or if it agrees with Marx's philosophy – particularly with regard to the existence of the peasants as a class.[1] One has to bear in mind that Kim was educated in the Soviet Union, and that Lenin played down the role of the peasant class by introducing the concept of the rural proletariat and placed the emphasis exclusively upon the antagonism between the capitalists and the working class.[2] The influence from Lenin must also be seen as including war communism, which almost seems like a blueprint for North Korea's economic policy,[3] with all production and distribution subordinated to state direction, all workers employed by the state, centralized supplies, etc. In addition, North Korea had abolished, if not money in the strict physical sense, at least the function of money in its normal meaning.

It is also striking how Lenin's line of argument in 1905 about 'socialist and democratic dictatorship'[4] seems to have been the model for the way in which the Korean reunification should be brought about. According to Lenin, communists should have supported the bourgeois 'democratic revolution', which sought to introduce a free political life and was forced to take the form of a 'democratic dictatorship' in order to prevent counter-revolution. Once this had happened, there would be an end to the cooperation with the bourgeois elements and it would be time to go on to the 'socialist revolution'. This mode of operation was clearly a model for the North Korean proposals on North–South discussions directly between the people and their organizations, in which category the government in Seoul was not included.[5] An appeal with this content, dated 25 January 1977, had been signed by the political and religious organizations in North Korea. As a comment, it will suffice to point out that the very idea of the existence of such organizations caused amusement among even the ambassadors of the communist countries. Several similar suggestions were to be repeated from Pyongyang's side in the following years. Such North–South discussions ought, from the North Korean point of view, to have been preceded by, or in themselves form, the 'democratic revolution' – with the task of repelling the counter-revolution of the Seoul regime. Later, this 'democratic revolution' would be extended to become the 'socialist revolution' that made reunification a reality. The justification for this was, as Lenin had pointed out in 1917, that 'the Soviet Republic is a higher form of democracy than an ordinary bourgeois republic'.[6]

Stalin's influence seems primarily to have been that of precursor in the choice of practical political paths. The collectivization of agriculture is one example, along with the enormous emphasis upon heavy industry and the cult of personality and the suffocating police and security services. It was, however, a foregone conclusion that de-Stalinization would not be tolerated, and nor would the thesis of peaceful coexistence. It was in such an atmosphere that it became expedient to introduce the *Juche* ideology. In many respects, this stands out as a form of surviving Stalinism that has been given an extended life.

The application of Marx's theses to a situation that they had never been intended to cover – i.e. to abuse the theory of development according to scientific laws by skipping the capitalist stage and carrying out the socialist revolution in a feudal society – must have led to them being reinterpreted in such a way that they became unrecognizable. Kim was not the first to come across that problem; rather, when it came to adapting the theories, he built upon a foundation that had already been laid by Lenin. While Lenin had been prepared to shorten the capitalist epoch by violence, Kim skipped it completely. Naturally, Kim's line of ideological reasoning, and particularly the 'primogeniture' of *Juche*, was seen as heretical by the Soviet communists. If they regarded their socialism as a science, then it must necessarily be universally applicable. They could not accept, or even take seriously, the possibility that others discovered or stipulated other laws for the science.

Korea's, and particularly North Korea's, dependence upon China has often been touched upon. It has been emphasized how the Chinese cultural influence over the centuries has been immeasurable and left its mark on trains of thought and habits. But when it came to communist ideology, I never experienced anything that contradicted the university vice-chancellor's concisely negative and categorical 'no' when he was asked whether the teaching of ideology also included Mao's writings.[7]

When he was young, Kim Il Sung could hardly have avoided being greatly influenced by the developments in China and by Mao's methods, which he evidently embraced as models for his own practical policy. The ideology, however, that directed the modern political construction of society was marked by the education Kim Il Sung had received in the Soviet Union during the Second World War. But later, he made himself into a creator of a renewed ideology who did not want to stand in the shadow of either Lenin or Mao. As previously mentioned, in the great square in Pyongyang there were three giant portraits, two large pictures of Marx and Lenin facing an even larger picture of Kim himself, but none of either Stalin or Mao.

The conclusion is obvious – not only Confucius, but even Marx and Lenin had met their match as ideologists, and there was no room for other prominent revolutionaries.

Bourgeois elements were never spoken of. North Korea prided itself upon being monolithic and so there could be no room for the forms of 'antagonisms' that Mao observed. As far as North Korea was concerned, they had already passed this stage because, from the very beginning, they had skipped capitalism and carried out the socialist revolution. There were, however, the rudiments of a common front and cooperation between parties. One of the vice-presidents of the country was not a member of the Korean Workers' Party but represented an otherwise unknown party –probably more to the point was the fact that he was a maternal uncle of Kim Il Sung. It was rumoured that this uncle had been a Free Church preacher in his youth. Perhaps he was the man behind the iconography surrounding Kim, which undeniably seemed to be inspired by examples from Christian Sunday schools. Nationalism would appear to be an area in which Kim was obviously influenced by Mao and his adaptation of Marxism, which clearly demanded that it be given a Chinese style and should be permeated by distinctive Chinese features. An equivalent Korean nationalism is plainly evident in the *Juche* ideology.

Communism has an inherent tendency to solve economic problems with political methods; this was most clearly expressed by the way in which political decisions could be made that violated economic realities. Kim's methods consisted of ruthless mass mobilization following the example of Mao's 'Great Leap' and Cultural Revolution – although the egalitarian content of the latter did not appeal to Kim. Nor did he embrace Mao's invocation of China's historical experiences, including Confucianism;[a] North Korea's history seemed, rather, to start in 1945. Furthermore, Kim gave preference to his own idea of class struggle in Korea, which meant transforming the peasants into a working class, rather than Mao's view of the key role of the peasants in the revolution.

When the domestic *Juche* ideology was developed, it was claimed to be the foundation for, and was considered superior to, Marxism–Leninism in the forms this had acquired in both Soviet Russia and China. With *Juche*, Kim Il Sung lay claim to being a thinker and teacher of world historic dimensions, which not only infringed upon recognition of Mao's revolutionary greatness but, if anything, seemed to be an attempt at outdoing Mao, indeed even at eclipsing Confucius, Marx and Engels. It is self-evident that such pretensions could hardly be expected to gain respect from the Chinese, so conscious of their history. But the habits of centuries had left their mark, and the North Koreans continued, in practice, to follow Chinese examples even when it came to the construction of communist society – but then chose to stick to this course even after the Chinese themselves had reconsidered their own choice of path.[b]

However, the circumstances of international politics lay outside the control of Pyongyang and the developments necessitated painful adjustments. In 1990, Gorbachev recognized South Korea, and with the dissolution of the Soviet Union one of North Korea's mainstays fell away. When China, too, in 1991 established trade and consular relations with South Korea, followed by diplomatic recognition in 1992, Pyongyang's isolation became apparent. In this connection China withdrew its veto against South Korea's membership of the UN and both Korean states were admitted in 1991. North Korea was obliged to soften its attitude towards

---

a   The free Chinese literature, distributed in a number of languages, included the title *Criticizing Lin Piao and Confucius*, in which a contemporary Communist deviator was attacked for praising Confucius (who lived in the sixth century BC) and criticizing the legalist school and the Emperor Chun Shih huang (who ruled 221–207 BC). This publication provides an excellent example of the difference between Chinese and Korean attitudes, because this sort of time perspective – stretching over thousands of years of living cultural heritage – was unthinkable in North Korea, where a purged politician would also have been weeded out from all official documentation.
b   In 1991, Maretzki claimed that nothing had changed in the methods of the centralized planned economy in thirty years; Maretzki, op. cit., p. 149.

the USA, Japan and South Korea, and particularly so when the food supply crisis made a request for international aid unavoidable. At this time, the North Koreans developed a considerable negotiating proficiency and succeeded both in establishing the longed-for direct contacts with the USA and in persuading its three arch-enemies to become involved in long-term aid programmes worth hundreds of millions of dollars. But this negotiating skill was characterized more by pigheadedness than by flexibility. It was never a question of anything other than tactical retreat; there was no new direction.

All societies in an acute modernizing phase have to wrestle with inevitable conflicts between the old and the new. As far as the North Koreans were concerned, it was apparent that their Confucian instincts were confronted with their communist-schooled brains. Now that communism, as an economic system, has been abandoned in the rest of the world, it will be impossible for little North Korea alone to carry out socialism or communism in *one* country. And when it, nevertheless, tried to do this during the 1990s, the poor economic development brought the country to famine and desperation. This ought, at least, to force the tradition-bound North Koreans – and, as I have described, even the most convinced supporters of the regime are still influenced by tradition – to ask themselves whether the present regime has lost its heavenly mandate. And who is prepared to rise up against the will of heaven?

If Confucian instincts turn out to be strong enough, they will surely, to a considerable extent, come to facilitate the break with Stalinist state socialism that not even North Korea will ultimately be able to avoid.

21

AS LONG AS THE GAME GOES ON ...

The number of Westerners who visited North Korea remained limited. No Western embassies, other than the Swedish one, were ever opened. Quite the opposite, as the staff of both the Western trade offices and the Swedish Embassy was cut down, and sometimes there was no staff at all. The number of Westerners with personal experience of both North and South Korea was even fewer because, although the authorities of neither country prohibited such visitors, they certainly did not particularly welcome them – and had their own subtle methods of making sure their views were respected. Within the Swedish Foreign Ministry, it was primarily the inspector and the medical adviser who had cause, which neither side could find objectionable, to have a good look at embassy working conditions on both sides of the demarcation line. These two found it incomprehensible that they were dealing with the same people.

In subsequent diplomatic posts I found the North Koreans to be afraid of contact. The exception was Geneva, where we gradually established relations – but the first time the North Korean quickly left the reception at which I had introduced myself. The South Koreans were consistently neither negative, nor positive, nor curious, but if anything programmatically indifferent. However, after the dissolution of the Soviet Union they became considerably more relaxed and open to discussion.

As the problems with, and the cost of, Germany's reunification came to light, it became noticeable that the South Koreans were starting to have doubts about a Korean reunification. There was naturally still a feeling of kinship between two halves of the nation, and the idea of reunification remained a categorical imperative, but now the differences came to the fore. South Korea's population was comparatively smaller in relation to North Korea's than West Germany's was to East Germany's. West Germany, with its market economy and the West German social institutions, was among the most stable and strongest nations in the world, whereas South Korea was still at the beginning of its democratic development.

Not least, one should bear in mind that the East Germans had been aware of their economic and political situation, were well informed about West German conditions and were positive about a reunification on market economy terms. The

North Koreans, on the other hand, lived in total isolation and were effectively indoctrinated into believing in the superiority of their own system. The South Koreans seemed, therefore, to begin to wonder whether the price of a Korean reunification might be too high, or at any rate whether the process should take place more gradually than was the case in Germany. Was it in fact even possible to foresee the problems surrounding reunification?

Japan and the East Asian 'tiger economies' had been integrated into the world economy, which automatically led to a continual adjustment to global conditions. These countries, too, were confronted with serious crises and setbacks, which did not, on the whole, differ from those that established market economies might meet with, and which could thus be solved within the framework of the global system. Through force of circumstance, however, the North Korean modernization programme had come about with state socialist inspiration. The system was well suited to organize a flying start but was, at the same time, ideologically fettered to such an extent that the very ability to think and act remained chained to the original choices and solutions. This development model required, for its realization, a totalitarian state that not only rejected the global system but even considered itself to be the better alternative with the future before it. With this conviction, the regime was doomed to failure.

The North Koreans' conviction that their choice of path and formulas were the final solutions meant that Marxism–Leninism in the form of *Juche* was the peak of human achievement – and this can even be explained as another version of the thesis of 'the end of history'. Adherents of a faith that preaches salvation naturally find it difficult to be convinced of the need to adjust their economic policy in the light of the tough lessons of reality. In the present-day situation, the hardened can also still hide behind the argument that they might have been in too much of a hurry but that history will prove them right. Communists have never been in the habit of making comparisons with their own times but compare today's market economy failings with tomorrow's socialist paradise – a designation that the North Koreans actually applied in advance.

When examining the state socialist system's mode of operation, there are difficulties in trying to fit it into the Marxist development scheme consisting of 'original society–slavery–feudalism–capitalism–socialism'. One common way to get round this problem has been to call it state capitalist. But the Soviet Russian system, in its Stalinist version, was also based upon slavery, which found its expression not least in the gulag archipelago. Similar conditions are said to exist still in North Korea.[a] Practice in both the Soviet Union and North Korea at that

a Interviewers of defectors who had served sentences in North Korean prison camps point out that the availability of information is unsatisfactory and that it is impossible to verify the testimonies. With the support of data from the South Korean Center for the Advancement of North Korean Human Rights, it is claimed that there are ten or so prison camps with about 200,000 prisoners, that the living conditions are decidedly severe, and that over the years an estimated 400,000 are thought to have died in them. As in the Soviet Union in the past, the camps form an integral part of the state production system; Diamond, L., 'Voices from the North Korean gulag', *Journal of Democracy*, Vol. 9, No. 3, 1998, 82–96.

time also suggests that the ordinary workforce could not really be regarded as consisting of free individuals. As I pointed out earlier, the North Korean workers' wages were little more than pocket money and they were bound to their workplaces for food, clothes and lodgings.[b]

In this context, it can be fruitful to compare the Korean situation with Elias' description of the way slavery works in a society:

> By letting the work be carried out by slaves, the society is tied to comparatively simple working tools, to technical material that can be used by slaves and, on account of that fact, any changes, improvements or adjustments to new situations of necessity involve comparatively great difficulties. The reproduction of capital is tied to the reproduction of slaves ... to the possibility of utilising the availability of slaves, and the reproduction of capital is thus never calculable in the same way as in a society in which one does not buy people for life, but in which one buys work-performance from people who are more or less free.[1]

Elias' description admittedly refers to the transition from antiquity to the Middle Ages, but it is nevertheless illustrative of the workings of an economic system based on tied labour, a command economy. In such an economy, the incentives for technical advance do not have the same positive role, a fact that helps to explain the inevitable way in which state socialism falls behind and stagnates. This tendency is aggravated by the thesis of the labour theory of value, i.e. that only labour power creates surplus value. Work under slave-like conditions, i.e. exploitation, is then logical. For the availability of labour power, by way of definition, sets the limits for economic development and it becomes more attractive to have cheap, rather than skilled, labour. And cheapest of all is forced labour.

There is, thus, a clear line from the labour theory of value to the gulag. But Marx had believed that 'the capitalist use of machinery' would, of necessity, lead to a transformation of society, which would then mean that 'free and associated work' would be achieved through the withering away of the state.[2] In the light of experience, it would seem more justified to claim that the socialist use of machinery led to exploitation under state direction, the result of which was economic stagnation.

The adherence to the ideological conviction that Marxism–Leninism was the final and ultimate product of all human thought meant an automatic rejection of all divergent research results. The discipline of economics had undeniably

---

b It is illuminating to read the reflections of defectors to South Korea: 'When I arrived in the South, I was amazed that this money could actually buy things. In the North you just don't carry money in your pocket. Shops don't even have any goods if you did,' and 'I am confused that every item seems to have a different price.'; Grinker, R. R., *Korea and Its Futures*, pp. 243–4.

137

developed since the days of Marx, but this was irrelevant as a consequence. As far as the North Koreans were concerned, one must also take into account the Confucian educational tradition, which did not seek to train experts but, rather, aspired to form morally untarnished leaders through the study of the writings of the classical thinkers. For the new generations that embraced the communist ideology, there was added a selective education in the natural sciences and technical subjects. On the ideological front, the Confucian classics were naturally replaced by Marxist works and, above all, by *Juche* according to the writings of Kim Il Sung and his son. It should, in this context, be observed that the development of *Juche* meant the abandonment of the international character of communist ideology in favour of an extremely nationalist, even isolationist, ideology of self-reliance. With this schooling, the system became immune to change and the leadership rejected all the warning signs and any intimation that the plotted course was leading them astray. So catastrophe was inevitable.

North Korea's situation was made gradually worse by a number of interacting external and internal factors, which in the 1990s led to a collapse of the food supply and health care systems. The dissolution of the Soviet Union had a crucial role in this as it led to the loss of the one trading partner whose importance was without comparison, not least as a supplier of oil. In addition, Moscow, in the second half of the 1980s, had supported Pyongyang with economic aid to a value of about a billion US dollars per year, as well as armaments worth about the same amount.[3] This support ended abruptly, which propelled the North Korean production apparatus from stagnation into a steep downward descent. 'Negative growth' (a euphemism for shrinking output) of about –5% annually leads to dreadful results within a few years. In the late 1950s, the annual per capita income in the North was double that in the South, but by the 1980s the situation had been reversed. Up to this point, both had increased – the North to around US$1,000 and the South to around US$2,000 –and continued to do so. However, by 1996 the North's per capita income had remained unchanged while South Korea's had grown to $11,000, although this dropped to $6,600 in 1998 on account of the South-East Asian economic crisis.[c] Another revealing comparison is to be found in the yearly *increase* in South Korea's gross national product (GNP), which by 1990 was already greater than the entire North Korean GNP.[4]

North Korea has no oil reserves of its own, and domestic energy production is based upon hydro-electric power and coal. When Russia refused to deliver oil

c The figures for the mid-1980s and 1996 are thus the same as regards North Korea, although in 1988 there was no particular shortage of food, while 1996 was a crisis year. The facts are quoted for illustrative purposes only as the GNP figures cannot simply be compared – rather they tend to distort, for example on account of different prices for food. With the same annual income as an African, an average Swede would starve to death early in the year; in the case of North Korea, there are obvious difficulties in estimating the market value of clothing, food, housing, etc. supplied by the state; Reese, *The Prospects of North Korea's Survival*, p. 25.

except against hard currency, imports were reduced by 75%. North Korea then turned to China, which, in 1993, followed the example of Russia. The repercussions were felt in all sectors of the economy. Transport capacity was immediately reduced, which particularly reduced the distribution of coal and also led to cutbacks in the use of tractors and agricultural machinery. The production of fertilizers fell. Consequently, both the production and distribution of foodstuffs were adversely affected. The regime was forced to turn a blind eye to the emergence of independent peasant markets and eventually found itself obliged to allow the local authorities to trade directly with Chinese companies.[5] Towards the end of the decade Kim Jong Il announced Chinese- and Vietnamese-style reforms in agricultural policy in order to meet the food shortages.[6] These developments towards limited private ownership and freedom of travel etc. are recognized in the new Constitution of 1998 – but simultaneously in April 1999 the Supreme People's Assembly made clear 'the intention to stick to their own socialism through the laws of the people's economic plans and rejecting the capitalist market economy'.[7] The words echo Lenin's reservations regarding the temporary character of the 'New Economic Policy'.[8]

One must also bear in mind the economic role played by the military. No facts are, of course, available, but the armed forces obviously have control of a considerable production capacity. It must be stressed that this sector has always been given priority and that it operates outside the ordinary planned economy – or, probably more correctly expressed, constitutes a parallel planned economy of its own. The procuration of arms has always been a priority within this priority, and the military apparently also operates the foreign trade in arms, both exports and imports. North Korean arms sales account for the lion's share of hard currency income, which, as a consequence, is used for importing arms rather than food. However, with eight years of compulsory military service the 'military–economic complex' has at its disposal a considerable workforce of able-bodied young men and women. Soldiers not only fight, but are also used for public works and harvesting.[9]

To these 'secondary' economies of the peasants' markets and the military shall be added the so-called 'court' economy, which 'sustains Kim Jong Il and the core party members', perhaps comprising as much as 5% of the population. As Oh and Hassig put it: 'The secondary economies combined are probably larger than the primary economy.'[10]

Other external factors consisted of catastrophic harvest failures as a consequence of large-scale flooding, which were further aggravated by internal phenomena. The road to catastrophe had been opened up with ideologically justified blunders of the same magnitude as had led to the destruction of the Aral Sea. It is not possible to apply the maxim 'politics equals will-power' in contrast to science and well-tried experience. The geneticist Lysenko had emphasized the importance of environment rather than genes and claimed that acquired skills could be inherited, and was thus favoured by Stalin who wanted to hear that the socialist system could create a new sort of person. The application of these theories to the cultivation of crops inevitably resulted in costly bad investments and failures.

North Korea evidently had continued on this road in its attempts at increasing food production. The way that all accessible land was put into cultivation was clearly a result more of a crusading spirit than a policy based on scientific experimentation and consideration. In the prevalent intellectual climate, no critical or cautious expert would presumably have dared put forward objections and point out the necessity of basing policy upon previous experience and advancing a step at a time instead of betting everything on a single card. Devastation of forested land, inappropriate terracing and an unbalanced mix of crops, together with drought and flooding, led to the topsoil being washed away and depleted. The construction of dykes and the creation of polders led to further setbacks on account of using the wrong methods for desalination. It remains to be seen if the ecological consequences will be so serious that in the future it will not – even in good years – be possible to gather harvests as large as before the crisis years.

The energy shortage led to an intensification of a demanding programme to develop nuclear power. Previously, in 1965 the Soviet Union had delivered two small research reactors, and in 1977 North Korea had been induced to sign an agreement with the International Atomic Energy Agency (IAEA), which gave the agency the right to carry out inspections – evidently more in principle than in practice. In 1984, with the help of surveillance satellites, the USA established that North Korea had built a larger reactor. The USA and the Soviet Union managed to persuade Pyongyang in 1985 to sign the non-proliferation treaty (NPT) intended to prevent the spread of nuclear weapons.

Undoubtedly, North Korea intended not only to generate atomic energy but also to build up its own nuclear arsenal in order to maintain its military advantage when faced with the fact that it could not afford to replace its enormous stocks of – as illustrated by the Gulf War – outdated conventional weapons. Nevertheless, this meant that further resources, which could have served to alleviate the food supply crisis, were being added to the already burdensome costs of the military apparatus. The military side of the programme was more or less confirmed in 1989. But Pyongyang succeeded in preventing IAEA inspection up until 1992, when six inspections were allowed to take place before the North Koreans withdrew their cooperation.

The concern of the outside world over North Korea's programme for developing atomic weapons was skilfully utilized by Pyongyang to realize its old aim of entering into direct negotiations with the USA. These negotiations went on throughout the 1990s and are still going on in various forms. The description in Chapter 10 of the Swedish–North Korean negotiations during the smuggling crisis can only give a little taste of all the chopping and changing that has characterized these top-level political issues over many years, with postponements, breaks, notices of withdrawal, and an endless amount of manoeuvring.[11] Thanks to the contribution of former US President Carter, who paid a visit to Pyongyang and, not to be neglected, to an indefatigable patience on the part of the US side, the negotiations resulted – just after Kim's death in the summer of 1994 – in an 'Agreed Framework' which covered aid within the energy sector (light-water reactors and oil deliveries in exchange for North Korea undertaking to abandon its own nuclear programme), as well as food from the USA, Japan and South Korea. These three countries formed a consortium called KEDO (the Korean Peninsula Energy Development Organization) to carry out the programme. The light-water reactors are estimated as costing US$4.6 billion and will be brought into production in 2003 at the earliest; it is only by then that North Korea must have dismantled its own sites.

The long-winded negotiations seem to suggest that North Korea does not consider itself to be in a poor negotiating position, despite the food crisis, and nor has the country's obvious isolation brought about any insight as to the need to start to adjust to the outside world. The KEDO project was more or less immediately affected by delays. These were caused by arguments as to what had actually been agreed, by disagreement about North Korea's commitments vis-à-vis IAEA, but also by North Korea's continued provocations. The demilitarized zone was not respected as a consequence of the armistice agreement being seen as being a thing of the past, and North Korean troops started to make intrusions into the area. A number of clandestine submarine operations along the South Korean coast were also exposed. The USA expressed its suspicions that North Korea had started to build an underground reactor in secret. In connection with the fiftieth anniversary of the People's Republic in 1998, the North Koreans tested a missile, which flew across Japan, and this, coupled with the latent threat of atomic weapons manufacture, caused a great deal of ill-feeling among North Korea's neighbours, especially Japan, and lessened their readiness to supply aid. The North Korean side complained that the light-water reactor programme was not following the agreed timetable and that promised oil deliveries had been delayed.

North Korea's food crisis developed over a long time without any radical measures being taken to try to improve things. At the same time as the regime asked the UN for US$500 million in emergency aid, the incursions in the demilitarized zone were taking place, as well as the clandestine submarine operations and even extensive manoeuvring exercises in 1997. The regime has thus long since lost any sort of legitimacy in the outside world. After the catastrophic famine of recent years, it risks a legitimacy crisis with its own population. But the regime's dilemma is that it is not prepared to accept the necessary economic reforms, because these would be a threat to its very survival as a totalitarian system.[12] Although the country has become dependent on aid from the market economy world for its daily bread, there are few encouraging signs that the leadership would be prepared to reconsider its policy. The North Korean regime is evidently unprepared to change track even when it is fighting for survival. However, international emergency assistance given to alleviate the lot of the starving population has been administered by a number of foreign governments, which were also given the task of ensuring that the food reached the needy and was not channelled to the armed forces. This led to innumerable contacts between common North Koreans and foreigners on a scale hitherto unknown. It is difficult to estimate the importance of these contacts, but they have, without doubt, helped to open up the country for the first time in history.

Despite everything, reality is likely to force a review of the situation eventually. North Korea's main foreign policy objective has always been the withdrawal of the US troops from South Korea, as these are seen as an absolute obstacle to reunification on Pyongyang's terms, and the reason why North Korea established one of the largest standing armies in the world. But now the time had come for misgivings, and for Pyongyang the presence of US troops ironically seemed to have changed character, so that they were now seen as being a defence against possible military ambitions on the South Korean side.[13] This attitude could, however, be largely hidden behind the demand for continued bilateral relations with the USA. Nor should it be forgotten that China sees the US military presence as a welcome counterweight to increased Japanese influence in the region.

For South Korea the development must indeed have seemed rather a double-edged sword. On the one hand, reunification is a categorical imperative. On the other, a premature reunification under Seoul's leadership would lead to economic overexertion of incalculable dimensions and just as incalculable socio-political complications such as mass flight from starvation. The costs of reunification have been estimated at between US$130 billion and US$2 trillion, with a compromise estimate of US$1 trillion.[14] More concrete cooperation between North and South has gradually been entered into,[15] and South Korea has also managed to avoid a situation in which the reunification itself could, in the eyes of the North Koreans, be made into a sort of scapegoat for the calamity.[16] Within the framework of the KEDO project, South Korea has also been given the chance of direct contact with North Korea, which has not prevented Seoul from demonstrating some misgivings against Pyongyang being allowed to achieve its objective of establishing direct contacts with Washington.

Because of what seems to be a permanent food crisis in North Korea, the reunification problem now involves practical consequences on such a large scale that they cannot be solved at peninsular level but must be dealt with internationally. For the donor countries, including South Korea, it has become necessary to keep North Korea afloat not only for humanitarian reasons but also for political ones, because if there is one thing the donors can agree on it is to avoid the situation on the peninsula developing into a crisis or a war, into which they would risk being drawn. North Korea must, in some way, be saved from chaos and instead be made to reform its economy. The North must also be persuaded to refrain from its subversive activity against the South and, quite simply, behave like a nation among all the other nations in the world community. It is in the interests of the rest of the world to facilitate this process because each and every one who is treated as an outcast or outlaw – whether this affects an individual or a country – reacts by asserting themselves or, in the worst case, by causing problems.

From this point of view, the election in 1998 of Kim Dae Jung as president of South Korea was of paramount importance. He launched what has been called the 'Sunshine Policy' towards North Korea, containing three guiding principles:

1   No toleration of armed provocation of any kind (deterrence).
2   No unification by absorption (no German-style unification).
3   Active promotion of inter-Korean reconciliation and cooperation, starting first with those areas of mutual interest on which both parties can most readily agree (functionalism).[17]

Without any doubt this policy has infused new life into the petrified Korean question. It has led to events of great symbolic value, such as the first summit meeting between Korea's two heads of state in June 2000 and the visit of US Secretary of State Madeleine Albright to Pyongyang in October of the same year. In a way these events can be compared to fireworks – the dark night is taken over by an impressive spectacle that draws everybody's attention but when it is over the night is as dark as usual. This is reflected in the newspapers, which present large headlines but remarkably thin reports. Nevertheless, these events are indispensable as signals for public opinion at home and abroad to look to the future with increased hope and to open the gates for a number of meetings at lower levels – but they can easily be misused to draw attention to one's own goodwill and the other party's perfidy. Kim Dae Jung consequently chose a risky policy and must be prepared to meet internal opposition and condescending accusations of being politically naive and adventurous, all the more so as he exposed himself and his country to an adversary well known for oversimplified self-righteousness. And during the first two years of Kim Dae Jung's presidency the North subjected him to a number of menacing challenges as well as simultaneous positive and negative signals – the decision-making process in Pyongyang still defies analysis.

South Korea promoted increased trade with the North, especially through investments in subcontracting for work and labour. A company in the South started a large tourist project in the famous Diamond ('Kumgang') mountains north of the demarcation line. Emergency assistance increased and reunion trips for divided families were organized – but overwhelmingly in one direction only. The investments have been a success as far as increased trade is concerned, but no investment is said ever to have yielded any profit, the reason being North Korean charges on tourist licences and workers' wages, thus eliminating the relative advantage of lower labour costs. Furthermore, local conditions are still characterized by erratic circumstances, making it, for instance, allegedly cheaper to transport goods from Seoul to Hamburg than to Nampo, the port town of Pyongyang. Many of these conditions plainly reflect North Korean greed and ineptitude in grasping economic calculations, but some, no doubt, indicate another mentality; the South is, for humanitarian reasons, prepared to pay for split-family meetings, but for the North each case appears to be a political question with a price tag.

143

During the period, contacts between the parties increased considerably such that four-party talks, involving the two Koreas, China and the USA, took place twice, in 1998 and 1999. Pyongyang also succeeded in establishing official relations with a number of hitherto reluctant countries, not least in Western Europe.

While the North broadened its cooperation with the South, it simultaneously continued its well-known strategies of confrontation. The nuclear negotiations went round, if not in circles, at least in spirals. The USA asked to inspect a nuclear site and after traditional bargaining was admitted at the price of a substantial amount of food aid. North Korea fired a new missile in August 1998 and, after further negotiations, abstained from firing another one. In return, Washington lifted some sanctions, mainly regarding trade and finance. The missile programme was seen as a part of the armament industry, which is controlled by the military and provides the armed forces with a considerable income from sales of weapons to Asian and African countries. Incursions of North Korean submarines or other spy-boats, incidents which in the past would have caused at least a temporary interruption of all contacts, now seemed to be grudgingly tolerated as part of the rules of the game. In June 1999, allegedly the most serious naval clash since 1953 took place on the west coast – while simultaneously on the east coast South Korean tourists were being ferried to the Diamond mountains. South Korean naval forces regularly drove intruders from the North back across the 'Northern Limit Line', but this time North Korean fishing and patrol boats stood their ground, which led to a minor naval battle. While the South suffered only a handful of minor casualties, the North lost one ship, several others were badly damaged and a few dozen seamen lost their lives. Both sides reacted with strong oral statements but the incident 'had no discernible impact on ... inter-Korean economic exchanges of all kinds.'[18]

Without any doubt, the 'Sunshine Policy' has brought about a decisive improvement in inter-Korean relations, and for this President Kim Dae Jung received the Nobel Peace Price. But the condition has been, and will continue to be, South Korean willingness not to let any North Korean provocations undermine its determination to pursue this policy. According to one observer: 'The military defeat suffered by North Korea in the West Sea, in June 1999, was ... the decisive turning point, because there has, generally speaking, been no repetition, since then, of the former, long-established, pattern of steps forward, followed by steps backwards, in North–South relations.'[19] Pyongyang has, quite simply, nothing to gain but very much to lose by returning to a policy of confrontation. This is the view held by most outsiders, but it must not be interpreted to mean that developments on the Korean peninsula are in any way predictable. The politics of North Korea have been formed by its unparalleled isolation and its lack of experience of international relations. Given time, the 'Sunshine Policy' will contribute to improve this state of affairs. It will then be necessary to be consistent and regard all North Korean contacts with the outside world as important and favourable, even if, in the short run, they merely serve Kim Jong Il's aspirations for international recognition. However, internal criticism of the 'Sunshine Policy' has apparently led President Kim Dae Jung to impose pressure on the media not to publish too many negative comments on northern politics and conditions? It might be a delicate venture to introduce compromise politics on the peninsula, but on the other hand a discriminating use of censorship would amount to a betrayal of the principles that the 'Sunshine Policy' aims at realizing.

It must also be recognized that North Korea is fighting for its survival, which gives the military great political influence; they might be prepared to fight for the preservation of the status qua. However, the world at large is not interested in contributing to the conservation of the totalitarian regime but is certainly willing to pay a price for peace and for emergency assistance in fighting famine and disease. Nor is any state prepared to take upon itself the costs and burden of administering the North Korean territory in the event of the collapse of the tpresent administration. But this administration is at present not capable of performing its duties - the people cannot survive without outside support, in concrete terms, mainly from South Korea, USA, Japan and the UN system. This means that the world at large has to share the responsibility for keeping the present administration functioning, and this task will rest mainly with the states mentioned. The obvious goal is to preserve peace in the peninsula - the responsibility of China and the USA- and to re-establish the ability of the northern part to feed its population. At present, there seems to be no solution other than to continue the trodden path of emergency assistance combined with efforts to modernize the economy and render it more effective, with all that this implies, not least in continuing endless and tiresome negotiations with the reluctant, and sometimes outright hostile, beneficiary, which cannot be allowed to sustain an administration that denies its subjects the rule of law, democracy and human rights. An experienced observer of Korean affairs during the last half-century has, in the case of a military putsch in South Korea, commented that: 'American officials had learned in previous crises [that] their power to affect Korean politics was limited when the stakes were high for the domestic actors involved? If the stakes were high for the South Korean actors when dealing with allies, they must be more than sky-high for the North Korean leaders in their present predicament. The task of dealing with them is both thankless and exasperating - but are there any options? The repetitive six power talks that have been introduced and are going on intermittently during the last years only serve to illustrate the obvious lack of alternative.

For most countries, the natural solution is probably seen as being market economy reforms ending in reunification under Seaul's leadership. But it is going to be extremely important to act in complete harmony with China because, as I have already pointed out a couple of times, Beijing has tolerated the status of, for example, Taiwan and Hang Kang, but in both 1895 and 1950 went to war against foreign invaders in northern Korea.

And then again, it is surely only reasonable to try to ascertain what North Korean subjects themselves want. What is actually known about any tacit opposition, composed of 'class enemies' and their descendants, for example, and of labour-camp prisoners? How many are they and to what extent can they assert their human rights under changing circumstances or in a disintegrating society? There are reports that during the establishment of the People's Republic an official but secret distribution was made of all subjects into forty-seven classes according to political reliability. The politically privileged class is said to constitute some 25–30% of the population, the lukewarm or unreliable middle class 40%, and the hostile sediment 30%. The last group is considered to be the victim of such discrimination that it constitutes a latent threat to the regime[22] – as is well known, the proletariat has nothing to lose but its shackles. Such a classification might have seemed logical if drawn up in the late 1940s. But its continued application after half a century in power and with all the bragging of the society's monolithic and monochromatic character in mind would imply a confession of such a monumental failure in having rallied round the Great Leader and his *Juche* that it is hard to believe – even when considering the stubborn habits of sticking to old decisions and disinclination to change direction. Nevertheless, it is most likely to reflect actual circumstances. It seems hardly likely, though, that the catastrophic famine will lead to insurrection, because historical experience tells us that famine leads to apathy rather than revolt. The famine in the Soviet Union, caused by Stalin's policies, did not lead to insurrection at the time. However, the famine and the isolation and the imminent threat of economic collapse in North Korea may perhaps result in some sort of settlement – with or without violence – within the ruling elite, which hopefully might venture upon a change of course, possibly ideologically camouflaged, for example by looking for inspiration from the NEP, Lenin's new economic policy.[23]

The power of the Confucian traditions over people's minds has previously been emphasized, and it has been noted that this does not only characterize the broad mass of people, but seems to still apply to leading circles, whose ideology is distinguished more by *Juche* than by communism. The question, then, is to what extent this also includes the unreflecting respect for the will of heaven. Again, people do not always practise what they preach, particularly when it comes to defending power and riches, and consequently the Confucian world is plagued by fractional battles and revolutions to the same extent as the rest of the world. It seems, however, incontrovertible that Confucian societies have shown a particular degree of social discipline and loyalty towards the people in power, towards the will of heaven. North Koreans ought, by now, to have learned from very costly experience that the regime in Pyongyang, including its 'President for Eternity', has evidently lost its heavenly mandate – and that to rise up against the Will of Heaven is pointless. Thus, it cannot be ruled out that the fate of the regime is regarded as already sealed, not only by the common people but also within leading circles. Many *Juche* disciples will certainly still retain a firm conviction, or at least a hope, that the mandate is not completely lost but can be regained, and they will be prepared to struggle for their cause. But if Confucian tradition is sufficiently anchored in the national soul, there is reason to assume that the opposition to a change of regime has lost its momentum. This does not necessarily mean, of course, that a change of regime would take place without violence or bloodshed. However, if a change of power could actually be carried through, then it would be accepted as a sign that the old regime had lost the mandate from heaven and that the victor had, by his very victory, proved that he had been granted that mandate.

Regardless of whether the old regime survives, or a new one succeeds in winning the heavenly mandate, it would have to be supported by foreign aid in order to combat starvation and avoid the entire society dissolving into anarchy. This will be particularly important if a new regime takes over, because it will then be a matter of preventing it from just being a link in a chain of lost heavenly mandates. But would it not then be the case that at the same time many other changes have to come about, for example the hermetically sealed border cutting right across the peninsula being replaced by a continuously enlarged form of peaceful coexistence? Even such reflections imply gazing into a crystal ball. Those who have lived in North Korea have learned never to take anything for granted because anything could happen at any time.[24] And perhaps something will have happened before this text is published. It does, however, seem fairly safe to claim that the Korean question will probably be with us for many years yet and demand from world society a great deal of aid, patience and willingness to cooperate with a disoriented, but stubborn and not particularly cooperative, opponent. Taking into account the scale of the problems of famine and adjustment, it is hard to believe that a Korea conference can be avoided in the long term. Regardless of whether such a conference is actually held, everyone should be open to the likelihood of the Korean conflict being solved according to principles other than clear-cut, Western agreements. For Westerners, light and darkness are in opposition. In the East, Yin and Yang are seen as complementary.

147

PART II
MARXISM–LENINISM RELEVANT
TO NORTH KOREA

22

A SUMMARY OF THE DOCTRINES OF MARX AND ENGELS

As a thinker and the creator of a philosophical system, Marx can be regarded as a product of English economics, French Enlightenment philosophy and German nineteenth-century thinking. His concept of history is based upon Hegel's version of the dialectic with its thesis, antithesis and synthesis as the formula with which one should be able to understand human and social development. But, unlike his ideological master, Marx was a materialistic determinist. While, for Hegel, world history was 'that gigantic drama, in which the spirit of the world – by way of the struggle of dialectic antagonisms – develops into an ever greater awareness and freedom',[1] Marx saw the explanation of historic events and political division as lying in the economic organization of society, in the conditions of ownership rights and production, while the role of the individual was restricted to being the result of these.

With examples taken from the basic sources, an attempt shall be made here to show how Marx and Engels applied their theory to historical events and how they considered that the laws that they had discovered pertaining to society gave them the possibility of sketching future development on a scientific basis. The starting point is an economic-deterministic variety of the dialectic process, according to which the history of mankind can be seen as follows:

1 Thesis – the original state of nature, before man formed proper societies.
2 Antithesis – the formation of societies characterized by state power and antagonisms between groups in society (classes).
3 Synthesis – the future stateless and classless society.

The social institutions are seen as being determined by the stage of development of, on the one hand, work, and, on the other, the family. In the period of the 'original condition', when work was organized to only a slight extent, social order was characterized by the extended family. But society developed, and with the arrival of private property and differences in wealth came 'the possibility of using outside labour power and thus the foundations for class antagonism'. Gradually, the old society was broken up 'in the clash between the newly developed social classes' and in its place came 'a new society, summed up in the state, the subservient parts of which are no longer family groupings, a society where the place of the family is entirely dependent upon property and where now those class antagonisms and class struggles develop freely that make up the content of all hitherto written history'.[2]

The doctrine of the class struggle, and the fact that the reasons for it are to be found in the economic organization of society, is a cornerstone in Marxist thinking. 'The history of existing society,' wrote Marx in *The Communist Manifesto*, 'has always been one of class antagonism, which has taken different forms in different periods. But whatever the form adopted, one factor has always been the same during past centuries, namely that one part of society has plundered another.'[3] And of the causes of class differences, Engels writes, 'that these social classes that struggle against each other have always been the creation of the conditions of production and exchange, or, simply expressed, of the economic conditions of their epoch'.[4] Antiquity was characterized by slavery, and this was replaced by feudalism, which was followed by capitalism, created by the expansion of the bourgeoisie, with the French Revolution of 1789 marking the definitive breakthrough of that class. The society of capitalism was, in its turn, going to disintegrate on account of the working class. These changes depended upon shifts in economic conditions:

> At a certain stage of their development, the material productive forces in society find themselves in antagonism to the existing production conditions, or, in what is just a legal expression for this, with the ownership conditions within which these productive forces have until then found themselves. From having been forms of development for the productive forces, these conditions are now transformed to chains for those same forces. A period of social revolution then begins.[5]

The real object of Marx's interest was the last of these revolutions, namely that which, in his opinion, decided his own contemporary times. Starting from the conditions sketched out above, he analysed contemporary capitalist society and the reasons why it must be replaced by socialist society. The character of property ownership was reflected in the formation of classes. According to the young Marx, they could, in practice, be reduced to two, bourgeois and proletarian,[6] but later he distinguished three, the last two, which he called the owners of capital and labour respectively, and, in addition, landowners.[7] The distinction is important, because when Lenin applied the theory to Russia he utilized the two-class theory and divided the peasants into a rural bourgeoisie and a rural proletariat, and in so doing disregarded the fact that the division into three made by an older Marx was probably associated with the way he, over time, distanced himself from his earlier revolutionary ideas. As shall be shown below, Kim Il Sung followed Lenin's two-class theory.

In order for a class to be counted as such, Marx demanded class awareness:

Provided that millions of families live under economic conditions which separate their way of living, their interests and their education from the other classes, and place them in an antagonistic relationship to those other classes, then they form a class of their own. Provided that there is only a local connection between the small-scale peasants, provided that the conformity of their interests does not create any sense of unity, any national connection and any political organization among them, they do not form a class.[8]

The necessary economic circumstances that mark the two main classes under capitalism are thus that one consists of owners of capital, and the other of owners of labour – in other words, on the one hand the owners of the means of production, and on the other, wage-earners, or the proletariat. The conditions for production which mark capitalist society most are the existence of means of production as private property. This, Marx taught, 'has, as a precondition, its opposite form which is the lack of property',[9] and the division into classes is thus clear. In order to abolish classes, the proletariat must therefore abolish private property: 'The proletariat ... is forced to abolish itself and its constituent opposite which makes it the proletariat, namely private property.'[10] By 'private property', Marx meant private ownership of the means of production, not all forms of ownership. So, in *The Communist Manifesto* one can read that: 'The proletariat shall use its political power to eventually take away all capital from the bourgeoisie, centralize all means of production in the hands of the state, i.e. in the hands of the proletariat which is now the ruling class'[11] and what is more, that 'communism does not take the power to acquire social products away from anybody, it only takes away the power to plunder the labour of others by virtue of this acquisition.'[12] And in his description of the Paris Commune, Marx wrote of the intentions of the communards:

> The commune wished to abolish that class ownership which transforms the labour of the many into the riches of the few. It intended to expropriate the expropriators. It wanted to make individual property a reality by transforming the means of production, land and capital, which at present are, above all, means of enslavement and exploiting labour, into being purely tools for free and associated labour.[13]

Under the capitalist system, the proletariat is reduced to poverty by unemployment and starvation. In order to survive, it must therefore break up the prevailing economic system and it is going to do so, because (expressed in Marxist terms) the existing forces of production will rise up against the existing conditions of production. That this increasing poverty for the large masses is the tendency of the development of capitalist society is proven by virtue of the theories of:

1   Centralization or concentration: companies become larger and fewer, and capital is accumulated in a few hands.[14] The development will go in favour of

the proletariat, which will come to make up the vast majority.

2   Impoverishment: the 'capitalist' utilization of machinery leads to a superfluous population of workers.[15] These impoverished people will become more and more numerous, because the middle class will sink down into the proletariat.[16]

3   Crises: through unplanned production and the increasingly obvious misorganization of the economic system, crises will arise, and these will become all the more severe and common.[17]

4   Catastrophe: workers rise up against society and join together; finally the great majority, consisting of the proletariat and groups allied to this, will overthrow the bourgeoisie in an open revolution and capture the forces of production of society by 'abolishing its own existing methods of acquisition and thereby the entire existing system of acquisition'.[18]

The impoverishment theory is worth looking at more closely, because it explains how the conditions of production of the capitalist system have become an obstacle for development and thus come to require that the whole system be broken up. The root cause of all evil is to be found in the distribution of the rights of ownership of the means of production. This results in exploitation, which through certain laws drives the capitalist system towards dissolution. This understanding is based on the labour theory of value with the law of the falling tendency of the rate of profit. The theory can be summarized as follows:

•   The value of a product is determined by the hours of work a worker has spent producing it.[19]

•   The employer's surplus, his profit, thus consists of the extortion of unpaid work from the workers, namely that part of the working day they are not reproducing the 'day-value' of their labour power,[20] or, simply expressed, in practice, that part of the price of a product that exceeds the wages of the workers (by which is really meant the cost of the survival of the workers' families).

•   As all profit has its basis in the extortion of unpaid labour from workers, the introduction of machinery with its concomitant savings in labour costs – 'the capitalist use of machinery' – means that the capitalist removes the source of his profit, because the means of production consist of work that has already been paid for and which thereby ceases to be a productive power that generates profit. This law of the falling rate of profit means that the profit can only be saved through the intensification or extension of working hours.[21]

Using the labour theory of value as a base, Marx explained why capitalist business pulsates in trade cycles. When the demand for workers increases, wages tend to go up, which leads to the capitalist trying to shift his investments to favour work-saving machines. But then the law of the falling profit rate comes into action and the capitalist, disappointed by profit not being forthcoming, limits his investments and cuts down on production. Already the work-saving innovations have led to workers being laid off and the decrease in production sends even more workers to the 'industrial army reserve'. A crisis is close, but it carries within it the seeds of its own solution. The increased unemployment has pushed the wage level down, which means both that less mechanized production methods are again profitable and that, in particular, it makes it possible to re-employ workers under conditions that are favourable to the capitalist. Production is thereby started up again and the process is repeated. Marx estimated the length of a trade cycle to be approximately ten years.[22]

As can be seen, these theories can only be applied to industrialized societies, and it is only in such societies that the revolution was expected to take place.

The result of the revolution is that the proletariat seizes political power, but its objectives are the economic remoulding of society and the abolition of classes and the state. This remoulding cannot take place immediately but only after a transitionary period, called the dictatorship of the proletariat. In his book about the Paris commune, Marx described this as a fully fledged example of the dictatorship of the proletariat, and of how the old society broke up: 'The commune should not be a parliamentary but rather a working corporation, executive and legislative at the same time.' Its 'first decree was about abolishing the standing army and replacing it with the common people who were to be armed', the police lost all their political functions and they could, as could all the officials of the various departments of the administration, be removed from their posts at any time. No official appointment entitled its holder to a higher income than a worker. The churches were dissolved and their property expropriated, while the priests were obliged to seek their keep from the believers. All educational establishments were made freely available to the people, without the interference of the state and church. The classes were to be abolished by 'the expropriators being expropriated' and, as steps on the way, night work in bakeries was abolished, employers were forbidden to levy fines on their workers and workshops and factories that were closed were handed over to cooperative associations of workers. The commune had no need of secrecy; instead, all speeches and documents were published.[23]

An important question is whether the revolution should be led by a discerning minority or carried along by the entire proletariat. Marx's opinion would have been decided by his understanding that the downfall of capitalism, through the revolution of the proletariat, was not a programme of action for the working class but an unavoidable event following the law of historical development. In *The Communist Manifesto* he wrote that 'the communists are, on the one hand, in practice the most advanced and determined section of all countries' working class parties. In terms of theory, they have come to a clear understanding, before the rest of the masses, of the conditions for, the course of, and the general results of the proletarian movement.' However, a couple of pages earlier, one can read that 'all earlier historical movements have been the movements of minorities or in the interests of minorities. The proletarian movement is an independent movement of the great majority, in the interests of the great majority.'[24]

These two statements do not necessarily contradict each other, but there is opportunity for different interpretations, and Lenin adopted, in practice, the standpoint of the discerning minority, which was to pull the masses along with it. This, however, is in contradiction to Marx and Engels' statements from the 1870s and 1890s. In an article from 1874, dealing with the disintegrating influence of the communards in exile, Marx pointed out that a revolution must be the work of the whole of the revolutionary class, and not a *coup d'état* staged by a minority.[25] Engels' opinion in 1895 is even more modified: 'The time has passed for revolutions that are carried out by small, knowledgeable minorities, leading unknowledgeable masses, the masses must understand what they want and why.' Instead of the obsolete revolutions with street battles, the proletariat had acquired a new weapon, universal suffrage, which gave them the possibility of legally gaining all important appointments, and the German Social Democratic Party was praised for the manner in which it had used this weapon.[26]

Allowing for the fact that the view of the elderly Engels has been regarded as being decidedly watered down, the preface to the 1872 edition of *The Communist Manifesto* shows that Marx and Engels already then were agreed on a revised opinion. They wrote that the conditions had greatly changed, and that:

> As a consequence there is no particular stress at all upon the … nearest revolutionary measures proposed; this manifesto, had it been written today, would in many respects have another form. The colossal development of modern industry during the last 25 years, the parallel and continuing organization of the working class into a party, and in addition the practical experiences that, first, the February revolution and even more the Paris Commune have given us – when the proletariat for the first time for two whole months was in possession of political power – all this means that the programme is now partly obsolete. In particular, the history of the Commune has shown that the working class can not simply take over the existing state machinery and put it into effect for its own purposes.

The reluctance of Marx and Engels to seek to hasten the revolution with the help of a putsch, would seem to be intimately related to their deterministic concept of history. According to this, a revolution cannot take place in a country before the economic conditions are ripe, after which it will take place. If a revolution does not take place, or fails, it must be because the society in question was not ready, and, to want to see a revolution take place, despite this, would be to frustrate those claims to scientific dignity that they considered the materialistic concept of history and scientific socialism entitled them to make, and instead reduce them to becoming simple prophets for a political programme.

The point of Marx's labour theory of value was, of course, to explain why owners of the means of production, i.e. capitalists, are not entitled to any share of the products that the workers produce with these means of production. This share can take a cooperative form, which does not give rise to ideological misgivings. It can also be expressed as a requirement for yield, i.e. interest on the cost of acquiring the means of production/machinery – but the whole of Marxist ideology is based upon the tenet that only work creates value and that machinery consists of a labour cost that has already been paid and that lacks the ability to create new value. If one peels away the ideological rhetoric, this means that the investment costs do not affect the value of a product. And, according to Marxist ideology, the consequence of demanding an interest yield in the production process, i.e. 'in the capitalist use of machinery', is the exploitation that with historic necessity leads to the socialist revolution.

From this point of view, we recognize the problem from religious preaching. On account of the Commandments laid down in the Old Testament,[27] the receipt of interest payments was long forbidden in Christianity, and still is by Islam, which does, however, accept the idea of a share. The Marxist theory of value is thus based not on any economic law, but instead on a morally motivated article of faith, namely that interest is the same as exploitation. This article of faith is intertwined in the materialistic concept of history as one of the laws for the progression of the capitalist society towards its fall. It was described above in connection with the impoverishment theory as 'the capitalist use of machinery' and formed the kernel of the capitalist system's intrinsic antagonism between labour and capital. This antagonism should, after the revolution of the working class, be solved by adopting a socialist method of production, in which exploitation was (by definition) abolished by virtue of the surplus value no longer ending up in the hands of individuals but going to society.

The final judgement was passed upon Marxism's economic theory by the collapse of communism. The greatness and strength of Marx lay on another level, namely as a sociologist and critic of society. His descriptions in *Capital* of the inhuman working conditions of industrial workers and, above all, of child workers amounted to a fiery and just accusation against early industrial society. But this did not lead him to become a social reformer; instead, he proposed an economic-materialistic concept of history in order to prove that the existing order was historically doomed to be cast into a violent revolution. With examples taken from the natural sciences, and especially from Darwin's theory of evolution, it was for this purpose that he determined the economic laws that governed social development.

But this 'scientific socialism' was based upon unreasonable conditions. The foundation-stone for the well-known theses about the class struggle – exploitation, mass production, the fall of capitalism and the dictatorship of the proletariat – is the labour theory of value. As shown above, this theory leads to the conclusion that only work creates value, while labour-saving machinery cannot generate profit – a conclusion that is obviously divorced from reality, and that is not applied to its logical conclusions either. This claimed state of opposition between what is termed 'constant' and 'variable' capital, between machinery and labour, embodies the self-contradiction of capitalism, which leads to it (as an absolute natural necessity) being replaced by 'free and associated labour'. By virtue of transferring the means of production to public ownership, the mass-production introduced under capitalism can come to benefit everyone in a classless society. State power will then no longer be necessary, and the state will accordingly wither away. In such a society, it would thus seem that capital goods generate surplus value – and the consequence of this can only be that the labour theory of value is not generally applicable.

An attempt to see the application of the ideology in practice as a system in which the state took the surplus value for the supposed benefit of its citizens would mean that capitalism survived as a system and is thus not in accordance with Marx's basic tenets. But this, in practice, was shown to be the unavoidable consequence of the theory, and it was realized during the Stalin epoch. These aspects are examined further in Chapter 25 on the ideology of the Soviet Union. The fundamental problem with the application of the value theory is that it is impossible to calculate profitability and thus impossible to optimize use of available resources.

According to Marx, the reason for the rise of class societies was that a minority in a society exploited the majority. This minority could thereby arrogate to itself the political – and its associated legislative – power. But the French anthropologist Pierre Clastres has shown that it is very likely that the opposite is true. According to Clastres, members of several primitive societies characterized by equality were fully aware that power is based on violence and therefore – in the final instance with violence – prevented someone from acquiring power. Chiefs could be given temporary power in war situations, but under normal circumstances their purpose was purely ceremonial or to mediate in conflicts between villagers. However, chiefs and medicine men could, by invoking contacts with higher powers and by controlling the demons of these higher powers (in practice, obedient villagers disguised in frightening masks and therefore unrecognizable) scare the majority into submission. Political power having been won in that way, it could then be used to exercise economic power. In this manner, the foundations were laid for transforming society into a state, and Clastres' conclusion is that 'the rise of the state determines the growth of the classes'.[28]

To this one can add another observation, namely that in some societies at a primitive economic level, for example among the nomads in the Sahara, there are obvious social differences between household slaves and their masters. However, the poor material conditions force a low and relatively equal standard of living upon all. This too, points towards political power's right of primogeniture.

One can object that the way classes arise no longer makes any difference, but that it is now a question of finding political solutions to actual problems. This is incontrovertible, and the argument has been put forward only to illustrate further how the Marxist intellectual construction is based upon inadequate analyses. Marx could, as stated earlier, inspire as a sociologist and a critic of society, but his economic theories can only be invoked selectively and after a conscientious examination. Above all, it is important to stress the difference between a market economy and the Marxist–Leninist system, which is sometimes called state capitalism. The market economy presupposes, and is based upon, mass-consumption, and it will enter a crisis if the buying power of the majority of the population weakens. It can only prosper in a situation of general well-being. This, in turn, is best attained by virtue of the people having the power to influence things. But democracy will have difficulties prospering in a society in which each and every one is dependent on a single employer, even if this were called 'public ownership'. Consequently, it is only in market economies that democratic welfare states have grown up. A good example of this is shown by the development of the two states on the Korean peninsula.

23

THE LENIN EPOCH

THE THEORIES ARE CONFRONTED
WITH THE PRACTICE

The theories of Marx exerted a great influence, particularly on the development of German socialism. At the end of the nineteenth century there was a break between the two tendencies within the German Social Democratic Party, one being more orthodox and the other revisionist. The latter saw itself as simply weeding out some clear excesses in Marx's teachings, such as the theories of surplus value, impoverishment, concentration and catastrophe, and it also wanted the Social Democrats to take part in parliamentary work in cooperation with other parties and carry out reforms within the framework of the existing society. As time went by, more and more of the disagreements between the two groupings disappeared, particularly after the Russian Revolution, when even the orthodox group clearly distanced itself from Lenin and his minority interpretation of the dictatorship of the proletariat.

In Russia, the revolutionary tradition was quite unlike that in Western Europe. It was maintained by the intelligentsia, and, with no industrial proletariat to count on, many intellectuals considered that the role of the workers would instead by played by the peasants. During the 1880s, the Social Democratic Party came into being, and at its congress in 1903, Lenin proposed a programme that involved extreme centralization and strict party discipline with unconditional submission to the central committee. The proposal split the congress into Bolsheviks (i.e. the majority) and Mensheviks (i.e. the minority). Before long, the latter group again, in fact, became the actual majority in the Party. They repudiated violent methods and, from the start, took part in the work of the Duma, in contrast to Lenin and the Bolsheviks, who in 1912 broke away and formed their own party.

Marx and Engels had devoted themselves to studying the conditions for when and where the revolution would occur but had never taken part in one. Lenin, however, was above all a practical revolutionary with a clear end in sight, and he let the end dictate the means. The way the theories were adapted, often with sophistry and decidedly Jesuitical arguments, is therefore best understood if one follows the course of his political actions as the development of Russia progressed. A good example of how Lenin differed from Marx and Engels in his approach to problems is his view on the peasant question. From a proletarian–revolutionary point of view, the position of the peasantry was of secondary interest, but as owners of the 'means of production' (land) they become enemies of the proletariat. Marx and Engels had also pointed out their reactionary influence, for example when Napoleon III took over power.[1] Lenin adapted his theories to Russian conditions, and demanded that allowances be made for the backwardness of Russia.

In the late nineteenth century, Lenin wrote in 1899, following the 1861 emancipation of the serfs, Russian agriculture had acquired a capitalist character with 'a rural bourgeoisie, little in number but with a powerful economic position, and a rural proletariat'.[2] The salvation of the rural proletariat lay, according to Lenin, in joining the workers in order to turn the land into the property of society. The task of the Social Democrats was thus to take the class struggle out into the countryside.[3] The fears that this would split their forces led Lenin to claim that they had to 'call upon the best part of the peasants if not to independent political struggle then at least to consciously supporting the liberation struggle of the working class'. The Party should not neglect the peasants for another important reason, i.e. it wished to stand out as being the leading force in the struggle against autocracy. But this should not be allowed to mean that it 'artificially protected the peasants from the growth of capitalism and the development of mass production' or took 'active revolutionary forces from the towns to the countryside'.[4] Nor should this imply any contradiction if the Party were to abolish its support in a later period of history, after the peasants had been satisfied through concessions from the landowners, because small farms increased productivity in the feudal day-work system but restricted it in the capitalist system, which strives for large-scale production and economies of scale.

The revolution of 1905 had a purely bourgeois character, wrote Lenin that same year, and the imminent development of capitalism lay in the interests of the proletariat and should thus be supported. But, for the bourgeoisie, it was advantageous if the changes took place slowly, more through reform than revolution, whereas for the proletariat it was the revolutionary path that was the quickest and the least painful. The task of the working class in the revolution was thus to 'extend its limits' by taking command and steering it past the aims of the bourgeoisie to serve its own interests.[5]

In works published in connection with the revolution of 1905, Lenin distinguished between 'the revolutionary democratic dictatorship of the proletariat and the peasantry' and 'socialist dictatorship of the proletariat'.[6] The difference was that the former aspired to the 'democratic revolution', namely the abolition of the autocracy and the introduction of a free political life because, as he pointed out, 'we must not forget, that there at present is not – and cannot be – any other means of coming closer to socialism than complete political freedom, the democratic republic and the revolutionary democratic dictatorship of the proletariat and the peasantry.'[7] He continued:

> This can only be a dictatorship, because the realization of the changes which are immediately and unconditionally necessary for the proletariat

and the peasantry will come to call forth desperate resistance from both estate-owners, the well-to-do bourgeoisie and Czarism. Without dictatorship, it will be impossible to crush this opposition and repel the counter revolutionary machinations. But it will naturally not be a socialist but a democratic dictatorship. It will not be able to shake the foundations of capitalism.[8]

Furthermore, he believed that the democratic revolution would be the end of the union 'between the wills of the proletariat and the peasant bourgeoisie';[9] the struggle for socialism would begin and thus the former allies would be abandoned.

Lenin's adamantly purposeful method was, thus, in 1905, already fully apparent. It was always a case of encouraging those forces that would lead to proletarian revolution under the leadership of the Bolsheviks – even if this meant that they must work towards shortening the capitalist epoch by 'extending' the bourgeois revolution to a socialist one. This declaration has many similarities with North Korean politics. When it was a case of simply skipping the capitalist epoch and directly introducing socialism, Kim Il Sung was inspired by Lenin. But even the tactics in the reunification question have distinct traces of a Leninist heritage – in brief, to realize 'democratic dictatorship' (i.e. wide-ranging cooperation between the North and South but with the South Korean regime eliminated) in order to bring about reunification under socialist control.

At the outbreak of war in 1914, to Lenin's great bitterness the socialist parties in all countries betrayed the cause of the proletariat, the task of which was, of course, 'to defend its class unity, its internationalism and its socialist conviction', and instead lent their support to their warmongering governments. The task of social democrats – by whom Lenin meant those who shared his opinion – must then be to oppose nationalism, each in his own country, and for the Russians 'there can be no doubt but that a defeat for Czarist monarchy ... would be the least evil for the working class and the workers among all the peoples of Russia.'[10]

When the Czar in February (March, in the new-style calendar) of 1917 dissolved the Duma, he removed the last barrier to revolution. The garrison of the capital became revolutionary, and, as in 1905, a soviet was convened that soon became a numerically strong congregation of workers' and soldiers' deputies from all the left parties with the Bolsheviks in the minority. In Petrograd, Lenin became quite isolated on account of his anti-government and extreme sentiments, which he published in the form of a number of theses. His programme had the following content:

1 end the war;
2 push the revolution forward from the first to the second stage, 'which must come to place power in the hands of the proletariat and the poorest peasants';
3 no support for the provisional government;
4 'explain to the masses that the soviets of workers' deputies are the only possible

form for revolutionary government' and propagate for an anti-bourgeois policy and win a majority in the soviets;

5 as the soviets had already been created, it would be a step backwards to retain the parliamentary republic, rather, it was now a question of 'a republic of soviets of workers' and peasants' deputies in the entire country, from the bottom and upwards';

6 nationalization of all land, which was to be placed at the disposal of local farm workers' and peasants' soviets;

7 nationalization of all banks;

8 'as our immediate task we do not have the 'implementation' of socialism, but only to immediately take over control of social production and the distribution of produce on the part of the soviets of workers' deputies';

9 tasks for the Party include changing the name to the Communist Party because the Social Democrats have betrayed socialism;

10 renewal of the International.[a,11]

Because of their involvement in the crushing of General Kornilov's revolt against the Kerensky government, the Bolsheviks became more popular. Most workers and soldiers supported them, which meant that both the Petrograd and the Moscow soviets acquired a Bolshevik majority. When the government realized that power was slipping out of its hands, it decided on 24 October (6 November) to take counter-measures. The premises of the Bolshevik newspaper *Pravda* were occupied, but were soon liberated by troops loyal to the Bolsheviks, who then occupied telegraph and railway stations, post offices and government buildings, and stormed the Winter Palace, the seat of the provisional government. Some days later, similar events took place in Moscow. Power was now in the hands of the Bolsheviks. The Great Socialist October Revolution was thus not a revolution at all but a *coup d'état*.

A month or so before the revolution, Lenin had written *State and Revolution*, in which he put forward the proletarian tactics in the battle against all opportunists, revisionists and anarchists. It was particularly with regard to the structure of the transitional period, of the dictatorship of the proletariat, that the diverging opinions became evident. Lenin claimed, with reference to *The Communist Manifesto*, that the socialist revolution would not mean the abolition of the state, but that the proletariat would win state power, and these two concepts became identical as 'the state, i.e. the (organized) proletariat that had become the ruling class'.[12] As a state is defined as an outer covering, for a class organization the transitional period must necessarily be a state, being characterized 'by exceedingly bitter class struggle, by exceedingly intensified forms of struggle', so that the state during this period must 'be in a new manner democratic (for the proletarians and the

---

a The Communist International, a Moscow directed organization for the coordination of the political activities of communist parties throughout the world.

poor in general) and in a new manner dictatorial (against the bourgeoisie)'. Even if the transitionary period could take a variety of forms, it was, in essence, a dictatorship of the proletariat.[13]

The final objective was communism, defined as 'from each according to ability, to each according to need', following the temporary stage of socialism, which was 'from each and to each according to achievement'.[14] Communism was distinguished by the fact that the state had gradually 'withered away', a term used by Engels,[15] and one chosen to emphasize the spontaneous nature of the process that will come to take place when society 'is ripe'. Lenin considered that the disappearance of the state also meant the disappearance of democracy, because democracy is not 'the same as that the minority has to subordinate itself to the majority. Democracy is a state, which recognizes the subordination of the minority to the majority, i.e. an organization in which one class systematically exercises violence against the other.'[16] The conclusion of these long-winded and scholastic interpretations seems to be that all forms of society, except the communist form, are, by definition, dictatorships. In Leninist vocabulary, it is but a minor detail whether modern Western forms of government are called dictatorial democracy or democratic dictatorship. The confusion of terminology and concept is little more than a political tactic, intended to make it impossible to debate types of society.

After taking over power, the first task was to form a government. This was renamed the Sovnarkom (the Council of People's Commissars) because of the revolutionary titles of its members. As a result of the previous government's decision, elections for the Constituent Assembly were held at the end of November. The election result was not favourable to the Bolsheviks, who only gained about 25% of the votes. The Assembly was therefore prevented, with violence, from holding a meeting and was abolished by a decree issued by the Sovnarkom. Ideologically, this way of going about things had been explained in advance by the observation that in a bourgeois republic a constitutional assembly is the highest form of democracy, but 'that the Soviet republic is a higher form of democratism than an ordinary bourgeois republic'.[17]

Lenin was an advocate of world revolution, and was convinced that a proletarian revolution in one country would be the signal for general revolution and the downfall of capitalism. Despite the fact that they could hardly deal with the situation in Russia, the Bolsheviks thus concerned themselves with fanning the flames of world revolution. This was the great objective, admittedly seen as historically unavoidable but nevertheless as being possible to prepare for. One cannot create a revolution, said Lenin in 1918, but one can work in favour of it.[18] But when world revolution was not seen to be a reality, it became of less interest in comparison with the work of consolidation in Russia. This meant that the original self-evident objective of world revolution had to be abandoned in favour of securing the socialist order in their own country – socialism in *one* country, which was hardly in line with Marx's intellectual construction.

The economic policy of the Bolsheviks in the years 1918–21 has been called 'war communism'; it had six main principles:

1 The state took over all the means of production and restricted private ownership even more by confiscating property and expensive items such as jewels.

2 The state controlled the work of every citizen and decreed by law that work was obligatory – Lenin recommended the introduction of a work and consumption book for every citizen.[19]

3 The state sought to concentrate all production to state-owned companies.

4 Extreme centralization.

5 The state sought to acquire a monopoly with regard not only to production but also to distribution. The People's Commissariat of Supply took what it could from industry and agriculture and distributed it according to its own regulations. As regards the distribution of foodstuffs, the class principle was decisive, which meant rationing on different scales, with workers being favoured.

6 An attempt was made to abolish money, by paying wages in kind and requisitioning without payment. Galloping inflation ensued, thus serving to finance the revolution and undermine capitalism.[20]

The results were catastrophic. Production decreased sharply, the quality of goods declined and the supply situation was untenable because the peasants preferred to leave their land uncultivated rather than be forced to deliver without being paid. This resulted in famine in the towns, which workers then abandoned in order to seek their 'daily bread' in the country areas. The civil war and the foreign blockade made things even worse, and by 1919 there were hardly any Russian exports at all.

For the duration of the civil war, it was possible to demand sacrifices, but opposition became more widespread when no improvements seemed imminent even after the defeat of the white armies. The decisive factor was the rebellion of the Kronstadt sailors in 1921, the same sailors who had once helped Lenin to power. They demanded new elections to the soviets with a secret ballot preceded by free agitation, freedom of speech, of the press and of assembly, the release of detained socialist politicians, etc. The rebellion was put down with cruel thoroughness after more than two weeks of fighting, but led to Lenin reconsidering the economic policy.

The result was the NEP, the new economic policy. Private enterprise was allowed within certain limits; heavy industry and the transport sector were kept in the hands of the state. Requisitioning from the peasants ceased and they were now made to pay a fixed tax, after which they could dispose of surplus production as they saw fit. Forced labour ceased, the value of money was stabilized, and a normal tax system was introduced. The first year of NEP was characterized by famine caused partly by drought and partly by the previous years' policy, but after that conditions slowly improved.

Lenin did not try to disguise his retreat, and admitted that they had gone too far and had been forced to make concessions.[21] The new order was simply a sort of state capitalism,[22] but the objective, about which there was to be no doubt, was that NEP Russia would be transformed into a socialist Russia.[23]

Lenin, as pointed out above, was a practical revolutionary with a particular end in mind, and he adjusted his theories and means to suit that end. But, by insisting that ideology was the guiding principle and source of inspiration, the foundations were laid for the monumental degree of discrepancy between words and deeds that became the special characteristic of the Soviet Union. With the new emphasis upon socialism in *one* country, he had betrayed and abandoned one of Marx's central ideas, namely the general and international character of scientific socialism. In its place, the programme of political action was put on the throne, which meant treachery against a basic thesis of Marxist ideology, i.e. the inevitable development of society in accordance with the materialistic concept of history. This showed that the causes of the Russian Revolution are to be found in Russia's own history and revolutionary traditions, and cannot be understood according to a social theory with such a defective base in reality as Marxism. Like most other revolutions, the Russian one was characterized by being a means for a small group to acquire the political, and thereby the economic, power.

24

THE STALIN EPOCH

Theory subordinated to practice

In January 1924, Lenin died, and a struggle for power ensued that was to last for many years; it ended, of course, with Stalin as victor, but his power was not consolidated until 1929. The Stalinist epoch was characterized by the collectivisation of agriculture, the five-year plans for industrialization, the purges and the cult of personality. The following description is, as far as is possible, restricted to the more decisive events and standpoints of the ideological development. I should perhaps emphasize at this juncture that the epoch, in that respect, is rather lacking in content, in part because Stalin was not a leading ideologue, but also because Marxism, to a growing extent, was restricted to playing the role of servant to the actual or desired development. This could, of course, only be done at the cost of further abusing the original ideas.

During the 1920s, Leninism became a concept, and it was defined by Stalin as 'Marxism in the epoch of imperialism and the proletarian revolution',[1] that is the development that Marxism had undergone in an advanced capitalist world, but not necessarily an adjustment of Marxism to Russian conditions.

When it became apparent that the revolution would not spread to other countries, it was still necessary to consolidate what had been won and make Russia stand out as the stronghold of world revolution. The programme meant carrying out socialism in the Soviet Union, socialism in *one* country, a slogan that aroused protests as it not only implied a major deviation from Marxist internationalism, but was also strictly speaking incompatible with the basic tenets of Marxism. The most influential opponent was Trotsky, with whom Stalin had clashed already during the civil war. Trotsky maintained that the victory of socialism meant world revolution, and this was called the theory of the permanent revolution. In addition, he attacked the NEP system, particularly the concessions to 'peasant-capitalism'. Trotsky led what was known as the left-opposition and was attacked by Stalin for overestimating the influence of capitalism in Russia, though this did not prevent Stalin – after the fall of Trotsky – from implementing large parts of the latter's programme.

Left-wing deviation had its counterpart in right-wing deviation, 'petit-bourgeois radicalism' and 'petit-bourgeois liberalism'.[2] Its leading advocates were Bucharin, after Lenin the leading theoretician in the party, and Rykov, who for a time was Lenin's deputy and later chairman of Sovnarkom, i.e. prime minister. These two were first used in the struggle against the men of the left but later came to share the same fate themselves. Bucharin was accused of having an 'incorrect, un-Marxist attitude on the question of the class struggle', in particular his 'theory of the kulaks growing into socialism'.[3]

In 1929, the NEP was abandoned in favour of the first five-year plan, which concentrated upon the collectivization of agriculture and rapid industrialization. The agricultural policy was intended to increase control over production and to abolish the class of landowning peasants. The consequences were the same as for 'war communism', so Stalin had to beat a temporary retreat. Industrialization, with strong emphasis upon heavy industry, was carried out at a previously unseen rate, but in that area too it was necessary to resort to ideological lapses. The levelling out of incomes was then abandoned, and in its place came a highly differentiated system of wages, one of the expressions of which was 'Stakhanovism'. This measure was justified by the (previously cited) definitions of socialism as 'to each and from each according to achievement' and communism as 'from each according to ability, to each according to need'. With regard to status and benefits, workers increasingly began to play second fiddle to the leaders of industry, some of whom were former bourgeois elements. Stalin's demand for a shift from collective to one-man management was a move in the same direction. In 1932 the death penalty was introduced for theft of state and collective property, and a year later for discussing strike action. In 1936 a standing army was established with officer ranks and marshals – an important step towards de-proletarization.

At the Party Congress in 1939, Stalin made an ideological statement of the greatest importance. He asked the question: why had the state not been abolished when the exploiting classes were eliminated and socialism, in the main, was in place? He answered the question himself by saying that it was not possible, because socialism had prevailed in only one country. Using an example from Engels, he showed that no such possibility had been contemplated and 'it thus follows that Engels' general thesis of the fate of the socialist state [withering away] can not generally be extended to the special and concrete case where socialism has prevailed in a single country', which, on account of the international situation, 'must have its own, sufficiently strong state to have the possibility of defending socialism's gains against attacks from outside'.

But, Stalin continued, the socialist state differed considerably from the capitalist state. While the latter's main function was its internal activity, 'keeping the exploited majority in check', in the socialist state 'the oppressing function' was replaced by

> the state's function of defending socialist property against thieves and embezzlers of the people's property. The function of protecting, with the aid of military force, the country from external aggression has been

retained to the full ... as have the penal organs and the security service, which are necessary to catch and punish spies, murderers and destructive elements that foreign espionage organs send to our country.

These Soviet organs 'no longer directed their activities inwards, but outwards, towards their external enemies'. To the question of whether the state would be retained even under communism, he replied: 'Yes, it will be retained, unless the danger of military attack from outside is neutralized,' and went on, 'It will wither away if the surrounding capitalist world is liquidated and this is replaced by a socialist world.' [4] Within the country, the main purpose of the state was 'to carry out peaceful economic-organizational and cultural-educational work'.

Although the idea of socialism in *one* country had been seen to be inapplicable in its original sense, Stalin was thus prepared to widen the theory to communism in *one* country. But if the state was to continue to exist even under communism, it meant that the 'withering away' no longer had its original spontaneous character, but had instead been subordinated to human planning. Stalin attempted to by-pass this difficulty with the statement that the activity of the socialist state was directed outwards, a statement that also explains why criminals and political opponents in the Soviet Union were so often accused of collaboration with foreign countries.

The dictatorship of the proletariat was to be the state authority during the transitional period from capitalism to socialism and would, in its turn, result in the classless and stateless society. But when Stalin declared the authority of the state to be permanent in the Soviet Union, the very content and purpose of all of Marx's ideology was betrayed – or, put another way, the thesis of socialism in *one* country was seen to be incompatible with Marxism.

The theory of the authority of the state under communism in *one* country, in fact, means a declaration of bankruptcy of the official ideology in its entirety. It amounts to an ideological contradiction and a conceptual absurdity, as it implies that the communist society was a class society – which it cannot be, by definition. It is proof, as good as any, of the absolute restriction of freedom of expression under Stalin's rule. This theory remaining unchallenged His exercise of authority extended to control of all aspects of society, political and economic, as well as cultural. The state was the only employer and, on principle, tolerated neither independent professionals nor self-employment. Every individual was thus dependent upon the state for his or her daily bread, and this economic monopoly made the state-socialist dictatorship probably the most totalitarian form of government in world history.

The development of events during and after the Second World War led to the Soviet Union annexing, or installing puppet regimes in, a number of Eastern

European states. This extension from socialism in *one* country to a socialist bloc was in no way a confirmation of the applicability of Marxism's deterministic concept of history but purely a result of armed Soviet Russian expansion. Officially, the process was interpreted as proof of the irresistible validity of the Marxist ideas – whereas these, in actual fact, had been degraded to the level of fancy dress disguise to conceal traditional Russian imperialism.

25

AFTER STALIN

Can theory and practice be united?

The Stalinist cult of personality could be carried out in a backward and isolated Russia, and could perhaps even be regarded as having served its purpose well. But the backwardness disappeared with the advance of the educational system and the increasing degree of industrialization, as did the feeling of isolation from a hostile outside world, when the people's democratic states and Red China were incorporated in the socialist camp. These developmental tendencies contributed to the feeling that, even during Stalin's lifetime, the Soviet Union was growing away from Stalinism, which was characterized in foreign policy by an irreconcilable attitude vis-à-vis the Western powers, and in domestic policy by the dominant role of the political police, by an emphasis upon the importance of heavy industry, and by the doctrinaire agricultural policy. In all of these areas, a reorientation was carried out by the men who took charge after Stalin's death in 1953.

The clearest change consisted of the introduction of collective leadership – and nothing could be easier to justify ideologically – in which one could distinguish different leaders for the party, government, military and the secret police. One of the first measures of the new regime, however, consisted in suppressing the secret police, which was under Beria's control. This was evidently not done purely on account of the latent threat to the rest of the leadership that the police minister's position of power implied, but also as a sign of the policy that meant a general softening with a deliberate attempt to improve the legal rights of citizens. A promise was thus made to revise the criminal law. Then, under Malenkov's leadership, there were signals of a swing in economic politics in the direction of greater production of consumer products and a less doctrinaire agricultural policy.

This softening-up policy was not without its opponents, and these became even more determined when the policy evidently led to a serious weakening of work discipline both inside and outside the Soviet Union. In East Germany, early in the summer of 1953, things even went so far that workers' demonstrations had to be suppressed with the help of tanks. Russian commitments to supply aid to China required increased exertion from heavy industry and differences arose among the leaders. Malenkov was pushed aside by Khrushchev but was temporarily allowed to retain an out-of-the-way position in the government, which may be seen as proof that the leadership wanted to show that purges were no longer seen as the only solution to a power struggle. But the leadership had not dared be so gentle with Beria and the other executed secret policemen, who had built up a considerable machinery of power.

A consistent element in the policies of Stalin's successors, was the abolition of the unlimited cult of personality. The very declaration of a collective leadership meant a break with the principles of the deceased leader, and this was followed by a greater emphasis on Lenin instead of Stalin. Full-scale de-Stalinization started at the twentieth congress of the Communist Party in 1956. Some of the party leaders were severely critical of the one-man domination, and Khrushchev in a secret report vehemently attacked Stalin, who was accused of having exercised a ruinous influence through his methods during the great purges, of having disregarded all the warnings concerning Hitler's intentions, and, as a result of his ignorance and dictatorial views, of having had a disastrous influence on military operations, of stealing the honour from others and of megalomania and paranoia.

Some practical measures were quickly undertaken in the field of foreign affairs. Closer ties were established with Yugoslavia through amnesty and the rehabilitation of Titoists and through weeding out Stalinists from prominent positions in the satellite states. The Communist Information Bureau (Cominform) was dissolved and, in connection with an invitation to Tito to visit Moscow, Molotov had to leave the post of foreign minister. But internally, this increase in freedom seems largely to have been restricted to the higher party echelons, while those lower down and the masses were governed as before. The question of whether such a policy was feasible, or whether it would be necessary to spread this increase of freedom or restrict it again, was answered by new disturbances in Eastern Europe. Workers in Poznan presumably had very little interest in the theoretical arguments but were, without doubt, sensitive to the possibilities for protesting about the low standard of living that they now enjoyed in the milder political climate. In 1956, Hungarians tried to go even further and use de-Stalinization to liberate themselves from the Russian grip. Order was restored with violence.

It thus became necessary to reconsider the gentler policy, as well as the de-Stalinization, which had been something of a flagship, but this did not mean that it was written off completely. De-Stalinization had come to acquire such a wide content that anything undertaken by Moscow could be branded as 'Stalinist' as soon as it did not contain a concession. The very cautious and partial rehabilitation of Stalin that actually took place ought therefore to be seen primarily as an attempt to give the de-Stalinization a form, the content of which was less dangerous for, and more suitable to, the Soviet Union.

From the point of view of the Russian leaders, the way the broad masses so willingly embraced the new strains must have been more than they had bargained for. Their inability to predict these perfectly natural reactions showed how they had become prisoners of their own ideology to such a degree that their grasp of reality was decidedly lacking in discernment. Khrushchev would later proclaim his conviction that communism would be victorious because the people in the poorer countries would be convinced by their stomachs as to the superiority of the system. There was no question of casting any doubt upon the basic theoretical theses, economic principles, or the main principles of foreign policy. In order to maintain the ideological regulation of society, they were still prepared to resort to violent means, as the events in Czechoslovakia in 1968 showed. And in order to promote the spread of world revolution – in a Soviet Russian sense – Moscow intervened militarily in several places in the Third World, for example Angola, Ethiopia, Cuba and Mozambique, and engaged in a proper war of aggression against Afghanistan.

During the Stalin epoch, ideology had degenerated to being a tool at the service of the cult of personality. As an element in the de-Stalinization process and the attempts at placing more emphasis on Lenin's importance, a need arose for a comprehensive survey of the 'proper' and original ideology. A group of Soviet academics put together a handbook entitled *Outlines of Marxism–Leninism*, which can thus be regarded as officially sanctioned. The handbook consisted of 800 pages but, despite that, claimed only to shed light upon the basics of the theory, though it was claimed that a successful study of these would lead to the acquisition of a solid philosophy. An account of the contents must here be restricted to an attempt at comparing the previously described tenets of Marx and Engels with the handbook's descriptions of the equivalent subjects.[1]

The handbook starts by stating that dialectical and historical materialism forms the unshakeable foundations for the entire construction of Marxism–Leninism. The scientific nature of materialism is particularly emphasized, as is the fact that it embraces a concept of society and its history. By discovering the material driving forces and the laws of the development of society, Marx and Engels transformed the study of the history of societies into a science. They also transformed materialist philosophy from an abstract theory into an effective means of restructuring society and an ideological weapon for the working class in its struggle for socialism and communism.

All phenomena seen in the world are, to a greater or lesser extent, firmly interconnected. The insight as to the necessary character of these contexts is the principle of determinism, which is said to be the cornerstone of every scientific explanation of the world and the fundamental principle behind all true scientific thinking.

The dialectical principle is presented in the following manner (here in highly summarized form): when studying any phenomenon in nature, in social conditions or in people's spiritual life, contradictions are discovered, i.e. collisions between opposing sides or tendencies. Development proceeds in such a way that the contradictions enter into a struggle with each other, which leads to the old forms being destroyed and new ones arising. Through the accumulation of quantitative changes, qualitative changes also take place and these happen by leaps. All development is characterized in the long term by progress.

Marx and Engels are said to have carried out the scientific feat of extending dialectic materialism to the study of society and its history and, by so doing, they created the materialist concept of history. They could do this because the historical conditions had arisen as a result of capitalism having exposed the material and economic roots of the class struggle. On the one hand, Marx and Engels established that people had created their own history, on the other, that this had taken place on the basis of objective, material conditions – history being a regulated process.

The most prominent place in society is occupied by 'production', and this always has a social character. It is through production that a division of work is developed among people, which results in the relationships between classes. As a result of this, conditions of ownership arise, and these have a decisive influence upon the formation of laws and political institutions – state authority is in the hands of the ruling class. But the conditions of ownership cannot keep up with the productive forces when these are developed, which results in a conflict. This is characteristic of every type of production before the socialist epoch, which is the first phase in the transition to communism. Before that, mankind has passed through four stages: the original society, the slave society, feudalism and capitalism.

The foundations of capitalist conditions of production consist of the capitalists' right of private ownership of the means of production. The capitalists exploit the waged workers, who are forced to sell their labour. The main classes in society thus become the capitalists and the workers. By main classes are meant classes without which the existing method of production would be impossible and which have arisen precisely on account of this method of production. Capitalist society also includes peasants, estate-owners, the intelligentsia, etc. The ruling class possesses the authority of the state in order to protect the existing conditions of ownership and production.

In order to introduce new, up-to-date conditions of production, it is necessary for the political power to pass into the hands of the new class, which is struggling for the modernization that development demands. The pressure from the exploited classes, i.e. a class struggle, thus becomes the driving force for the development of society. Revolutions are periods in which the critical stage of the class struggle reaches its peak, which in the development theory corresponds to the requirement of qualitative changes taking place in leaps, if not necessarily with violence.

While previous revolutions had meant only that one form of exploitation was replaced by another, the socialist revolution of the working class brings the exploitation to an end in all respects, and leads to the abolition of all classes. This comes about by replacing the capitalist form of private ownership of the means of production with a public, socialist ownership and socialist conditions of production.

The labour theory of value is described in the handbook primarily in the same way as in Marx's *Capital*, with the exception of the law of the falling rate of profit, which is conspicuous by its absence. It is established that 'products' are

176

only those products of work that enter consumption through exchange. The products become values as a materialization of the labour power that has been put into them. The value is not, however, decided by the labour that has gone into making the particular item, but by the labour that is, on average, used in society for the production of the type of product in question. This type of labour can be measured in working hours and is called socially necessary labour. While the value of a product is created by the labour used to produce it, this value is expressed only in the exchange.

The theory of centralization is described in the following way: under the influence of the law of value, the price of products is drawn towards the level of their value. However, because of continual fluctuations in supply and demand, prices are always deviating from the true value. Should supply exceed demand, the price will fall below par – and if price should exceed value, this generates an increase in production, which leads to the price sinking below the level of value. In capitalist society, the continual fluctuations in price lead to the less competitive producers succumbing while the stronger ones strengthen their positions and, finally, capitalists become a numerically negligible minority.

The essentials that a worker needs to support himself and his family decide the value of labour power. This requires, say, six hours of work, but if the worker has a twelve-hour working day, then he is delivering six hours of unpaid surplus labour to the capitalist. Surplus value is created; capital grows. The capitalists are interested not in producing goods beneficial to society, but in extracting the greatest possible surplus value. The increase in this can be achieved either by lengthening the working day or – most commonly – by intensifying work or by reducing the number of working hours required, i.e. by reducing the price of the essentials that decide the value of labour power. This, Marx's theory of surplus value, is seen as exposing the manner in which the capitalist's exploitation of the workers takes place in a bourgeois society.

As was pointed out above, the law of the falling rate of profit is not described. It is, however, stated that one must distinguish between the two parts of capital: constant capital, i.e. the means of production, and variable capital, i.e. labour power. When the means of production participates in production, it does not create any new value, whereas variable capital in the production process creates a surplus value. The greater the part that variable capital represents in relation to constant capital in an industrial branch, the greater will be the surplus value that is extracted. It is also noted in the handbook that it is meaningless for the capitalist to invest in an industrial branch in which the extraction of surplus value is lower than in another branch. However, it is further observed that invested capital, regardless of this, gives a more or less similar profit. This is said to be because there is competition for the most profitable capital investment. Capital leaves those branches in which an overproduction of goods is observed and is directed towards those branches in which a shortage of goods has caused a rise in price. In this manner, an average profit rate arises.

The theory of crises was also covered in the handbook in a way that differs somewhat from the original sources. The starting point is the capitalist's striving towards an unlimited increase in production, while at the same time consumption is limited by the insufficient buying power of the masses. The capitalist's way out is to increase the production of the means of production, but, because the goal of all production is the production of consumer goods, this results in crises of overproduction. Overproduction results in difficulties in selling goods, a fall in prices, a decrease in production, a reduction in wages, and unemployment. With the aim of raising work productivity to make profit even with the low prices, the capitalist starts to renew the equipment in his companies. This generates a demand for means of production, which eventually results in an upswing, after which the whole process is repeated.

A prerequisite of the crisis theory is the limited consumer ability of the masses, i.e. the theory of impoverishment. But the original meaning of this theory must be regarded as having been abandoned in the handbook, which emphatically denies that there is a continuous worsening of the living conditions of the workers under capitalism. This is because the class struggle leads to positive results. However, the relative position of the working class is worsened, i.e. its share of the national income decreases.

The catastrophe theory, on the other hand, is dealt with in the handbook: capital is centralized, which leads to the development of the deliberate application of science in production with planned exploitation of land, and the transformation of working tools to means that can only be used by the collective. The antagonism between the social character of production and the private capitalist appropriation becomes more acute, as the capitalist method of production acts as a fetter for the development of society's productive forces. It thus becomes necessary to convert the decisive means of production into public ownership. This takes place when the masses, under the leadership of the working class, rise up in a struggle against capital. Both the necessity of capitalist society's revolutionary transformation into socialist society and the manner in which this shall happen Marx is considered as having deduced from the objective law of the development of capitalist society.

Lenin introduced the concept of 'imperialism as the highest stadium of capitalism'. As the section on Lenin was, as far as possible, restricted to considering that part of his ideological innovation that was connected with the internal process in Russia, it might well be relevant to summarize the handbook's description of imperialism. As a result of centralization – or concentration as it is also called – production becomes all the more dominated by large companies, which inevitably leads to the emergence of monopolies. The first and most important singularity of imperialism is that it constitutes monopolistic capitalism. The monopoly arises from the free competition, but does not set aside the competitive struggle; on the contrary, it makes the struggle even more bitter and destructive. The monopolies do not set aside the anarchy and chaos of capitalist production.

The concentration of production is accompanied by the centralization of bank capital. This leads to the emergence of a bank monopoly. The monopolistic bank capital merges together with the monopolistic industrial capital, thus giving rise to finance capital. The domination of finance capital in the most developed capitalist countries leads inevitably to a situation in which a small number of imperialist states dominate the entire capitalist world. An important tool in this context is the export of capital, i.e. the placing of capital abroad in order to appropriate the surplus value that is created by the workers of other countries.

Besides dividing up the world economically by means of cooperation between capitalists from different countries, the world was also divided up territorially among the imperialist countries during the period preceding the First World War. Even states that, in a formal sense, were politically independent were thus often considered as being ensnared in a net of financial and diplomatic dependence. This is said to explain how the USA, without owning a single colony, could develop into the de facto largest colonial power.

The emergence of large companies as producers and distributors for entire populations marks a development in the public character of production. But the appropriation remains private. The main contradictions of capitalism become thus all the more acute with the development of monopolistic capitalism. This means that imperialism is dying capitalism, because the increasingly monopolistic character of capitalism is a sign of the beginning of its transition into socialism. It is in this manner that Lenin is said to have come to the scientifically based conclusion that imperialism is the threshold of the socialist revolution.

The handbook also explains why Marx and Engels' thesis that the revolution could only be victorious simultaneously in all nations, or at least in the leading capitalist countries, has not stood the test of time. The ideological fathers based their conclusion upon the study of pre-monopoly capitalism, whereas the handbook introduces the law of the unequal character of economic and political development, which should apply under imperialism. At the end of the nineteenth century, Great Britain's monopolistic position was undermined by the rapid development in the USA, Germany and eventually in Japan, too. This shows that some countries developed in leaps, whereas the development of others was more restrained. The different manner of economic development is associated with differences in political development too, in the way that the political conditions for the victory of the socialist revolution do not 'mature' at the same time.

An analysis of these conditions led Lenin to the conclusion that the revolution could not be victorious in all countries at the same time, rather the opposite, in that it could be victorious in just a few countries or even in a single country. The differences in the temporal maturity of the revolution in different countries would make it possible to break through the chain of imperialism at its weakest link.

As can be seen, Stalin was not accorded a place in the development of Marxism–Leninism – except perhaps indirectly through the conclusion of the explanation of the rise of socialism in *one* country. This, however, means a manifestly essential concession to the inexorable reality that emphatically showed that socialist revolutions took place not in economically developed countries but, rather, in underdeveloped countries such as Russia, China and Cuba. Other concessions to reality were also made, for example that the theory of impoverishment should be interpreted no longer literally but relatively – the workers in the capitalist countries were recognized as having improved their living standard instead of becoming impoverished but their share of the national income diminished. This particular statement in the handbook is debatable, as are several others, some seeming even to be mutually incompatible.

It is, however, more important to note that attempts are made to keep the labour theory of value as intact as possible. It is admittedly recognized that the value is influenced by modified concepts such as 'socially necessary work' and that the price is influenced by supply and demand. But the relationship between value and price remains elusive. And it is still maintained that it is only the labour power, and not the means of production, that creates any surplus value. Could it be so, that former Russian conditions contributed to this attitude? The wealth of the landowning aristocracy in Russia was based not upon the value of their property, the land, but on the number of serfs tied to that land.[2]

At the end of the chapter on Marx and Engels, I stated that the mechanism of capitalist exploitation was claimed to consist of the demand that interest be paid on the investment costs that were part of the production process. Really, the Soviet form of socialism ought rather to be called state capitalism and, by definition, exploitation did not cease. Despite this, it was claimed that they had created a society free from exploitation and class antagonism. In reality, in the Soviet system, the differences in living standard between the rulers and the ruled were greater than in other industrialized societies. However, this depended only partly on the way in which the economic system's poor capacity led to narrower borders within which any policy of redistribution would have to function. The main reason was of a political nature, namely the lack of democratic institutions for which there was no breeding ground in a society in which the state had made itself all-powerful by virtue of being the sole employer.

Economic capacity was fettered by prejudice, by the fact that calculations of profitability met with ideological opposition that counteracted an effective use of resources. The labour theory of value, and the way interest costs and exploitation were seen as being the same thing, prevented a clear recognition of the manifest role that technology and technical improvements had as a factor in the creation of value. And how could one apply the labour theory of value to the costs of, for example, environmental pollution and maintenance? Without any comparable basis for calculating all the contributory costs, not just labour but also raw materials acquisition, energy production, transport, infrastructure, maintenance, environmental conservation, etc., not only was there no basis for optimal utilization of available resources, but also all barriers against wasteful use of resources were removed. This basic Marxist philosophy must have effectively contributed to the

Soviet form of socialism never being able to fulfil Khrushchev's promise of catching up with, and surpassing, the industrial societies within the market economy. The same basic philosophy had been instilled in Kim Il Sung and it determined his economic policy – a policy characterized by a waste of resources that led the country to economic collapse.

26

THE ROAD TO RUIN

A problem that must have become all the more pressing for the Soviet leaders could be called the end of ideology. Over time, an increasing number of stated objectives were eventually realized, albeit at a frighteningly slow pace when compared with the West. But the empty promises of the ideology that the Soviet Union would overtake the West in wealth and freedom remained empty promises, and it became all the more obvious that they could not be fulfilled. The result was that the ideology lost credibility and started out on the road to ruin.

The reason for this failure is presumably, to a not inconsiderable degree, to be found in the way in which the fundamental labour theory of value stipulated that it is solely the labour input that creates value. State socialist economic thinking was thereby fettered with obsessions, the practical consequence of which was that economic growth was created more by a greater allocation of labour-related resources than by efficiency measures. In the absence of the well-worked-out market economy methods of measuring cost-efficiency, the state socialist system thus led to waste and the ruthless exploitation of resources because it lacked – and even went as far as denying the existence of – an applicable yardstick. The idea that work alone creates value also leads to a lack of respect for the value of natural resources, the consequence of which is environmental pollution.

Additional problems included the centralized decision-making system and the mutual isolation of the various branches of industry, imposed by the security services. The development or, more correctly speaking, the lack of development thus continued in its well-worn tracks. It was increasingly obvious that the economic gap between the socialist camp and the advanced market economy countries (joined, in time, by a growing number of former underdeveloped countries) was continually widening and that the countries of the Third World were becoming increasingly convinced that the socialist system did not offer the solution to their problems. Apart from this, ecological catastrophes were rife, and the war in Afghanistan was both ideologically and economically costly. Soviet trade and industry encountered increasing difficulties and could only function thanks to 'fixers'. Corruption was prevalent and a steadily growing cynicism was spreading.

During the last decades of its existence, the Soviet Union came to resemble increasingly the form of a traditional dictatorship in which ideological motivation became petrified in an unfruitful ritual. The hierarchical system produced elderly leaders, who were unable to free themselves from the economic and political conditions of the Stalin epoch. It was not until Gorbachev that a leader came into power who was from the generation born after the Revolution and who realized that the system demanded thorough change. But even he evidently believed, right up to the very end, in the possibility of limited and gradual reforms without questioning the foundations of the system.

The entire construction of the state and society was built upon an ideology that denied economic realities. This thwarted attempts at changing course within the framework of the system and had slowed down the economic development to such a degree that one could use Marx's own, previously cited, words to explain the Soviet Union's inevitable path to economic collapse: 'At a certain stage of their development, the material productive forces in society find themselves in antagonism to the existing production conditions, or, in what is just a legal expression for this, with the ownership conditions within which these productive forces have until then found themselves. From having been forms of development for the productive forces, these conditions are now transformed to chains for those same forces. A period of social revolution is then entered into.'[1]

If one applies Marx's theory of the origin and development of bourgeois society, one finds (as Deutscher pointed out[2]) that the Russian industrialization during the Stalin epoch showed great similarities to Great Britain's industrial revolution, as Marx had described it in such black terms in *Capital*. From a Marxist point of view, the Russian Revolution of 1917 should really be termed a bourgeois revolution, an equivalent to the great French Revolution of 1789. With this way of looking at things, in its best days the Soviet Union would have been a bourgeois state in full prosperity. And, to use the language of Marx, it did indeed have the typical attributes of such a state: a standing army and police force, a powerful government and imperialist policy.

An orthodox Marxist could thus have ample reason to claim that the Marxist concept of history was not repudiated by the rise and fall of the Soviet Union. Lenin and the Bolsheviks chose to ignore Marxism's characteristic of expressing a concept of history and transforming it into a political action programme and, in so doing, the original meaning disappeared. The Russian Revolution's character of bourgeois revolution would instead, if anything, confirm the relevance of Marx's understanding of history, for Lenin did not succeed in his purpose of 'extending the limits of the bourgeois revolution' and making it socialist because the time was not ripe. The experiment of the Soviet Union failed for the reason that it is impossible to skip a historical epoch.

Such reasoning may well be correct, but it does not follow that the Marxist concept of history thus stands on a firm foundation. History cannot be explained by Marxism's simplified scheme of things. It should suffice to point out that the slave society did not collapse through revolutions in which the slaves turned themselves into feudal masters, and indeed that the feudal system was abolished through a genuine revolution only in France and Russia and, possibly, China.

Nowadays it is no longer appropriate to try to subordinate historical scholarship and social sciences to fixed laws in the manner of the natural sciences. But in the economic field, certain guiding lines and laws must be respected in order to maintain growth and thereby build up welfare states. In this respect, the Soviet Union's example and fate convincingly show that Marx's economic theories, even ignoring the fact that they were artificially intertwined with metaphysical 'laws' for the development and prosperity of society, did not form a practicable basis for an economic policy that encourages growth and welfare. The system simply ground to a halt, and virtually every communist country embarked upon an arduous and trying transition to a market economy. The conspicuous exception was North Korea, which as recently as 1988 still indignantly denied the need for perestroika in its country and has continued since then to persevere along the old road. The developments in the Eastern European countries showed that the reforms were hard earned. But, by not following their example, Kim Il Sung and his successor led North Korea not only to economic collapse but also to famine.

NOTES

1 HISTORICAL REVIEW

1 Henriksen, T. H. and Mo, J. E., *North Korea after Kim Il Sung*, p. xxii.
2 Hunter, H. L. *Kim Il-song's North Korea*.

3 DIPLOMACY IN THE TWENTIETH CENTURY

1 Djilas, M. *The New Class*, p. 163.

18 THE IDEOLOGICAL ISSUE

1 For a full explanation, see pp. 168 and 170.
2 For a more detailed description, see p. 157.
3 Marx's doctrines have been thoroughly criticized. The basic thesis that political power originally stems from economic power has been contested by, for example, Pierre Clastres, who demonstrates that the reverse appears more likely; see p. 158.
4 For a more detailed description of 'war communism', see pp. 165–6.
5 Buzo, A., *The Guerilla Dynasty*, p. 118.
6 A comprehensive summary of the handbook is given on pp. 175–9.

19 CONFUCIANISM AND COMMUNISM

1 According to Maretzki, his actual name was Kim Song Chu, while the real Kim Il Sung was a considerably older and prominent partisan leader who was killed in 1936; Maretzki, op. cit., p. 14; see also Fairbank *et al.*, *East Asia: Tradition and Transformation*, p. 882.
2 Fairbank *et al.* even call a chapter of their book 'Yi Dynasty Korea: a model Confucian society'; Fairbank *et al.*, op. cit., p. 301.
3 The rumours about an elder brother from an earlier marriage circulated openly among Eastern Europeans in Pyongyang. They cannot, however, be confirmed and there is no mention of a brother in the available biographies of Kim Il Sung, for example Suh, D. S., *Kim Il Sung: The North Korean Leader*.
4 According to Hunter, university students taking the most advanced scientific courses have to devote some 20% of their time to studies in ideology; for those taking lower courses the percentage is considerably higher; Hunter, op. cit., p. 214.
5 Reese, D., *The Prospects for North Korea's Survival*, p. 15.

NOTES

20 KIM IL SUNG'S MARXISM

1 See p. 152.
2 See pp. 161–2.
3 See p. 114 and pp. 165–6.
4 See pp. 162–3.
5 See p. 80 and p. 163.
6 See p. 165.
7 See p. 13.

21 AS LONG AS THE GAME GOES ON …

1 Elias, N., *Über den Prozess der Zivilisation, Zweiter Band* (Swedish edn), p. 73.
2 The theory of the 'withering away of the state' is briefly dealt with on p. 158 and p. 170.
3 Eberstadt N., 'North Korea's Reunification Policy', *Korea and World Affairs*, Vol. 3, 1996, 425.
4 Buzo, op. cit., pp. 174–5.
5 Reese, op. cit., pp. 27 and 32 ff.
6 Harrison, S. S., 'US policy toward North Korea', in Suh, D. S. and Lin, C.-J. (eds), *North Korea after Kim Il Sung*, p. 67.
7 Jonsson, G., *Towards a Breakthrough in Inter-Korean Relations*, p. 24.
8 See p. 115 and pp. 166–7.
9 Noland, M., 'Prospects for the North Korean economy', in Suh, D. S. and Lin, C.-J., op. cit., p. 34; see also Hunter, op. cit., p. 41.
10 Oh, K. and Hassig, R. (1999) 'North Korea between collapse and reform', *Asian Survey*, Vol. XXXIX, No. 2, 1999, 290.
11 For a general description of the negotiations see Reese, op. cit., Ch. 2; and Henriksen and Mo, op. cit., Ch. 11.
12 Kim, G.-N., (1996) 'The uncertain future of North Korea', *Korea and World Affairs*, Vol. 4, 1996, 633.
13 Lee, C. J., 'US policy towards North Korea', *Korea and World Affairs*, Vol. 3, 1996, p. 363.
14 Reese, op. cit., p. 60.
15 Lee, J.-S., *Rethinking the Korean Reunification Problem*, p. 138 ff.
16 See p. 107.
17 Kim, S. S., 'North Korea in 1999', *Asian Survey*, Vol. XL, No. 1, 2000, 159.
18 ibid., p. 161.
19 Jonsson, op. cit., p. 33.
20 Hoon, S. J., 'The moral cost of engagement', *Far Eastern Economic Review*, 4 Jan. 2001.
21 Oberdorfer, D., *The Two Koreas: A Contemporary History*, p. 110.
22 Hunter, op. cit., Ch. 1.
23 See p. 115 and pp. 165–6.
24 An insightful description of the confusing multitude of considerations connected with North Korea's future is to be found in Levin, N. D., 'What if North Korea survives', *Survival*, Vol. 39, No. 4, Winter 1997–8, 156–74.

22 A SUMMARY OF THE DOCTRINES OF MARX AND ENGELS

1 Ahlberg, A., *Filosofins historia*, p. 605.
2 Engels, F., *The Origin of the Family, Private Property and the State* (Swedish edn), p. 8.

NOTES

3 Marx, K. and Engels, F., *The Communist Manifesto* (Swedish edn) p. 29.
4 Engels, F., *The Development of Socialism from Utopia to Science* (Swedish edn), p. 42.
5 Marx, K., *A Contribution to the Critique of Political Economy* (Swedish edn), p. 7.
6 Marx, K. and Engels, F., *The Communist Manifesto* (Swedish edn), p. 10.
7 Marx, K., *Capital III: 2* (Swedish edn), p. 835.
8 Marx, K., *The 18th Brumaire of Louis Bonaparte* (Swedish edn), p. 140 f.
9 Marx, K., *A Contribution to the Critique of Political Economy* (Swedish edn), p. 241.
10 Marx, K. and Engels, F., *Gesamtausgabe*, Vol. I.3, *Die heilige Familie*, p. 205 f.
11 Marx, K. and Engels, F., *The Communist Manifesto* (Swedish edn), p. 20).
12 ibid., p. 25.
13 Marx, K., *The Paris Commune* (Swedish edn), p. 75.
14 Marx, K., *Capital I* (Swedish edn), p. 588.
15 ibid., pp. 371 and 599.
16 Marx, K. and Engels, F., *The Communist Manifesto* (Swedish edn), p. 17.
17 Marx, K., *Captal I* (Swedish edn), p. 595; and *The Communist Manifesto* (Swedish edn), p. 15.
18 Marx, K. and Engels, F., *The Communist Manifesto* (Swedish edn), pp. 17–21.
19 Marx, K., *Capital I* (Swedish edn), p. 22 ff.
20 ibid., p. 188 ff.
21 ibid., p. 370 ff.
22 ibid., p. 595.
23 Marx, K., *The Paris Commune* (Swedish edn), p. 75.
24 Marx, K. and Engels, F., *The Communist Manifesto* (Swedish edn), pp. 20 and 22.
25 Programme of the Blanquist Refugees of the Commune, Volkstaat 1874; quoted from Carew Hunt, R. N., *Marxism Past and Present*, p. 144.
26 From Engels' introduction to Marx, K., *The Class Struggles in France*.
27 Deuteronomy 23:19–20.
28 Clastres, P., *Samhället mot staten* (*Society vs State*), p. 147.

23 THE LENIN EPOCH: THE THEORIES ARE CONFRONTED WITH THE PRACTICE

1 Marx, K., *The 18th Brumaire of Louis Bonaparte*; and Engels, F., *On the Peasant Question*.
2 Lenin, V. I., *The Agrarian Question in Russia at the End of the 19th Century* (*Lenins samlade skrifter i urval* [LSU], Swedish edn, LSU: Vol. 1), p. 193.
3 Lenin, V. I., *The Workers' Party and the Peasants, 1901* (Swedish edn, LSU:3), p. 263.
4 ibid., p. 267.
5 Lenin, V. I., *Social Democracy's Two Tactics in the Democratic Revolution, 1905* (Swedish edn, LSU:5), pp. 79 and 83 ff).
6 ibid., pp. 106–12; and Lenin, V. I., *Social Democracy and the Provisional Revolutionary Government, 1905* (Swedish edn, LSU:5), p. 26.
7 Lenin, V. I., *Social Democracy's Two Tactics in the Democratic Revolution, 1905* (Swedish edn, LSU:5), p. 234.
8 ibid., p. 91.
9 ibid., p. 109.
10 Lenin, V. I., *On the Defeat of Our Own Government in the Imperialist War, August 1915* (Swedish edn, LSU:9), p. 32.
11 Lenin, V. I., *The Power Crisis, May 1917* (Swedish edn, LSU:11), p. 14.

NOTES

12 Marx, K. and Engels, F., *The Communist Manifesto* (Swedish edn), p. 29; and Lenin, V. I., *State and Revolution* (Swedish edn, LSU:12), p. 26.
13 Lenin, ibid., p. 35.
14 ibid., pp. 100 and 96 ff; see also Marx, K., *Critique of the Gotha Programme.*
15 Engels, F., *The Development of Socialism from Utopia to Science* (Swedish edn), p. 66.
16 Lenin, V. I., *State and Revolution* (Swedish edn, LSU:12), p. 85.
17 Lenin, V. I., *Thesis on the Constituent Assembly, Dec 1917* (Swedish edn, LSU:11), p. 391.
18 Lenin, V. I., *Final words of the Report on the Contemporary Situation on June 28, 1918* (Swedish edn, LSU:13), p. 195.
19 Lenin, V. I., *The Immediate Tasks of Soviet Power* (Swedish edn, LSU:13), p. 85.
20 Chamberlain, W. H., *The Russian Revolution II*, p. 97 ff.
21 Lenin, V. I., *On the International Situation of the Soviet Republic, 6 March 1922* (Swedish edn, LSU:16), p 18.
22 Lenin, V. I., *Political Report of the Central Committee of the RCP(b)'s XI Congress on 27 March 1922* (Swedish edn, LSU:16), p. 53.
23 Lenin, V. I., *Speech to the Plenum of the Moscow Soviet on 20 November 1922* (Swedish edn, LSU:16), p. 10.

24 THE STALIN EPOCH: THEORY SUBORDINATED TO PRACTICE

1 Stalin, J. V., *Our Theory and Practice* (Swedish edn), p. 151.
2 Stalin, J. V., *The Basic Questions of Leninism* (Swedish edn), p. 184.
3 Stalin, J. V., *Our Theory and Practice* (Swedish edn), p. 322.
4 ibid., pp. 818–39.

25 AFTER STALIN: CAN THEORY AND PRACTICE BE UNITED?

1 The description follows the handbook, and it has thus been deemed unnecessary to use notes. With the help of the detailed table of contents in the handbook it is easy to find the equivalent chapter.
2 See footnote on p. 117 regarding Gogol's *Dead Souls*.

26 THE ROAD TO RUIN

1 Marx, K., *A Contribution to the Critique of Political Economy* (Swedish edn), p. 7.
2 Deutscher, I., *Stalin* (Swedish edn), p. 371 ff.

BIBLIOGRAPHY

Ahlberg, A., *Filosofins historia*, Stockholm: Natur och Kultur, 1952.

Buzo, A., *The Guerilla Dynasty*, Boulder, CO: Westview, 1999.

Carew Hunt, R. N., *Marxism Past and Present*, London: Geoffrey Bles, 1954.

Chamberlain, W. H., *The Russian Revolution*, London: Martin Lawrence, 1935.

Cha, V. D., 'Engaging North Korea credibly', *Survival*, Vol. 42, No. 2, Summer 2000.

Clastres, P., *Samhället mot staten* [Society vs State] Stockholm: Nordan, 1974.

Deutscher, I., *Stalin – en politisk biografi* [Stalin – A Political Biography] Stockholm: Norstedts, 1951.

Diamond, L., 'Voices from the North Korean gulag', *Journal of Democracy*, Vol. 9, No. 3, 1998, 82–96.

Djilas, M., *The New Class*, London: Harcourt, Brace & World, 1962.

Eberstadt, N., 'North Korea's unification policy; a long, failed gamble', *Korea and World Affairs*, Vol. 3, 1996, 406–30.

Elias, N., *Från svärdet till plikten* [Über den Prozess der Zivilisation II, Wandlungen der Gesellschaft] Stockholm: Atlantis, 1992.

Engels, F., *Socialismens utveckling från utopi till vetenskap* [The Development of Socialism from Utopia to Science] Stockholm: Arbetarkultur, 1938.

Engels, F., *Familjens, privategendomens och statens ursprung* [The Origin of the Family, Private Property and the State] Stockholm: Arbetarkultur, 1939.

Engels, F., *I bondefrågan* [On the Peasant Question] Stockholm: Arbetarkultur, 1946.

Fairbank, J. K., Reischauer, E. O. and Craig, A. M., *East Asia: Tradition and Transformation*, London: Allen & Unwin, 1973.

Fong Y.-L., *Précis d'Histoire de la Philosophie Chinoise*, Paris: Payot, 1952.

Foreign Language Press, *Criticizing Lin Piao and Confucius*, Beijing, 1975.

Gogol, N., *Döda själar* [Dead Souls] Stockholm, 1948 (an English edition is published by Penguin Classics, London, 1972).

Granqvist, H., *Filosofi i Kina* [Philosophy in China] Stockholm: Svenska Förlaget, 2000.

Grinker, R. R., *Korea and its Futures*, New York, NY: St Martin's Press, 1998.

Henriksen, T. H. and Mo, J. E., *North Korea after Kim Il Sung*, Stanford, CA: Hoover Institution, Stanford University Press, 1997.

Henthorn, W. E., *A History of Korea*, New York, NY: Free Press, 1971.

Hessler, C. A., *De sanna riddersmännens stat* [The State of the True Knights] Stockholm: Norstedts, 1979.

Hunter, H.-L., *Kim Il-song's North Korea*, Westport, CT: Praeger, 1999.

BIBLIOGRAPHY

Jonsson, G., *Towards a Breakdown in Inter-Korean relations*, Stockholm: Center for Pacific Asia Studies, University of Stockholm, 2000.
Kim, B.-L., 'Human rights in North Korea', *Korea and World Affairs*, Vol. 3, 1996, 431–50.
Kim, C. N., 'The uncertain future of North Korea', *Korea and World Affairs*, Vol. 4, 1996, 623–36.
Kim, C. J. E. and Kim, H.-K., *Korea and the Politics of Imperialism 1876–1910*, Berkeley, CA: University of California Press, 1967.
Kim, I. I., *Communist Policies in North Korea*, New York, NY: Praeger, 1975.
Kim, J. A., *Divided Korea: The Politics of Development 1945–1972*, Cambridge, MA: Harvard University Press, 1975.
Koh, B. C., *The Foreign Policy Systems of North and South Korea*, Berkeley, CA: University of California Press, 1984.
Lee, J.-S., *Rethinking the Korean Unification Question*, Ph.D. thesis, Stockholm: University of Stockholm, 1996 (this thesis contains a comprehensive bibliography, including works in Korean).
Lee, C.-J., 'US policy towards North Korea', *Korea And World Affairs*, Vol. 3, 1996, 357–79.
Lenin, V. I., *Lenins samlade skrifter i urval 1–20* [Selected Works in 20 Volumes, Swedish edn] Stockholm: Arbetarkultur, 1932–43.
Levin N. D., 'What if North Korea survives?', *Survival*, Vol. 39, No. 4, Winter 1997–8, 156–74.
Maretzki, H., *Kimismus in Nordkorea. Analyse des letzten DDR-Botschafters in Pjöngyang*, Böblingen: Tykve Verlag, 1991.
Marx, K., *The Class Struggles in France*, London: Martin Lawrence, 1934.
Marx, K., *Kapitalet I–III* [Capital I–III] Stockholm: Tiden, 1930–32.
Marx, K., *Kritik av Gothaprogrammet* [Critique of the Gotha Programme] Stockholm: Arbetarkultur, 1938.
Marx, K., *Louis Bonapartes 18:e Brumaire* [The 18th Brumaire of Louis Bonaparte] Stockholm: Arbetarkultur, 1939.
Marx, K., *Till kritiken av den politiska ekonomien* [A Contribution to the Critique of Political Economy] Stockholm: Arbetarkultur, 1943.
Marx, K., *Pariskommunen* [The Paris Commune] Stockholm: Arbetarkultur, 1946.
Marx, K. and Engels, F., *Gesamtausgabe*, Frankfurt: [MEGA], 1927–41.
Marx, K. and Engels, F., *Det kommunistiska manifestet* [*The Communist Manifesto*] Stockholm: Tiden, 1946.
[The Outlines of Marxism–Leninism] *Marxismen–leninismens grunder*, Moscow: Förlaget för litteratur på frammande språk, no year of publication given [probably 1959].
Oberdorfer, D., *The Two Koreas: A Contemporary History*, Reading, MA: Addison Wesley, 1997.
Oh, K. and Hassig, R., 'North Korea between collapse and reform', *Asian Survey*, Vol. XXXIX, No. 2, March–April 1999.
Reese, D., *The Prospects for North Korea's Survival*, Adelphi Paper 323, Oxford: Oxford University Press, 1998.
Scalapino, R. A. and Lee, C. S., *Communism in Korea 1–2*, Berkeley, CA: University of California Press, 1972.
Shmitt, E: *Konfuzius*, Berlin: Deutsche Bibliotek, 1925.

Simmons, R. R., *The Strained Alliance, Beijing, Pyongyang, Moscow and the Politics of the Korean War*, London: Macmillan, 1975.

Stalin, J. V., *Leninismens grundfrågor* [The Basic Questions of Leninism] Stockholm: Arbetarkultur, 1935–8.

Stalin, J. V., *Vår teori och praktik* [Our Theory and Practice] Stockholm: Arbetarkultur, 1943.

Suh, D.-S., *Kim Il Sung: The North Korean leader*, New York, NY: Columbia University Press, 1988.

Suh, D.-S. and Lee, C.-J. (eds), *North Korea after Kim Il Sung*, Boulder, CO: Rienner, 1998.

Sörbom, P., *Tao och de tiotusen tingen* [Tao and Ten Thousand Things] Stockholm: Norstedts, 1979.

INDEX

Abu Dhabi 87
Afghanistan 117, 175, 183
Albania 25, 88
Albright, M. 143
Algeria 25, 44, 67, 71, 79, 108
Angola 44, 117, 175
Australia 57–60, 79
Austria 6, 25

Bamako 97
Benin 44
Beria, L. 173–4
Bhutto, Z. 79
Björk, K. 12
Bongo, O. 38
British Commonwealth 57
Bucharin, N. 115, 169–70

Cambodia 25, 67
Carter, J. 145
China 3, 4, 10, 11, 21, 25, 42, 53, 57, 64,
    67, 70, 72, 75–8, 81–4, 88–9, 102–3,
    106, 109–12, 119–21, 126–7, 132–3,
    139, 142, 144–5, 173, 180, 185,
Chou Enlai 101, 127
Christianity 120, 123, 129, 132, 157
Clastres, P. 158
Colombo 44, 61
Comecon 4, 6, 41–2, 76–77, 122
Confucius, Confucianism 105, 110–11,
    119–21, 132–4, 138, 146
Congo *see* Zaire
Cuba 11, 25, 27, 67, 77, 117, 175, 180
Czechoslovakia 4, 26, 117, 175

Darwin, C. R. 157
Denmark 62, 64

Deutscher, I. 184
Djilas, M. 23

East Germany 7 25, 28, 61, 65, 90, 116,
    135, 173
Egypt 25, 44
Elias, N. 137
Engels, F. 109, 114, 133, 151–9, 161–2,
    170, 175–6, 179–80
Ethiopia 44, 88, 117, 175

Finland 6, 25, 65
France 152, 184–5

Gabon 25, 38, 88
Germany 3, 7, 72, 102, 135–6, 179
Gogol, N. 117
Gorbachev, M. 8, 103, 106, 117, 133, 184
Great Britain 179, 184

Hegel, F. 151
Hitler, A. 174
Ho Chi Minh 101
Hong Kong 4, 76, 110
Hungary 26, 103, 117, 174

IAEA (International Atomic Energy
    Agency) 140–1
India 25–6, 102
Indonesia 21, 25
Iran 88
Iraq 25, 88
Islam 157

Japan 3, 5, 10, 20, 41, 69, 70, 75, 78,
    80–4, 91, 93, 110, 119, 122, 134, 136,
    141–2, 145, 179